The David Discovery
A Novel

By Eric Rozenman

The David Discovery
A Novel

By Eric Rozenman

Academica Press
Washington

Library of Congress Cataloging-in-Publication Data
Names: Rozenman, Eric (author)
Title: The david discovery | Rozenman, Eric
Description: Washington : Academica Press, 2025. | Includes references.
Identifiers: LCCN 2025940824 |
ISBN 9781680533545 (hardcover) | 9781680533569 (paperback) |
9781680533552 (e-book)
Copyright 2025 Eric Rozenman

Dedication: To Melinda, My Chief Muse and Editor

The David Discovery is a work of fiction. It refers to historical figures and events only as part of a fictional story. Dialogue for the Great Disputation between Nachmanides and Paulus Christiani (Barcelona, 1263) is based on records of that disputation.

Contents

Chapter One:
Manhattan, the Present: 1

Chapter Two:
Persia—632 C.E. 25

Chapter Three:
Jerusalem, the Present 39

Chapter Four:
702 C.E., Aures Mountains 49

Chapter Five:
New York City, The Present 59

Chapter Six:
Havana, Cuba, the Present 63

Chapter Seven:
Cairo to Baghdad, 915 C.E. 71

Chapter Eight:
Pechora, 1944/New York City, 1969 89

Chapter Eight, (continued):
New York City, the Present 97

Chapter Nine:
Smartest Man in Brooklyn, the Present 101

Chapter Ten:
Mainz, 1096 109

Chapter Eleven:
Key West, Florida, the Present 119

Chapter Twelve:
Jerusalem, 1099 123

Chapter Thirteen:
Narbonne, 1136 127

Chapter Fourteen:
New York City, the Present 133

Chapter Fifteen:
Barcelona, Spain, 1263 145

Chapter Sixteen:
New York City, the Present 159

Chapter Seventeen:
Speyer, Holy Roman Empire (Germany), 1352 171

Chapter Eighteen:
New York City, the Present 177

Chapter Nineteen:
Havana, Cuba, the Present 181

Chapter Twenty:
Lisbon, Portugal, 1492 185

Chapter Twenty-One:
New York City, the Present 205

Chapter Twenty-Two:
New Amsterdam, 1655 213

Chapter Twenty-Three:
Jerusalem, the Present 219

Chapter Twenty-Three, (continued):
New York City, the Present 223

Chapter Twenty-Four:
The Holy Land, 1799 227

Chapter Twenty-Five:
Havana, Cuba, the Present 237

Chapter Twenty-Six:
Burlington, Vermont, 1901 247

Chapter Twenty-Seven:
Las Vegas, Nevada, 1979 253

Chapter Twenty-Eight:
New York City, the Present 259

Chapter Twenty-Nine:
Efrat, Israel, 1998 269

Chapter Thirty:
New York City, the Present 277

Chapter Thirty-One:
Jerusalem and New York City, the Present 299

Chapter One:

Manhattan, the Present:

"So, a messiah lives in each generation? Is that what you're saying?" The young scholar was incredulous.

"Not *a* messiah, or even *the* Messiah, perhaps but certainly possible candidates," the rabbi replied.

Perplexed, the scholar—Joshua Golden, senior lecturer and all-but-dissertation in philosophy at Columbia University—asked, "there are, or have been, multiple messiahs?"

"Of course not," said the older man, stroking his prematurely gray, intentionally untrimmed beard. "Think of them as potential messiahs, or messiahs-in-waiting."

This man, the scholar thought, looks like a guitarist from that old power trio, ZZ Top. If ZZ Top wore black suits, white shirts, dark ties and black fedoras, that is.

"If you're into sports," the rabbi was saying, "they're high draft picks. But since we're talking about a Jewish concept, let's use Hebrew terminology: *Mosiach*, to be exact. 'Messiah' is that oratorio from Handel." His eyes twinkled in the dangerous manner his followers had learned to recognize as equal parts amusement and triumph.

"But then what determines which of them manifests as the recognized savior of the Jews, and not coincidentally, humanity?" Golden probed.

The twinkle looked ready to burst into a grin. "Let's not get ahead of ourselves. First, *Mosiach* as restorer of the House of David, the Davidic dynasty, on earth. King Mosiach. Then leading the Jews, opening the way for the Kingdom of God on Earth and the redemption of all people. In that order. But not a savior. That job's already taken, and has been since creation, by the Creator Himself."

With that the rabbi rose, or more accurately sprung from his chair. He began to pace his study. His square frame and agile steps gave evidence of the collegiate wrestler he'd once been.

"First, let's specify terms. We ought to do so with every important matter in life. From buying groceries—potatoes or sweet potatoes? onions or shallots?—to choosing a mate—tall or short; learned or unlearned; pretty or plain, insightful or self-blinded, to recognizing *Mosiach* or not—there is a difference. Definitions matter.

"In Judaism," the rabbi continued, "messiah and savior, or better, messiah and redeemer, are two different terms. The former refers to the human messenger, a descendant of and heir to King David, who will inaugurate the imminent coming of *Ha-Shem's*—The Name, or God's—earthly kingdom. He, and the Jewish understanding is that the messiah must be a man—he is to be king, after all, not queen—should not be confused with the redeemer of Israel. *Ha Ga-el*, the Redeemer, is none other than God Himself. Curious that the older English term for jail was *gaol*, and from which prisoners could be redeemed. Regardless, it's crucial to keep our distinction in mind. *Mosiach*: human messenger and leader; Redeemer: God, the supreme being Who acts through history in ways humans can only begin to infer."

"Okay, messiah one thing, redeemer or savior another. Why don't we recognize these human messengers/kings in each generation? Why the wait for the messiah if candidates abound?"

"Good questions," the rabbi said enthusiastically. "In the generation just passed, there were at least three obvious and incredibly learned potential *moshiachs*. They were also wonderfully articulate, accessible to scholar and layman alike. One was Rabbi Adin Steinsaltz in Jerusalem, and outside *eretz Yisrael*, Rabbi Lord Jonathan Sacks in London. And just before them, the Lubavitcher Rebbe, Rabbi Menachem Mendel Schneerson, right here in Brooklyn."

"So, *moshiach* must be a rabbi?" the scholar asked.

'Not at all!" the rabbi replied. "Just a true *mensch*, his generation's recognized epitome of the righteous, charitable, just, wise, compassionate and broadly inspirational individual who teaches Torah to the world in his generation. And married, of course."

"That's all? A royal, Jewish Billy Graham?" the scholar said sardonically.

"You see," the rabbi answered, the twinkle again bright, "your tone reveals that crippling cynicism which, generation-wide, prevents the messianic manifestation."

"But if we're too credulous …"

"Yes, false messiahs—like the David Reuvenis, Shabbataei Zvis, Jakob Franks of old—will sprout like forest mushrooms after a spring rain. Each will have a podcast, YouTube channel, Twitter account and Instagram messages…."

"Not an *influencer*!" Golden laughed.

"No, please God!" the rabbi chuckled. "The trick—not yet understood, let alone mastered by an entire generation—is to be skeptical yet not cynical. Learnedly skeptical, not ignorantly cynical."

"I begin to see why the messiah has not yet shown up," the scholar said dryly.

"No, remember—every generation has its likely candidate, or even candidates, for *moshiach*. But no generation has yet been worthy and therefore has not yet been fully able to recognize him."

"So, all it would take is a more messianically-minded, or better informed, messianically-minded generation and Bingo! he'd be here?"

"I wouldn't put it quite that way, but yes," the rabbi replied. He stopped pacing and sat down again at his desk.

"Well, it seems to me there's an 800-pound gorilla in the middle of this messianic room," Joshua Golden said.

"And that is?" the rabbi invited, that little smile again playing on his lips.

"There are somewhere around two and a-half billion Christians, or at least people raised in and if not religious, then certainly products of an essentially Christian social and cultural environment," Golden said. "They believe, many fervently, others at a minimum tacitly, that Jesus Christ was the messiah, that he came once and will come a second time, heralding the end of days, final judgment and the start of heaven on earth. They cite scripture, including Torah—for example the book of Ruth, the story of a convert who nevertheless became the ancestor of King David. Doesn't that make your concept of *mosiach* something of a relic?"

"It would, if we were talking about a popularity contest. Which in terms not only of theology and philosophy but also of spirituality we are not. But the difficulty you suggest is more apparent than real."

"How so?" Golden challenged.

"Christians believe that Jesus—Yeshua—was himself of the Davidic line. Ruth, as you mention, was a Moabite woman who, widowed herself, stayed with Naomi, her widowed mother-in-law, instead of returning to her own land, and ended up remarrying an Israelite. She actually became the great-grandmother of King David. We Jews too, recognize Ruth as David's forebearer. But while that could be said to put Jesus in the line of succession, it would have done the same for his siblings."

Joshua Golden looked askance.

"You didn't know that the Jesus of Christianity had brothers and sisters? It's not surprising that many Jews do not. After all, this story is not part of our Torah, which we know as holistic. It belongs entirely to the New Testament, which from our perspective is about other matters, those touched on in books not in the Hebrew Bible. But that Jesus had a brother James, that is, Jacob, is recorded in Matthew, who must have been called Matityahu in his day, and John, that is Yonatan, mentioned in other books of the Christian Bible. In fact, James is said to have eventually led the nascent church.

"Perhaps less well known generally is that the Christian messiah had three other brothers, Simon, Joseph and Judas, as well as at least two sisters who are not named. Christians may differ over this familial structure, many Catholics for example holding to the belief that these are not siblings at all but, in view of the asserted perpetual virginity of Mary—who must have been called Miriam—cousins. In any case, in terms of searching for Jewish descendants of King David, whose great-grandmother indeed was Ruth, it could have been possible that Simon, Joseph, Judas or one of the sisters had a son or sons, who themselves had a son or sons and so on, at least one of whose descendants turned up as a link in the chain that led to the last of the Exilarchs."

"Or," said Joshua provocatively, "even Jesus himself?

"Possibly," replied the rabbi. "Possibly Yeshua himself married and fathered a son. After all, it would have been unusual for an unmarried man to have held much sway among Jews of Temple and even post-Temple times. In fact, marriage was a requirement for the priesthood—one foot in heaven and one rooted on earth, so to speak. But, of course, there is no assertion or even minor alternate tradition asserting such a development in normative Christianity."

"Okay, so for discussion's sake let's accept that the blood of Jesus Christ's family members, or even of the Christian savior himself, still runs in the veins of a potential Jewish *mosiach*. What about Maimonides' assertion that in the time of the messiah, the House of David—the line of the legitimate kings of Israel—will be restored? Even if a wholly righteous generation proclaims its *mosiach*, how will it sort through pretenders to the re-established throne?"

Softly, Rabbi Reuven Samson said, "In fact, we know who this generation's potential messianic candidates are right now. The Organization has known in each generation for more than a millennium."

****

About two miles away, a pleasant walk and then ferry ride across the East River, a middle-aged man sat at the counter of a small coffeeshop. Tucked among the office towers of lower Manhattan, the breakfast and lunch spot sold the best bagels within eight or ten blocks—and this being New York City, that included a lot of competition. Busy all morning and into the early afternoon, the shop was nearly deserted now, half an hour before 3 p.m. closing. The plate glass window, smashed the week before by Jew-haters *The New York Times* called "pro-Palestinian," had been replaced. And now protected by a metal grate.

Among the few lingerers was the man at the counter, well-dressed in a dark suit, crisp white shirt and new, fashionable red-patterned tie. His expensive Italian loafers, however, needed a shine. The contrast between clothes and shoes suggested the man's attention was not quite fully on his appearance. He swiveled back and forth a little on his stool, sipping his coffee—good, as usual—and chewing through his bagel. Perfection in simple things, he thought for the umpteenth time. They paved the way for perfection in bigger things. A rueful smile played on his lips. And my decision, he considered yet again, is anything but simple.

Not quite behind him, at the corner of his peripheral vision, another man sat alone in a booth, almost toying with his own coffee and bagel. A copy of *Investors Business Daily* lay on the table in front of him, but a close observer would have seen he was not reading. Instead, his eyes were on the man at the counter. But so ordinary, so common-place in appearance was he—was that hair dark brown or black, were those eyes green or brown, was his suit pressed or a little wrinkled?—that the fellow at the counter barely noticed him.

Just before 3 o'clock, the first man rose, placed some money next to his cup, idly spun the wedding band around his ring finger, softly patted his hands together twice, as if he'd reach a decision of some sort, and left. He was barely out the door when the man from the booth stepped onto the sidewalk behind him, anonymously ordinary, and continued following. *Investors Business Daily* rolled up in one hand, he trailed the first man four or five blocks to one of the newer high-rises, a building occupied primarily by medical suites. Looking into the lobby he watched as the subject stepped into an elevator. The fellow under surveillance was keeping his weekly psychiatric appointment.

On the plaza outside the revolving door, the observer sat at a nearby bench, inserted an ear bud, and touched an app logo on his cell phone. Once more he marveled at the sensitivity and clarity of the organization's Everywhere All-the-Time Audio app. His subject was saying "when will we ever tell the truth?"

"About what?" the female psychiatrist asked.

"You know about what," Gerry Meyer said. "About what really counts. About Chosen People, Promised Land."

"You're not able to let this thing go, even for a while?" she inquired. "It might do your overall mental state good to step back a bit, take a break, and reevaluate. After all, you have other important considerations in your life."

"You sound more like my lawyer than my therapist," he replied. "This is not a passing interest. It wasn't sparked by any advertisement. 'Need to unwind? Call Marla's Massage.'

"What this is, is some sort of calling. God knows I didn't ask for it." Then Gerry Meyer laughed. "Yes, only God knows. Why me, why now?"

Professionally empathetic yet professionally and personally dubious, the psychiatrist replied: "You've considered that only a week or two after you admit your marriage is in trouble, your job no longer fulfilling, your children are spending their high school years slacking off, and that your next birthday will be the big 5-0, you hear the word of God to go prophesy to the Jews? You don't think that's quite a coincidence?"

"Sure, it's a coincidence," Gerry Meyer said. "After twenty-five years of looking for something to believe in, something to give my life a bit of transcendence that environmentalism and president of the condo association board, for heaven's sake did not, I stopped looking. Given my successes on Wall Street, my partnership in Berger, Berliner, Boroetz and Whitson Investments, LLC, I told myself I didn't need it. I told myself transcendence was for losers. But something kept gnawing at me. Then, bam! That something found me."

On the sidewalk bench the ordinary-looking fellow apparently scrolling through messages on his cell phone adjusted his ear bud. This one's going to be more difficult than most, he thought. Generally, they don't have a clue, at least not until later and then externally, not internally. That makes them a little easier to conduct surveillance over, a little easier to manage, if and when necessary.

Mid-life crisis. Or crises, the psychiatrist was thinking to herself. Big crises.

What she said, softly, warmly, like an old friend whose $400 per 50-minute session charge was but a minor after-thought in her tastefully decorated office in a high-rent building was this: "Perhaps first, you *should* see your lawyer. Get your legal and financial affairs, joint custody terms, all that in order if you're really going to file for divorce. Then find a place to live, as close to your home as possible so as not to disrupt the children's routines, and your own, any more than unavoidable. As nice a place as you'll be able to afford, considering inescapable support payments. And hold off buying yourself that new car you've been talking about—Ferrari, Lamborghini was it?—since we first met until things sort themselves out. And one more thing, Gerry ..."

"Yes?"

"Are you meditating, 20 minutes a day, twice a day? As I mentioned before, some of my clients find it helpful, or at the least, relaxing. Instead of tranquilizers, if possible, in parallel if not."

"I started. It's easy for me to go into that semi-trace. But to stay there? After only a few minutes I start focusing on my mission. Anyway, I'm not stressed out; I don't feel undue pressure. I don't have vivid dreams. I just get impressions, realizations that come into my head fully-formed, in broad daylight. Realizations of what's about to happen—not in my personal life, not in the stock market, not with the Jets—never the Jets, thank God—but to the Jews, to America. About things beyond my education or, up until now, much interest."

"What is your Jewish education?" the man on the bench heard the psychiatrist ask.

"The usual," her patient said. "Bar mitzvah, then Hebrew school dropout, college atheist, graduate school agnostic, new-father deist. Why?"

"As you take care of the other things I've suggested, you might want to make a little time for study with someone who knows."

"Knows what?"

"If you think you are really are being called to prophesy, then the necessary foundation—Torah, Talmud, Jewish history," the psychiatrist said. "My father was a rabbi. For a while. Before he became a lawyer. Yeshiva, law school, or the Talmud and U.S. Code—a lot of similarities."

She's sharp, thought the ordinary-looking man sitting on the sidewalk bench, pretending to examine his cellphone. Maybe there's a way the Organization can use her. But for now, the question was did this patient—they'd been calling them clients for years, though the revised nomenclature hadn't seemed to change treatment outcomes, psychotropic drugs did that—did this Gerry Meyer really hear the call? Determining that was above his pay grade. His job was to watch, follow and, if necessary, protect. Which he did as the man shortly exited the building.

****

"The 'organization?' What organization—this one, the Jewish Outreach and Learning Organization?" the scholar asked, a little too aggressively, he thought to himself.

"No, not this one," the rabbi said. "An offshoot, you could say." You could say, he mused, because you'd be unlikely to get it right. "An organization that attempts to identify messianic candidates in each generation, and, if necessary, makes every effort to guide them."

"Identify and guide them?" the scholar asked, nonplussed.

"By *halachic* standards," the rabbi said, referring to Jewish law as rendered and handed down, generation to generation, by sage-like decisors. "It's long-established that the messiah can't proclaim himself. Instead, he must be recognized more or less spontaneously and widely by the Jewish people of his day. He must be both saintly and a man of positive action, bringing justice and compassion to the world, and a direct descendant of King David. That is, he must possess an unbroken, 3,000-year-old royal lineage."

Golden looked doubtful, to put it mildly. The rabbi's eyes, however, still twinkled. "Remember," he said, "the lineage was confirmed for the first 1,500 years and more, even after the second Roman exile following the defeat of the Bar Kochba revolt in 135 C.E., through the exilarchs of the great Babylonian *yeshivot* up to roughly 1,000 C.E. So, the Organization only has to account for the past millennium."

"Right. What could be so hard about that, given the travails, disruptions, wanderings and massacres repeatedly imposed on the Jews across those centuries?" replied the younger man.

"If you keep tripping over your own irony," the older man said, "I'm afraid you'll never reach your destination. Now, I'm also afraid, we must halt today's discussion." Looking at his watch, he added, "I've another appointment that won't wait. Until next week, then."

"Next week," the scholar answered as he rose and softly closed the study's heavy, polished wooden door behind him. As the latch clicked shut, the rabbi turned in his swivel chair and looked directly at one of the recessed ceiling lights behind his desk. The glowing outer ring enclosed a slightly convex lens and adjacent microphone.

"You have Mr. Golden under surveillance?"

"Yes, by two agents, following separately."

The voice in the rabbi's ear, via an apparent hearing aid, was that of the institute's security director. Uri Stein spoke from a control room of sorts, located almost exactly in the center of the hulking, five-story, nearly block-square structure that housed the charity's manifold activities and even a mid-sized synagogue. A vault in the sub-basement, known only to a handful of JOLO senior staff, held some ancient treasures, including one or two popularly but mistakenly rumored to be in possession of the Vatican. Stein, with an assistant beside him, scanned a bank of high-resolution monitors. They showed activity on surrounding streets and sidewalks, in the basement and tunnels running under the building and in the sky overhead. There had been four attacks at the headquarters in the past month: vandalism, attempted arson, assault on people entering or leaving, even a drone with a Molotov cocktail attached. That compared to three in an entire year before Jews in Israel went to war to defend themselves against fanatic murderers. Israelis fight back and Jews around the world are attacked.

"What about the other candidates?" he asked.

"We're shadowing them as well. There's the old Talmudist in Jerusalem, the teenager in Havana and that Gerry Meyer fellow here in New York."

"Good," the rabbi said. "Keep watching—and guarding—and update me daily, more often if necessary."

"Of course," Uri Stein replied.

The rabbi swiveled back, propped his elbows on the desk, interlaced his fingers and rested his chin on his hands. He closed his eyes and mused. There were four men now alive known to his organization to be direct descendants of the last king of Judea, and eventually of the last exilarchs, who were direct descendants of King David. There could be others, of course. But given the smallness of the world's Jewish population, maybe 16 million out of eight billion-plus human beings on Earth, or barely one quarter of one percent, that seemed unlikely. Reuven Samson believed the young scholar, likely to be offered a permanent teaching post at Columbia University, should he defend his dissertation successfully, to be the most plausible candidate. That was so even though Joshua Golden had no idea and only now was learning about the concept in any detail.

Better at this point that he did not have any fixed idea. As often had been the case over the centuries with such candidates, this one had put himself, or found himself on the right track without knowing it. Of course, this newly-visible, peculiarly self-directed contender, Mr. Gerry Meyer, also could be genuine. Or, the rabbi mused, just one more troubled middle-aged man in Manhattan.

It was one thing to be an heir—there had been more than 150 in the past 1,400 years—and quite another to have demonstrated, without ever personally hinting, let alone proclaiming, that one possessed the foretold qualities requisite in God's chosen messenger. And what word, what earth-shaking if not heaven-shattering proclamation, would that messenger bring? This was a question the rabbi and his predecessors stretching back 43 generations, had repeatedly prepared themselves to answer. They had been playing a long game, the longest game, in fact. The contest would end, not abruptly, but in a process rather than a moment.

Here the rabbi allowed himself the hint of a smile. It would end not with a second coming but the first, not with the sudden imposition of a kingdom of God on Earth but rather the footsteps of *Mosiach*, the messenger and anointed king. More than a few in *eretz Yisrael*—the land of Israel from snow-capped Mt. Hermon in the north to what Arab nomads once called Um Ras Ras, that is, modern Eilat on the Red Sea in the south, from the eastern banks of the Jordan River to the Mediterranean Sea on the west—heard those approaching footsteps immediately after the miraculous 1967 Six-Day War. But that was two generations ago.

When those footsteps really drew near the dynastic successor to biblical King David would be crowned and resume the reign of the Davidic lineage from Jerusalem and the whole of *eretz Yisrael*. Acknowledged by the reunited descendants of the tribes founded by Jacob's 12 sons, *moshiach* would herald the imminent redemption of human life, all human lives. And manifestation of this mystical prophesy would become progressively evident. So, the rabbi believed, and, if asked, would say he knew.

Perfection being possible only in heaven, in *Olam ha-Ba*—the world to come—back on earth even after *mosiach* there still would be disease and death, but less of the former, later for the latter. Likewise, poverty and war, not as crushing or extensive. Human beings would still be humans, perfecting but never perfect. Utopias, on the other hand, however envisioned by dreamers, almost always became blood-soaked revolutions raised by self-appointed elites on behalf of manipulated masses and institutionalized by tyrants. There had, the rabbi knew, been two modern exceptions—modern being post-Enlightenment—in which a revolution did not devour its children: the American, and the Zionist. Otherwise, the word utopia lived up to its original Greek meaning—nowhere.

But in the days of *mosiach*, Rabbi Samson believed deep in his heart, his bachelor's degree in computer science from City College of New York notwithstanding, the difference would begin with most of humanity—Jew or Christian, Muslim or Hindu, Buddhist or non-believer, saying one to another, as Isaiah and Micah prophesied more than 2,500 years before in, for and from the Holy Land, "'Come ye, and let us go up to the mountain of the Lord, To the house of the God of Jacob; And He will teach us of His ways, And we will walk in His paths. … For out of Zion shall go forth the law, And the word of the Lord from Jerusalem …"

****

"Tell me about this rabbi," she said, dangling one high-heeled shoe off her toes. "You've been spending a lot of time with him. Almost as much as with me."

"Not so. An hour a week, that's all," Joshua Golden protested. "Our conversations, his insights, help me with my dissertation. And," he smiled, "I spend as much time with you as your schedule permits."

Jamming both feet into her shoes, Rachel Shapiro stretched, inhaled—a Vogue-cover sort of traffic-stopping display in the little trattoria on Lexington Avenue at 30th Street in the Murray Hill neighborhood—and leaned forward on the small table covered with empty plates and mostly empty glasses of her wine and his beer. "An hour a week," she snorted. "Only if you discount the hours of reading you do before your rabbinic tete-a-tetes, mostly old religious texts as near as I can tell, not your philosophy works, and the hour or two of compulsive note-writing that follow. It's almost as if he were your adviser and you are trying out your dissertation on him. Over and over."

Rachel Shapiro wasn't hostile to religion, certainly not to Judaism. After all, her grandfather had been cantor at the Conservative B'nai Jeshurun Congregation on the Upper West Side, and she still dropped in on Friday night services there once in a while. Women sometimes danced and sang in the aisles, and the current cantor played guitar. But no cellphones in use. Not on Shabbat. You've got to draw the line between sacred and profane somewhere, sometime.

Whatever, she couldn't figure out what was going on with this man across the little table from her, finishing his Peroni. He wasn't coming clean with her, not quite, about this rabbi in Brooklyn, Crown Heights no less.

Rachel Shapiro and Joshua Golden were a pair. Both 30 years old, they had been dating for two years and were seriously discussing moving in together—they couldn't agree on whose apartment was preferable. She was vice president for client acquisition at Securitized, a cybersecurity risk management firm. A start-up four years ago, when she'd joined on the strength of a recommendation from a former college roommate, Securitized now employed more than 60 people in New York, London and Madrid, with dedicated tech support from what she envisioned as a digital sweatshop in Mumbai. Her responsibilities, titles and salary had grown with the company and she could now afford her one-bedroom, one bathroom apartment in a new high-rise with its view of the Statue of Liberty down the Hudson River to the south. Joshua's apartment further north, in Morningside Heights near the university, was in a post-World War II midrise that needed maintenance dating, it seemed, to the Korean War. But he had two bedrooms, one serving as a book-filled study, and rent control. If they moved in together, she intended to be married a year later and deciding in which preschool to enroll their as-yet-unborn child. And Mr. Professor Golden should have figured that out by now, she thought.

What she said was, "Lunch was great. Now I've got to get back to my office. Come over tonight for dinner, around seven. We'll have left-overs."

He stood and kissed her lightly on the lips.

"Not like that," she said. "Like this." Once again, she had the trattoria's attention and Joshua Golden's. And, though not as obviously, that of one young man on a barstool nursing a beer, another sipping an espresso in a rear booth. Both wore ear buds.

It wasn't leftovers Rachel Shapiro and Joshua Golden dined on that night at her apartment. They'd picked up a pizza from the popular Vezzo's and took back one of the thin crust pies dressed with a savory, house-made tomato sauce for which the place was known, mozzarella cheese and plentiful toppings, and an abundant salad with the signature oil-and-vinegar dressing. Vezzo's was one of those places of which the great New York Yankees' catcher Yogi Berra might have said, "it's so popular no one goes there anymore," except, of course, they did. And most of them seemed to be singles within about five years either side of Rachel and Joshua in age.

"The red pepper, please," Rachel said through a mouthful of pizza.

"Certainly," Joshua replied. Before handing over the shaker he sprinkled a few of the flakes onto his next slice. She just dumped them. There was truth in their private joke that she was the spicier of the two.

"I think I want to talk to this rabbi of yours," Rachel said.

Joshua stopped chewing and, buying time to think, sipped his iced tea. Rachel and Rabbi Samson in conversation. Could this be good, even if he could arrange it?

Outside her apartment, a delivery van marked "J and J Florists—We Make New York Bloom" squeezed into a space. Two men sat inside. One was behind the steering wheel, arm out the open window motioning other drivers to pass. In the front passenger seat sat the other, a bouquet of flowers across his lap, headphones over his ears. After a pause, he heard the man say, "I'll see if I can set it up. Although, given the strictures of his movement, he won't meet with you alone. Not because you are a beautiful, single woman, but because you are woman, period. Some other female, probably his wife, will have to be there."

"How Amish!" Rachel said. "Above suspicion, purer than Caesar's wife and all that. I figured as much. Reputational risk reduction. No problem."

"What should I say you want to talk to him about?"

"You, for starters. His role in your work; I aim to see you a professor, dissertation and all, and just want to be sure he's helping you focus, not diverting your attention. And, as a female descendant of a noted Jewish leader, I've always wanted to question someone knowledgeable about this ancient business of the messiah having to be a man, no women permitted. Also, and most important, the old question: How can one be a committed Jew in the modern world, active in that world, without being swallowed by or at a minimum unduly compromised by the things of that world?"

"You'll only get an hour, at best," Joshua said. "And it doesn't sound like that'll be nearly enough."

A week later, Rachel found herself sitting in Rabbi Samson's office, with him and his wife.

"Joshua tells me you are an executive in a risk analysis and management firm," the rabbi said to Rachel Shapiro. "You are, what, five or six years out of university? You have risen quickly."

"Eight years," Rachel corrected. She smoothed her knee-length skirt. After some consideration, she'd chosen a navy-blue skirt and matching jacket over a white blouse, beige mid-heel pumps and the barest touch of red lipstick. As an unmarried woman, unlike that of most married women within six blocks of the rabbi's office, her hair, thick and wavy auburn, was covered by neither a scarf nor *sheitel* (wig). "The first year, with a major in psychology and a minor in Jewish studies, I worked as a cocktail waitress. Two more years teaching Hebrew in a day school. I felt I was going nowhere.

"Then a friend told me about this start-up he was involved with. In the beginning there were only four of us, and I did a little of everything, mostly sales. Or attempted sales, to be honest. But we struggled on and developed a couple of algorithms to help companies like banks, insurance, real estate, tech firms identify and block attempted cyber infiltrations. That's the new Wild West of crime, sort of the modern version of stagecoach robberies, and for some reason—sometimes I think whoever's supposed to be in charge prefers it this way—official sheriffs are few and far between. So, we're a digital posse for our clients.

"In four-plus years we've grown to 60 people here and overseas. I'm now 'vice president for client relations.'" Rachel laughed. "That means I hold hands with the especially anxious or demanding customers who need extra care and feeding."

"So, you travel a lot?" the rabbi asked.

"Five to ten days a month," she answered. "Mostly two- or three-day trips, usually in the States or Canada, but sometimes Europe too."

"You and Joshua are …" here the rabbi searched for the word he wanted "… a pair?"

"Definitely a pair," Rachel smiled. "A pair, partners, a team, lovers." She didn't expect that last to startle him, and it didn't.

"There's something there," he replied, "but are you *b'sherit*?" Are you fated to be together? he meant.

"I think so. But I wonder sometimes if Joshua realizes it."

"Is that why you wanted to see me?"

"Not really. If I can't handle that part of the relationship, then maybe we're not *b'sherit*. Actually," Rachel continued, "I wanted to find out about your relationship with Joshua."

"Mine?" the rabbi asked.

"Yes," Rachel said. "I'm starting to wonder if the time he spends with you isn't getting in the way of his completing his dissertation and preparing to defend it."

"Because you expect him to become a tenure-track professor, marry you and father your children, all in the next few years?" the rabbi said.

Startled, Rachel answered simply, "Yes."

"Miss Shapiro," the rabbi said, not yet glancing at his wife, who sat in a wing-backed chair a few feet to the right and behind the rabbi, "what do you think of Joshua's dissertation topic?"

That question she didn't expect. "The origins of natural law theory? From what he tells me, and the little I remember about the subject from my undergraduate history classes, it's the cornerstone of English and American political philosophy, the source of the Declaration of Independence's assertion about individual rights and 'life, liberty and the pursuit of happiness'—that sort of thing."

"Quite so," Rabbi Samson said. "And I doubt many people, whatever their academic or professional backgrounds, could put it as succinctly as you have."

"Thanks," she said. "Probably osmosis. After all, I practically live with the guy …"

Oops, she thought, stopping herself. A blunder.

"You know," the rabbi said evenly, "other things being equal, couples who cohabitate before marriage have markedly higher divorce rates than those who don't. Apparently, something about not first taking sacred vows reinforces feelings and even expectations of more easily severable intimate relationships. More transitory partnerships, you might say. But we can talk about that another time."

Oh, we can talk about it, can we? Rachel thought. Here they were on the verge of combining households and this rabbi seemed to be intruding.

"I was 22 when I asked my mother to find me a bride," he went on. "She went to work, contacting her sisters and their friends. They all knew me and they knew my family. When you marry, of course, you don't just wed a spouse. You join a second family. Compatibility is key, not just for the two of you, but to the greatest extent possible, all of you.

"In a few weeks, I was introduced to a young woman from our community. Our community here in Brooklyn is large, so though I'd heard of her family, I did not know her. We met, chaperoned of course, and talked. We met a second time, and she decided I was not for her.

"A month or two later, one of my aunts arranged for me to meet a second young woman. I'll let her tell the rest."

The rabbi's wife stood up and took a few steps to her husband's chair. She was almost as tall as Rachel herself, probably about five feet, six inches. A little on the stocky side, but not unattractive and with a smile that seemed to radiate light.

"My name is also Rachel. My mother was a schoolmate of Reuven's aunt, so she was familiar with his family. You might say, with only a little exaggeration, that my family and his had been tracking each other since before either of us were born. Anyway, after we met the first time, I told my mother 'He's the one.'"

"How old were you then?" Rachel asked.

"Twenty. Almost 21."

"So young. How could either of you be certain?"

"You might say we'd already been checked and cross-checked, vetted by our parents, our relatives and their friends, by our community. And we have different expectations than young people in society in general. Compatibility—including mutual aspirations, a shared way of life defined by a transcendent belief system—comes first. Then marriage is not just living together, but making a life together that involves love, children, and family," *Rebbetzin* Samson said.

"It's been 38 years now," the rabbi smiled. "Thirty-eight years, six children, so far 11 grandchildren …"

"*Baruch ha-Shem*," his wife interjected. God be blessed.

"*Baruch ha-Shem*," the rabbi affirmed. Then, shifting gears, "Miss Shapiro, the closer Joshua gets to the day he defends his dissertation before a panel of five professors, the more problematic he will find his premise about natural law."

"What do you mean?" Rachel asked, for the first time during the interview feeling alarm.

"For Western political scientists and political philosophers, natural law theory is less theory than certainty, the Rosetta stone of their discipline. But for philosophers of what many Western political scientists call Judeo-Christian ethics, for people like myself, whom you might call practicing theologians—though I don't care for the term—natural law is less Rosetta stone than substitution, a theory necessitated by the hole in their bagel."

"Rabbi, I'll tell you what I tell some of our clients: You're going to have to be more specific if you want me to understand the problem."

"Certainly. In the Declaration of Independence, Jefferson—giving voice to the Founders' vision of individual rights and liberty—placed Americans in the natural law tradition. This tradition understood that the concept of right and wrong within society expressed a higher law, one that did not come from kings or legislatures but rather a greater, 'self-evident' source. But unlike for the British, the Founders needed something both more precise yet beyond human manipulation. Hence, individuals' rights were 'endowed by their Creator.' Humans could reason their way to this truth.

"Joshua, in the mainstream of natural law tradition, traces these ideas from the Roman writer Seneca though Hobbs and Locke to America's revolutionary Founders, drawing on Anglo-Saxon common law along the way. From the Declaration's 'life, liberty and pursuit of happiness' ordained by the Creator to the Constitution's 'we, the people,' a people—free individuals who nevertheless constitute a particular nation—born with rights. A government's job is to help us secure those rights, not define, let alone limit or erase them.

"But this no longer works well in the United States, let alone the home of Anglo-Saxon common law, Great Britain. Americans are torn between progressives and conservatives. Progressives, since at least Franklin Roosevelt and the New Deal if not Woodrow Wilson and his 'New Freedoms,' and even earlier, the hyper-active Teddy Roosevelt, look to government to lead and shape society. Of course, today's 'progressives' often are something else, functional reactionaries heavily influenced, consciously or not, by neo-Marxist rigidities. Today's conservatives still believe, however inarticulately, in the private sector over the public sector—in which individuals remain largely free to choose."

"But rabbi," asked Rachel, a little exasperated, "what has this to do with Joshua's dissertation?"

"From what I understand, based on our conversations, Joshua is coming to realize the edifice of natural law theory, which he seeks to first defend and then add his own contemporary updates, is hollow. That is, nature's law really is 'survival of the fittest,' the strong over the weak. Hobbs himself famously described nature as 'red in tooth and claw.' Among humans, following only natural law likely leads less to life, liberty and happiness than, more probably and historically, emperors, kings and aristocracies or dictators and the party. They lord it over 'the people,' if not enslaving them then tightly regulating. Or perhaps, their subjects materially swaddled, they can treat the people as perpetual adolescents, consumers dependent on paternalistic government.

"Unless we recognize that people's rights came not from nature but from Sinai, when Moses brought down the law for human beings created in God's image—not looking like God, of course, but rather each with a godly spark that makes his or her life and liberty sacred—then there are no rights at all, only privileges that can be cancelled as well as granted. Joshua's dissertation, as he has discussed it, has no Creator as the source of liberty, no transcendent gyroscope. And this is hardly a theoretical or academic problem alone. In a country in which at least twenty-five percent of the public no longer identifies with any religion, the idea of a Creator and God-given rights becomes progressively harder to sustain. Without creation's Creator front and center, natural law is a conceit, not a concept."

For a rabbi, he knows his political theory, Rachel thought. What she said was, "Do you mean, at the 11th hour, Joshua should toss his dissertation and start over?" Rachel could not hide her anxiety.

"No. Something more challenging. Ideally, he will show that the political philosopher's natural law follows directly from the revelation at Sinai, that without revelation of the Law, without the Creator, the one in the Declaration of Independence who endowed each member of mankind with certain unalienable rights, natural law is more hypothesis than law. My relationship with Joshua is about helping him resolve this contradiction," the rabbi said, telling Rachel part of the truth.

The *rebbetzin* interrupted them. "My husband and I will be pleased to attend your wedding," she smiled. "When you and Joshua become husband and wife in the eyes of God, the people Israel and of course the state of New York. But let me ask you this: Do you really believe, in your heart of hearts, that Joshua's calling is to be a professor of philosophy?"

Here it is, Rachel thought. Now we're getting to it. This rabbi, for all his amiability, all his erudition, and his wife, for all her maternal solicitude, want something else for Joshua. My Joshua, not theirs.

"What else?" she replied coolly.

The rabbi answered. "A tenured professorship, perhaps. But not necessarily of philosophy," he said, still pleasant. "After all, that was a Greek specialty, to which the French and Germans contributed so much. The Germans …" The rabbi stopped for moment, as if lost in thought. Then he resumed, "Kant, Nietzsche, Hegel, Wittgenstein—and, of course, Marx and Engels. All, eventually, to the torment and death of so many souls. No, I was thinking—and, Miss Shapiro, I have not said this to him—

that Joshua, with his intellectual curiosity, rare depth of analysis and gift for self-expression, could make a greater contribution, perhaps much greater, as a theologian. A Jewish theologian in particular, though the word theology, like the word religion itself, does not quite square with the essence of Judaism as a system, or better, way of life built on ethical monotheism as practiced by a community of practical believers.

"Either way," the rabbi said, eyes twinkling, "I suspect Joshua will find his calling, and attract a following."

Rachel was surprised. And a little confused. She did not get to ask about a female messiah. At least, not then.

****

Gerry Meyer tried to follow his psychiatrist's advice. At least for a couple of months. He enrolled in two 12-week courses at Agudat Yeshurim, The Park Avenue Synagogue on Park at 87th Street. Both were taught by assistant rabbis. "Re-Introduction to Judaism," by Rabbi Dov Franco for an hour and a-half on Tuesday evenings and "Talmud for Today's Decision-Makers," by Rabbi Amy Maggid for another 90 minutes Thursday nights.

Meyer enjoyed the former. It reawakened old lessons and lapsed practices and usually left him with a glow of nostalgia. The class conjured imagines of childhood Friday night dinners, his mother lighting the Shabbat candles, his father blessing the wine before the meal. More than once he imagined he smelled warm *challah*, or at least recalled the promising and comforting aroma of the freshly-baked twisted loaves. Which, he told himself, was of course impossible since his mother did not bake. She purchased the loaves at the big kosher Seven Mile Supermarket near their home in Pikesville, a suburb of Baltimore. Still, he was pretty sure that when he thought about those long-ago evenings, he smelled that bread.

But in terms of enjoyment, Talmud study was another matter. Even in a pop-psychology, self-help format, he found the subject matter abstruse, esoteric and hard to follow. Several times during the 12-week session he had to pinch himself to remain awake.

"So, no final exam," Rabbi Maggid ("Call me Amy") smiled near the close of their last class. "But a little oral review. Rafi," she said, nodding to one of the five men in the 11-person class, "why do we even need the Talmud, all 37 tractates of the Babylonian Talmud …"

"Or 39 of the Jerusalem Talmud." Michael the Obsessive interrupting again, Gerry Meyer grumbled to himself.

"… right, Michael," the rabbi continued unruffled, "with its 2,711 pages…"

"And nearly countless commentaries," Michael interjected again. What a *nebbish*, Gerry Meyer thought, almost ready to lash out at the round-faced, round-bodied retired accountant.

"Let's stay focused," Rabbi Amy said evenly. "Why do we need them?"

"First of all," Gerry Meyer was saying, almost before the rabbi had stopped speaking and preempting Raphael Rothstein, professor emeritus of Byzantine history at New York University, "biblical, like modern Hebrew, is based on words with three-letter—sometimes just two—roots, all consonants. To be certain of the meaning of a particular word, one must understand it in context of the surrounding phrase, essentially supplying the proper vowels mentally. It makes the language exceedingly regular—but only once one has 'the code.' That's why the drivers of cars with those bumper stickers you see occasionally that read 'The Bible says it, I believe it, and that settles it' don't have a clue. To get at the meaning of the Torah, not just the plain surface meaning but the nuances and subtleties, we rely on the old sages and their Talmudic interpretations."

"Very good," Rabbi Amy started. "It's like recognizing six-sided, red-and-white road signs the world over that had the letters STP but no 'O' and reading 'Stop' …" But Gerry Meyer wasn't finished. "… And there's another, bigger reason," he continued. "Traditional Judaism believes that God gave the Oral Law to Moses along with handing him the Written Law, the Torah itself, at Mt. Sinai. The Torah hints at this several times, when God tells Moses to carry out certain commandments 'as I told you.' And we are to believe that the Talmud reflects the Oral Law.

"But I find this an exasperating concept," he continued. Now Rabbi Amy was frowning. "I'm a lawyer who became a financial consultant, advising pretty large-sized banking and real estate firms in the city. Very little business gets done in this industry of billions of dollars on the basis of a conversation and handshake commitment. We have an entire legal structure, laws, contracts, tax codes and when necessary, courts founded on written words. Talmudic reasoning may well have had a great deal to do with the success of Jews in the law, but the laws themselves are and must be written, not oral. And written with vowels as well as consonants."

Before Rabbi Amy could respond, Michael the Obsessive was clapping his hands and practically shouting. "Well said, well said! This 'Oral Law' thing has troubled me all session."

"Me too," added Lisa Lenkowitz, a well-dressed widow as slender as Michael was rotund.

"I believe there must have been an Oral Law to complement the Written, as Mr. Meyer has acknowledged, but because it was told just to Moses and can only be inferred from fragments of Torah, we hardly can justify 37 tractates and 2,711 pages of Talmud," the usually quiet, even shy Judith Krakower put in. Was this still shapely blonde, a woman who seemed quite the loner, looking at him admiringly? Gerry wondered.

Some of the other students shifted uncomfortably in their seats. Rabbi Amy felt the summary, and perhaps the course, slipping away from her in its closing moments. Her rescue, such as it was, came from an unlikely source.

"I think," boomed the deep voice of Ido Tabatchnik, a burly if none-too-tall Russian Jew by way of Israel where he had worked as a security guard and who, though a regular attendee, previously had little to say, "we should respect what our leader, Rabbi Amy, has taught. There was, and is,"—here his voice dropped even lower—"the Written Law and the Oral Law. Both handed down by God to Moses and interpreted, when necessary, by the learned men who compiled the Talmud. Otherwise, the Written Law alone would have turned to stone long ago."

After class that night Gerry Meyer, Judith Krakower, Lisa Lenkowitz, Michael the Obsessive and Ido Tabatchnik were sitting in a late-hours café on 86th street, sipping coffee and eating cake. Meyer was relieved that Tabatchnik, who until his outburst that evening had said next to nothing during the entire course session but had not missed a class, always sitting just behind and to the right of him, came along. This Ido struck him as some sort of study hall monitor who had politely, almost deferentially, agreed to join them. In times like these—the coffee shop, owned by an Israeli-American, had been fire-bombed and newly-placed red, black and green Palestinian flag stickers reading "Crush Zionists, Globalize the Intifada!" obscured the front window—it couldn't hurt to have a man like Tabatchnik around. Meyer did not notice the Russian-Israeli-American nod almost imperceptibly to a man leaning against the doorway across the street as the classmates had exited Agudat Yeshurim.

"I'm so glad you said what you did tonight," Lisa Lenkowitz was telling Gerry Meyer. "I'd been thinking the same thing but was afraid to say so." "I'm glad too," Michael jumped in. "Yes, I am. Very glad too."

"And I would like to hear a little more," Judy Krakower said softly.

Their eyes met, briefly. And Gerry Meyer had a thought, two really. One, Lisa Lenkowitz, with her perfectly coiffed silver hair and just-so eye shadow and lipstick, looked like she could have been a model once. And two, Judy Krakower looked ready.

Chapter Two:
Persia—632 C.E.

It was spring, 632 C.E. Passover, in fact. And the ruling Sassanian emperor, newly-ascended Yazdegerd III, sent holiday greetings to the Jewish exilarch. The Sassanids long ago had revived Zoroastrianism as the state religion. Nevertheless, they generally tolerated their Jewish, Christian, Manichaean, Buddhist and other religious minorities. Occasionally, their aristocrats even took Jewish or Christian spouses. So, the exilarch was not surprised to receive the annual declaration or the court delegation that delivered it. In fact, he was quite expecting it.

"To the Reish Galuta," it began; the Exilarch did not mind the Babylonian/Persian transliteration of the Hebrew *rosh galut*—head of the captives or exiles—"Greetings from His Highness, Yazdegerd, Emperor of all Persians. In remembrance of the days when the Prophet Moses led the Israelites from Egypt, We share your happiness ...."

Bustanai ben Haninai finished reading the holiday proclamation with satisfaction, especially the line emphasizing that "the Emperor and all His Subjects wish you much joy at this season." Since the emperor, then a prince, had given one of his daughters, Lady Dara Izdadwar, to ben Haninai in marriage some years earlier, and the princess still seemed a happy woman, an amiable wife—one supported to be sure by at least a dozen servants, the exilarch could never keep track—he assumed the royal communique was sincere as well as pro forma.

"You know," Princess Dara said to her husband when he showed her the proclamation, "my father hopes to maintain support among the minorities of his realm. We are in trouble, though most of his advisors, sycophants that they are, hope to curry favor by telling him otherwise."

"What do you mean, my wife and grand vizier?" ben Haninai jokingly replied.

"You know what I mean. Pretending otherwise when danger threatens only makes it worse."

He knew. He just didn't want to dwell on it. The Sassanids had barely ended four years of conflict with the Parthians immediately to the west. The internecine fighting had weakened both former partners in the confederated empire. And this could not have happened at a worse time; Arab armies, energized by the new belief they called Islam—meaning *submission*—were pouring out of the Arabian peninsula. They already had wrested Yemen, what Westerners called the fabled lands of Sheba, from Sassanid control and were battling their way into Mesopotamia.

Still, the Arabs were upstarts, ben Haninai thought. The empire's mighty armies, led by the heavy cavalry that long ago had stopped even the eastward advance of imperial Rome, eventually would quash them. After all, they were merely desert raiders in light armor, riding camels—unpredictable beasts at best—and relying on archers against veteran, armored knights on large, imposing horses. The Arabs' leader, the one they called Muhammad the prophet, had just died. Several Arab tribes he had conquered already were in revolt. No, the exilarch thought, his wife worried too much. Things would continue well with the empire, with its Jews and himself. Authority to levy communal taxes and administer community courts, tolerance—and not grudgingly, either—under the Zoroastrians, all would continue. The Jews in the Sassanid Empire might be in *galut*, exile, spiritually, but they certainly did not feel like exiles, let alone captives, he told himself. Again.

****

"Now what?" Emperor Yazdegerd III demanded of his councilors. Among them, feeling a bit out of place and increasingly vulnerable, was Exilarch Bustanai ben Haninai. It was shortly after Passover, 651 C.E. and what was left of the royal court met in the oasis city of Merv. Merv and its environs constituted most of what remained of the Sassanid Empire. The 400-year-old realm once stretched from the Mediterranean Sea to central Asia. Now after two decades of successive and expanding Arab invasions, it comprised no more than a few hundred square miles of Turkmenistan, north of Persia proper.

"We can organize a caravan, guarded by the royal cavalry, and—taking as much of the remaining treasury as possible—quickly make for Byzantium through northern Syria," urged one.

"Too far, too dangerous," said another. "Byzantium has been an enemy and we would have to cross a still-festering Parthia. China is almost as close."

"Almost," said a third, "but the terrain is more inhospitable." The squabbling continued.

"Byzantium!" the emperor finally shouted. "How soon can we be ready to go?"

As the councilors resumed arguing, this time about preparations, Bustanai ben Haninai slipped out of the room. Much closer than Byzantium, China or God knows where else, he thought, was the army of Abd'-Allah ibn Amir, 100,000 men or more. It already had sacked Estakar and slaughtered 40,000 of its defenders in the process. If the exilarch was to make a separate peace for himself and his community with Muhammad's successor, Caliph Uthman ibn Affan, now was the time. Or the time to die trying.

Back at the latest dwelling they had occupied in the long retreat ahead of the advancing Arabs—now more like flight—ben Haninai was nearly out of breath. Twice he had got turned around hurrying through unfamiliar passageways.

"Do what you must for the rest of the Jews," Lady Dara said after hearing him out. "I'm going to do what I must for our son."

"Which is?" asked ben Haninai.

"Get him to Aleppo. Or maybe even Jerusalem."

"Impossible! How do you imagine you could do this?"

"My lady-in-waiting, Esther bat-Sholom ha-Dimashq, knows how. She was born there. Her family is from Damascus and they are traders. There is a network."

****

"So, you are the Exilarch?" It was less a question than an assertion, one with a tone of menace. It came from General Abd'-Allah ibn Amir. The leader of Caliph Uthman's Army of the Northeast—the caliph seemed to have armies everywhere—sat on the makeshift throne recently warmed by Yazdegerd III, last ruler of the 400-year Sassanid Empire.

Disguised now as a poor trader, in shabby robes and attended to by a remnant handful of devoted servants, with the way to Byzantium blocked, Yazdegerd fled toward China. He had found refuge there once before, at the height of the Parthian revolt. That time he had returned triumphantly, at the head of his regrouped, enlarged forces. This time he would be murdered by a Turkman miller enraged at his haggling over the price of a bag of grain.

General ibn-Amir did not have to question the man standing before him as to his biography. The general had not won battle after battle by being unprepared. So, he already knew a great deal about Bustanai ben-Haninai, leader of the Jews in exile, heir to the role of High Priest at the Temple in Jerusalem, direct descendant of Daoud the King and his son, the great King Sulieman who had built the First Temple. No, he questioned ben-Haninai to see, by his manner as much as his answers, what kind of man he was.

"Not many Jews live in Merv. What was your home city after we conquered the capital, Ctesiphon?"

"Khorasan, Excellency."

"If I let you and your Jews live—People of the Book, yes, but cursed by Allah for killing Isa and fighting the Prophet—what would you have?" the general asked, in hard, flat words.

Bustanai ben Haninai considered. He was not sure he would leave this interview with General Abd'-Allah alive; in addition to the throng of advisors and courtiers standing to the sides and below the throne were guards from an elite corps of fighters. They were tall, muscular men—some said eunuchs but ben Haninai doubted that—with the curved swords of finely honed Damascus steel that were able to separate a man's head from his shoulders by a single, one-armed swing. Yet now the general asked him what he wanted, in addition to his own life.

The exilarch bowed toward the general, not for the first time during their conversation. "If your Excellency pleases, I would ask only for the continuation of the academies at Pumbedita and Sura." These were the premier centers of diaspora Jewish scholarship, home to some of the greatest rabbinic sages, seedbeds of the Babylonian Talmud.

Ben Haninai did not like the way the general looked, or more accurately, glared at him. Finally, the other man asked, "How many studied in the academies before?"

"Many. Hundreds, perhaps even thousands," the exilarch replied.

The general considered. Several advisors moved to whisper to him. He stopped them with a raised hand.

"Granted," he said. "On these conditions: Not hundreds of students and certainly not thousands. Fifty at most, in each of the two places. And, as everywhere else, the Jews as *dhimmi* people—protected so long as they know their place and pay the yearly *jizya* head tax; they will not construct buildings higher than those of the Muslims; they will bow to Muslims in the street; the word of two Jews will be inferior to that of one Muslim in court; Jewish women will be given to Muslim men as wives if the Muslim pays the bride-price; and orphaned Jewish children will be raised by Muslim families in the one true religion."

The exilarch stopped himself from objecting. To object might well mean not only his own execution but the death of entire exile communities so he cast his eyes down and bowed.

"And one other thing," General Abd'-Allah said. "When you reach your new home in Pumbedita, you will not leave it, ever. You will communicate through messengers. Agreed?"

"Agreed."

After the exilarch had gone, the general's advisors remonstrated with him. "You were too generous," said one. "The Jew deserved to die. He only bowed; he did not prostrate himself."

"They are the killers of prophets, falsifiers of the holy book," reminded another. "Armiah, Isa, even Muhammad," he said, meaning Jeremiah and Jesus as well as the Islamic prophet, "they murdered, or tried to murder them all. They wrote that the progeny of Itzhaq, not Ishmael, would inherit the Word."

The general smiled. "In the present, I was lenient. But in the future, you will see, I will squeeze them. There are Jews all over what was Babylonia, in some cities the majority. But this is no longer Babylonia, no longer part of *dar al-harb*, the world of war, but of *dar al-Islam*, the world of Islam. And as time passes, there will be fewer and fewer of them but more and more Muslims whose ancestors were Jews. You will see, and if not, your children will."

****

In the wagon, Esther bat-Shlomo ha-Dimashq huddled over the small boy. In a blanket, he curled up on her lap, crying softly. "Hush, Yosef. Hush," she said. "It will be all right." The wagon rattled on over the rocky road. It was less a road than a track, winding ever westward, slopping gently upward.

It would get stepper soon, but at the rate they traveled, not soon enough, thought Yehuda ha-Gadol—Judah the Large. That was his nickname. If anyone knew his real name, they didn't utter it.

Glancing over his shoulder yet again, Yehuda watched as what had been a smudge grew into a cloud ascending from the eastern horizon below. A troop of cavalry, gaining on them. His little band of refugees had no more than an hour's lead, maybe less.

As the track rose higher and became narrower, Yehuda found the kind of place he was looking for. "Halt!" he shouted. The wagon and its outriders, perhaps thirty in all, came to a stop.

"We cannot outrun them so long as we have the wagon. Esther, the boy will ride with me. You'll be right behind with Benjamin on his horse. Take one sack of jewels from the chest. Just ahead, where the road narrows so that a wagon can barely pass, we'll turn it over for a barricade. Then we'll scatter the rest of the jewels, gold and silver on the trail in front of it. Ten men will dismount in the rocks above on each side. Just before they reach the wagon—it won't be much more than half an hour from now—and fall upon the treasure, you will ambush them. First with arrows, then charging into the survivors swinging your swords. The rest of us are going on, as fast as possible, to Damascus." He had never disclosed that Aleppo, not Damascus, was their destination in case any of the men were captured and made to talk.

"I will ask for volunteers first. Who will fight here, and then follow after the ambush?"

All thirty raised their swords, knowing that another word for this ambush was suicide.

"I thought so," Yehuda said. "You are men." He then selected the ten riders whom he knew to be the swiftest to continue with Esther, the boy, Benjamin and himself.

It was a strange, and sorry little band—six horsemen plus a woman and boy—that straggled into Aleppo on January 2, 662 C.E. Dust-covered, clothes tattered, horses worn nearly to skin and bones, they looked at the end of their strength. A mother and child, seeing these apparitions round a corner, shrunk back against a stone wall. But the meager party kept moving. Two horses carried a rider and a passenger each. On the first a small boy clung to a big man holding the reins, on the second a woman held tight behind the rider's waist. The animals tottered as if the merest breeze might fell them. Still, they pushed deep into the city. On a narrow, twisting street they drew up finally in front of a large private house, its stone front gray with age, heavy wooden front door locked, its windows shuttered.

Dating from the fourth millennium B.C.E., Aleppo was one of the world's oldest continuously inhabited places. If not quite as antique as Jericho and Damascus, it nevertheless bustled down through most of the subsequent centuries, submitting to and then growing with and ultimately outlasting conquerors including Amorites, Hittites, Egyptians, Mitannai, Assyrians and Persians. Now the Arabs ruled, but what mattered to the eight strangers dismounting in front of the shuttered stone house was that for the previous 700 years, since around 100 B.C.E., Aleppo had been home to an active, if necessarily inconspicuous, Jewish community.

The residence to which they now begged admittance was the home of one of the community's leaders, a prosperous merchant named Eliezer ben-Haddad. Eliezer was a Hebrew name meaning "my God's help," going back to that of the Damascus-born servant Abraham trusted to return to Mesopotamia and find a wife for his son Isaac, a wife who would turn out to be Rebekah. Haddad was something else. The name of the storm god of the Amorites, Akkadians and Canaanites, it signified Eliezer ben-Haddad was a man of his place, that he belonged. And so he was treated, most of the time. Aleppo had largely recovered from the burning and pillaging by conquering Arabs in 637 C.E., and, human beings always needing to trade with one another, the ben-Haddad family fortune and local standing recovered with it.

"This is the boy?" ben-Haddad asked Yehuda ha-Gadol once the travelers had been admitted and the door closed and barred behind them.

"Yes," the visitor said.

"His name?" their host asked.

"Yosef ben-Hanania."

"The Exilarch's son?

"Youngest son. His sole surviving child," replied Yehuda ha-Gadol.

"And the woman caring for him—who is she?"

"Esther bat-Shlomo ha-Dimashq, the princess' favorite lady-in-waiting."

"Former princess," ben-Haddad said, almost to himself. "I know this Esther's family well. We have often done business together. But things are worse in Damascus now than here in Aleppo. For pagans, Christians, especially for the Jews."

"We know. That was one reason we came here and not to Damascus, even though it is Esther's hometown." Yehuda ha-Gadol did not say so but even more critical in the decision to bring the boy to Aleppo and not the larger city of Damascus was the presence in the former of Eliezer ben-Haddad.

"Well," ben-Hadad said, "we will do everything possible to support Yosef in the way his father meant for him, in the way we all need him to traverse. He will learn from the city's best teachers—and they are quite good—train with someone appropriate, perhaps yourself, and, of course, be given a new name, new outward identity. The world at large must not know he is the last son of the exilarch. As it is said, we will bring him to Torah, to marriage, to good deeds and teach him to swim." The three traditional essentials; as to the last, as it also is said, one never knows.

Ever so slightly, the other man bowed.

****

As he grew, Yosef ben Hanania took naturally to his studies. The program was rigorous—up before sunrise to be ready for morning prayers, followed by two hours of Talmud study prior to midmorning breakfast. Then three more hours of Talmud until late lunch. An hour of Arabic to supplement his native Farsi and Hebrew followed. This was succeeded by afternoon prayers and an hour of Torah. A light dinner, evening prayers, and finally, on three nights, general history—Jewish, Greek, Roman, Persian, Byzantine and Arab. Alternating, on three others, something Yehuda ha-Gadol called "physicality."

"All else you study is intellectual and spiritual. But remember, the body is vessel for the soul. You must train it too." That meant long walks around the city, always in company with Yehuda and one of his assistants, mock jousting with padded poles, archery and, when political and social conditions were sufficiently calm to permit, horseback riding outside the city walls. This was the program, six days and evenings a week. Seven hours of sleep was all, and enough. The seventh day, of course, was Shabbat, the holy day of rest God gave the Israelites, so sacred Moses brought it down from Sinai as the Fourth Commandment. In Eliezer ben-Haddad's household it meant the special Shabbat morning prayers, the weekly Torah reading followed by a festive meal, and afternoon rest, informal study, and a lighter late afternoon meal. At sundown, the short Havdalah service to close the sacred day and separate it from the mundane rest of the week with the three-wicked entwined candle, smelling clove, cinnamon and other sweet spices and sip of the smoothest wine. And maybe a smile from Miriam, the youngest of the three ben-Haddad sisters.

Yosef found his life rigorous but not onerous. His Talmud and Torah study was exacting but not beyond him, esoteric at times but nonetheless intriguing. He thought his teacher, Eliezer ben-Haddad's younger son Hezekiah, a worthy scholar. His *chevrusha*, study partner, was a distant ben-Haddad cousin called Avner, younger but diligent. The three of them, Hezekiah, Avner and himself comprised what Yosef privately thought of as the Aleppo Academy. But what he enjoyed most of all, even above galloping alongside Yehuda across farmlands beyond the city, was the company of Miriam. The sisters and their mother sometimes took their evening meals with the men of the family and, of course, every Friday Shabbat dinner. It was then that Miriam and Yosef exchanged glances, and once in a while, usually after Havdalah, a word or two…

Time passes at two speeds, Yehuda ha-Gadol thought. There is the mundane, the day-to-day plod, with its routine tasks, habitually preformed, interspersed with occasional moments of surprise, of joy and sorrow, but overall stretching with a certain sameness both reassuring and tedious. It threads continually through the days, weeks and into the lengthening years.

But there is the other pace, the ever-accelerating unreeling of time, blowing through life like an oncoming storm. The older one gets, the faster it goes. Yehuda, when compelled, gave his age at 47, but in fact was 56. This was old for most men, especially those battered by life and time as he had been. Nevertheless, if a little bent, Yehuda still stood a bit bigger and stronger than most.

He let his mount lag behind just a bit, watching Yosef ben Hananiah spur his own horse over the next hill. The two of them had been out for more than half an hour, riding over the rolling hills outside Aleppo's walls. Along farmers' trails and across open pastures they went under a late summer sun, sometimes letting the horses walk, at others spurring them into a gallop. They both enjoyed these excursions, for the sport and more, for the sense of freedom. Yosef, as he had grown almost into manhood at age 17 increasingly came to take their rides together for granted. Yehuda, whom life had taught to expect the worst and plan for it to appear all of a sudden, knew better.

The boy slowed his mount and as Yehuda drew alongside, asked, "Shall we water the horses at the stream ahead?"

"No," said Yehuda. "We'll cross upstream on the way back. We can stop then."

"What's wrong?" Yosef asked.

He's learning, the big man thought appreciatively. He's becoming more observant. But soon enough?

"What have you noticed since we've been out?" Yehuda asked him.

"In the past few minutes, you mean?"

"Yes."

"A little dust cloud above the trees along the stream bank. But it's almost gone now," Yosef said.

"Good," said Yehuda. "What does that tell you?"

"There's almost no wind today. So, something, or someone, must have caused the dust to rise," the boy answered.

"Maybe some grazing cattle come down to the bank to drink. Or perhaps people, people with horses," Yehuda said. "How many, do you think?"

"The cloud was small. If caused by a man, or men, on horseback, maybe one. No more than three," Yosef said.

"That would be my guess," Yehuda said approvingly. They wheeled their horses and began to trot back toward the city. As they did, not one, not three but four horsemen broke from the tree line along the stream and galloped toward them, shouting and swinging swords.

Yehuda smoothly reached for the short, laminated cavalry bow attached to his saddle, fitted an arrow into the bowstring, and let it fly. The rider nearest them, no more than 50 yards off, screamed, plummeted to the ground and lay still. The other three continued toward them, closing to roughly 30 yards before Yehuda brought down another, who managed to rise to his feet, cursing in pain as he grasped one arm with the other.

Now the remaining two were on them. Swords clanged against swords. A man screamed as blood spurted from his shoulder. Yehuda's blade had slashed deep, through muscle, tendon and an artery. But the big man could not turn quickly enough to intercept the fourth attacker before the latter's sword tip found his ribs.

Yosef struggled to control his mount. Unlike Yehuda's, it never before had smelled the sweat, blood, fear and elation of humans on horseback furiously attempting to kill each other. It reared twice before Yosef finally pulled close enough to jab his short blade into the back of the man struggling with Yehuda. The man, whose leather head covering slid off, revealing a face that looked to be no older than Yosef's, rolled his eyes up under their lids and, without a sound, dropped to the hard-baked earth and lay motionless.

"Go!" Yehuda told Yosef. "Go on ahead. At the city gate, give the password—'*wardat jamila al yawm*'—rose of the day. I will come after you." Yehuda paused, then wheezed a command: "Go, now!"

The big man sat almost upright on his horse. But Yosef saw the red smear spreading across the side of his garment, saw Yehuda's left hand clutching his horse's mane for support. He opened his mouth to speak.

"Leave me! Now!" Yosef had never heard Yehuda's voice so thin before. He turned and rode toward the city, crying.

"*Wardat jamila al yawm,*" he sobbed to the watchman.

****

"There are too many bandits! Too many and now too bold!" thundered Ali ibn-Sharif, viceroy of Aleppo. "Raids once in a while, small affairs, we can swat them away or merely ignore them. But weekly, sometimes daily? It's too much! It unsettles the people and it disrupts trade, which means it undercuts taxes."

"Yes, but putting down the bandits—sending troops to scour the hill country for what probably would turn out to be a long campaign since the bandits won't stay put—that too would unsettle the public, acknowledging we have a problem. Also," said Hussein ibn-Hussein, one of the viceroy's closest advisors, "it would be expensive, requiring us to redirect funds, raise taxes again, or both. There must be an alternative."

"There always is," the viceroy sighed. "We can crackdown on the Jews one more time."

"Of course," said ibn-Hussein, "the bandits are mostly secret pagans, not real Muslims. And some are Christians. But there are more pretend Muslims and more Christians in Aleppo than there are Jews, even if Jews are some of the wealthiest merchants. So, we make an example of the children of Israel, and the others will get the message."

"We'll increase the *jizya* tax and raise more revenue. We need the money anyway," Ali ibn-Sharif said. "Still, I wonder how many more times we can squeeze this particular goose."

"Someday we might find it is once too many," ibn-Hussein conceded. "But the Jews are comparatively few, weak. That always makes me wonder: Why are they hated so?"

"Just because they are few and weak," the viceroy said. "But not only that. I have thought about this many times. It's not enough to say the Muslims, the Christians, the Arabs hate the Jews because they are few and weak—that might be a reason to tolerate them. No, there's something more. It's because the Jews, even in their small numbers, their inability to stand against their enemies, nevertheless consider themselves our equals, if not our betters. Not because tomorrow we couldn't crush them all; they know that. But because they were given the law that Allah bequeathed to Musa on the mountain, they and no one else. Those laws make us more than animals, raise us up as humans. Because they were the original custodians, they feel superior in their spirit, in their minds, even if we make them inferior in their bodies, in their life. They know it and we feel it. So, they go on being Jews, even when oppressed, and we go on hating them, even though in power."

"Yes, what would we do without our Jews?" ibn-Hussein mused.

"Fight each other, even more frequently," Ali ibn-Sharif said.

Chapter Three:
Jerusalem, the Present

Aaron Yehezkieli closed the book in front of him, took off his glasses, laid them beside the leather-bound volume on the table and rubbed his eyes. This Thursday afternoon he had taken an hour off teaching to re-read parsha *Vayigash*, the weekly Torah portion dealing with the reunion of Joseph—by then viceroy of Egypt—with his brothers twenty-two years after they had sold him into slavery. Rabbi Yehezkieli had been reading, or rather pouring over Torah and Talmud for nearly 70 years, since childhood. And each time he took them up, he found the truth asserted by the words of the ancient sage Ben Bag-Bag, "turn it and turn it"—*turn to it and return to it*. In the very old there was always something new.

Rabbi Yehezkieli propounded the late Rabbi Lord Jonathan Sacks' view of the *parsha*. Queen Elizabeth II had made Sacks a life peer in the House of Lords in 2005. He then styled himself "Rabbi Lord" Sacks, not "Lord Rabbi Sacks," jesting that he wanted to keep the order straight. According to Sacks, the concept of forgiveness entered the Torah, in fact entered written history, for the first time in *Vayigash*. Joseph forgives his brothers when he sees their reluctance to take their youngest sibling, Benjamin, favorite of his father Ya'akov, from the old man in Cana'an and bring him to Egypt as Joseph insists. Joseph realizes their hesitation stems from recognition and regret over an earlier transgression. That had come when they jealously ripped him, their father's first favored son, from Ya'akov's side more than two decades before.

Sacks taught that forgiveness, when earned by the transgressor and granted by the victim, restored and tended to equalize both. It was, he insisted, possible only in a guilt-and-forgiveness culture like that of the Israelites, and adopted later by Christianity. To shame-and-honor cultures such as those of the Greeks and other earlier, ancient, pagan societies surrounding the twelve tribes descendant from Ya'akov, forgiveness was foreign. Acknowledging one's guilty action and genuinely seeking forgiveness was, in Sacks' view, necessary for an individual to fully realize his or her humanity. Shame-and-honor societies, on the other hand, defaulted to appeasement or retribution. These denied human equality and so perpetuated unequal power relationships and conflicts. Like the conflict many Arabs, many Muslims have with us, Rabbi Yehezkieli mused.

Generally, rabbis paid less attention to the *haftorahs*, the short companion selections usually from the Prophets, read aloud each Shabbat morning after the Torah portion. But Rabbi Yehezkieli found that of his name-sake, Ezekiel, Chapter 37, verses 18 to 29, chosen by the sages to follow *Vayigash*, compelling. It relates the Jews' return to Judea from Babylonian captivity, as recalled not only in the Torah but also on the Cyrus Seal long held in the British Museum. In the *parsha*, Joseph forgave his brothers, and in the *haftorah* God announced through the prophet that He was forgiving and restoring the Jews.

In chapter 37, Ezekiel—both a member of the priesthood and a prophet, an immediate successor of Jeremiah and who, his book relates, conveyed God's word to the captives in Babylonia after the fall of the First Temple in 586 B.C.E.—envisions the valley of dry bones reanimated. First, he inspired the dispirited exiles with this vision of the Jewish nation revived. Then, with a second conceptualization, he promises reunification of the remaining two tribes in Judea, Judah and Benjamin, with the so-called lost ten tribes. These were Dan, Naphtali, Issachar, Gad, Reuben, Asher, Simeon, Zebulon, Manasseh and Ephraim. Historically, they had not been lost but exiled and scattered from 733 to 722 B.C.E. by the Assyrians, who replaced them in what had been their northern kingdom of Israel, in Hebrew *Shomron* (Samaria) with other peoples. Ezekiel forecast not only the restoration of the Jews to life but the nation to prominence:

"So says the Lord God: 'Behold, I will take the children of Israel from among the nations, where they are gone, and gather them on every side, and bring them into their own land; and I will make them one nation in the land, upon the mountains of Israel, and one king shall be king to them all. … And My servant David shall be king over them." David's heirs shall reign forever, Ezekiel says, relating God's vow and his words that "the nations shall know that I am the Lord that sanctify Israel, when My sanctuary shall be in the midst of them forever.'" So, the Third Temple—brought down from the heavens, not built up from the ground by man—said the prophet.

Ezekiel's fantastical visions, beginning immediately in chapter one with God's flashing, jewel-like chariot, the airborne Merkava with its crew of four-faced creatures that passed before him along the banks of the Euphrates River, eventually provided material for 20th century science fiction. Much earlier, it unsettled some of the rabbinic authorities who ultimately canonized the Hebrew Bible by roughly 100 C.E. It unsettled them so much that they had considered omitting it. Best that they had not, thought Rabbi Yehezkieli, and not for the first time. Bizarre-sounding though some of Ezekiel could be on first reading, the rabbi returned and returned again to the work as to a familiar friend. That Israeli armor officers in 1979 had named their new main battle tank—now in its fourth generation—the Merkava, both amused and cautioned him.

Rabbi Yehezkieli felt at times that his lifelong study and teaching of Torah and Talmud—the extensive commentary on the Hebrew Bible compiled from discussions, debates and rulings by rabbinic sages from roughly 400 B.C.E. to nearly 500 C.E.—had trained him as an archaeologist. An archaeologist of Judaism, sifting through successive layers of commentary and interpretation down through the centuries, trying, always delicately, like an archaeologist on a dig, gently brushing the dust of ages off what would be revealed as a glittering coin or legible shard. A coin or shard from when the Second Temple—or perhaps even the First—had stood, high priests had prayed, prophets spoken and kings ruled from Jerusalem.

A fifth-generation Jerusalemite and current head of the Yehezkieli rabbinic dynasty originally from Baghdad, the rabbi stood and stretched. It would soon be sundown, not enough light left to continue reading in the little courtyard of the *Or Zahav* (Golden Light) *Yeshiva* Rabbi Yehezkieli led. The school occupied an old but still-elegant late Ottoman-era stone structure in the Rehavia neighborhood just west of central Jerusalem. The interior of the building featured arched passageways along ground floor corridors on each side of the square, three-story building. The arches opened into the bougainvillea-lined courtyard. There an old, delicately carved stone fountain burbled in the center. Sundown was time for the evening *Ma'ariv* prayers.

With 108 students Or Zahav was not a large school, especially not as Jerusalem *yeshivot* went. But the rabbi, as *rosh yeshiva,* head of the institute, thought it about perfect. At that number, he, his two rabbinical assistants and the school's four other teachers were able to maintain close relationships with every student. They guided their studies, interactions with each other and, as much as possible, their spiritual as well as intellectual growth.

Besides, 108 was a multiple by six of 18, *chai* in Hebrew numerology. *Chai* meant life. The rabbi had been one of six children. Brothers and sisters became doctors, lawyers, army officers, fathers, wives and mothers. The black sheep among them worked as an accountant. But the rabbi was his generation's only religious scholar, its link in the Yehezkieli dynastic chain. So, 108 students—between the ages of 18 and 30—it was. A majority of *yeshivot* taught students from primary school age to—in many cases—the rest of their lives, their families receiving government subsidies often resented by more secular Israelis. But Rabbi Yehezkieli gave more than lip service to the Talmudic injunction that one studied in order to be active in the world, not to withdraw from the world in order to become learned. Of course, one was properly most active in the world when learned, on the basis of Torah study.

Paraphrasing Maimonides, Rabbi Yehezkieli taught that one studied Torah for its own sake, yes, but having studied it one then performed its teachings, its *mitzvot*, the commandments, in the world. Not meditating alone on some mountain peak, but involved in daily life. Involved the right way, the sanctified way. That was how one made the world a better place. Which was, after all, the Jew's job description, he mused yet again. Whether the world wanted be improved, to be disturbed, jarred from its indulgences and complacencies and sanctified or not.

"Aaron, the *talmidim* are waiting to *daven*," his wife, Rebbetzin P'nina Yehezkieli, reminded him, referring to the students. The rebbetzin stood under one of the arches, holding an envelope. A scholar in her own right, she taught classes three times a week, for women only. She also wrote a twice-monthly column on family matters for *Israel HaYom* (Israel Today), aimed at readers observant, secular and in-between.

The rabbi and his wife had a small family by the standards of very observant Jews in Jerusalem—only five children. There were three girls and two boys, all married adults. Which meant that Aaron and P'nina already lovingly indulged 16 grandchildren, many of whom could be found along with their parents at their grandparents' Shabbat dinner table, a long "T"-shaped affair that extruded from dining room into the living room. They were there for the food, blessings and conversation. In summer when sundown came late and dinner later, the talk extended to midnight and beyond. This was western Jerusalem; families walking home in the wee hours of Saturday morning, even pushing young children asleep in strollers under fragrant pines, were common.

"You might want to read this before you start," P'nina said, handing the envelope to her husband. "It just came, by messenger."

The envelope bore the embossed insignia of the prime minister's office. The single line on heavy, cream-colored stationery read, "I would like to speak with you *motzei* Shabbat regarding my coming trip to the United States." The prime minister's thick but legible signature scrawl ran underneath it.

Three evenings later, after Shabbat, Rabbi Yehezkieli strolled the few blocks from Ohr Zahav to the prime minister's official residence on Balfour Street. Israel was a small country, barely 10 million people, almost eight million Jews among them, on a pencil-thin land stretching just 260 miles from Lebanon at the north to the Red Sea on the south, rarely more than 35 miles east to west. Its capital, modern Jerusalem, itself a sprawling city, nevertheless was assembled, puzzle-like, from a series of compact, interlocking neighborhoods. So, such a stroll was unremarkable, especially among senior members of overlapping circles in government, commerce, academia, journalism and religion. Scent from evergreens reminded him of hiking as a youth along the Carmel range near Haifa. So long ago and yet recent in his memory. Time had fled from him through his children and now into his grandchildren. With great-grandchildren to come it fled faster.

The city was returning to secular life after the profound quiet of Shabbat; restaurants and taverns reopened, motorcycles and automobiles—when not blocked by Egged transit buses—cruised along the streets. Sidewalks filled with people, many of them young. An answer to his unspoken question of what the prime minister wanted this time was not long in coming.

Despite the long history between the two men—they had known each other as boys growing up in *Achuza*, a pleasant neighborhood in upper Haifa atop the Carmel ridge—there was no preliminary conversation about family or friends or even a sip or two of premium American bourbon. The prime minister started immediately. "How should I use my meetings with the president and secretaries of state and defense?" Alon Meir asked him. "I'd like to give them hell. It worked for Harry Truman, of course, when dealing with his political opponents. And God knows my hosts deserve it for their cowardice and double-dealing regarding us and our enemies. They've violated more than one written agreement between our two countries, including the most recent military Memorandum of Understanding to continue helping us maintain our qualitative edge in weaponry. And they've trashed more than one unwritten pledge, including to use the American veto in the U.N. Security Council when a resolution directly threatens Israel's right to defend itself or right to administer its own sovereign territory. Of course, in such cases they are not doing anything the first Bush, Obama and Biden administrations did not do. Administrations always go their own ways, unless Congress keeps their feet to the fire."

The prime minister paused and, hands clasped behind him, stared out an office window at twinkling city lights. Rabbi Yehezkieli stood by quietly.

"Or," Meir resumed, "should I try conciliation? Although—judging by some of their staff members, people who in the past never would have seen the inside of the White House or Pentagon except on a guided tour but who now, activists for this or that cause, rise unhindered by achievement—one cannot reconcile irreconcilables. There's the old diplomatic balance, 'on the one hand, this; on the other hand, that,' but it rarely gets small nations anything but good press. And not even that for this small one."

Still, Rabbi Yehezkieli said nothing.

"My quandary is that the ultimate audience is not the White House, Foggy Bottom or Pentagon, important as they are. My real audience is Congress and ultimately the American public. The administration undermines its allies by trying to appease its enemies, a pattern set in the past with Ukraine and Taiwan—hell, as far back as with South Vietnam, and with us cyclicallly versus the Palestinian Arabs. It sees us as a problem as much as it does part of the solution. Thank God that we still have friends in the Defense Department, if not in the defense secretary's office."

"*Baruch HaShem*," the rabbi finally said, breaking his silence. Bless the Lord, Thank God. "What I think ... that's all it is, what I think. I'm sure you've already spoken with your advisers, cabinet members and so on about this ..."

"Yes, Aaron" the prime minister said impatiently. "That's why I want to hear from you."

"I'll tell you what the Lubavitcher Rebbe, Rabbi Schneerson of blessed memory, told a young Bibi Netanyahu when he started as ambassador to the United Nations in the mid-1980s. 'You are going to a place of great darkness. Light a candle. Even a small source of light dispels much darkness.'

"The United States is not the same place it used to be. You attended university there. I have made several trips to America, on some occasions for months at a time, to study and teach. When it was a place where an Israeli graduate student from a politically prominent family could safely walk an Ivy League campus, where a man with a beard, wearing a dark suit and fedora—a man looking quite like an Orthodox rabbi—could ride the New York subway without incident, where synagogues did not need security guards or Jewish cemeteries surveillance cameras lest the tombstones be toppled.

"It's hardly a country full of Jew-haters of course. But revolutions are carried out by small, well-organized, cult-like members of ruthless ideological movements. And the United States today is full of such people. They block doors to synagogues, beat participants at Jewish book fairs, throw red paint on the homes of pro-Israel members of Congress and scream at parents dropping their children at Jewish day schools. And those who do so are rarely arrested and even less frequently prosecuted and jailed. This indulgence granted such antisemites allows other psychological descendants of such *Hitlerjugend* and *Komsomol* members to stab Jews on New York sidewalks and shoot them on the very streets of Washington, D.C.

"Somehow," Rabbi Yehezkieli told the prime minister, "you need to make Americans understand that our fight is their fight, for the values that made their country what Lincoln called 'mankind's last best hope,' values that came originally from Sinai."

"Yes," Alon Meir agreed. "That's why Lincoln also called the United States 'the almost promised land.'"

"When are you going?" the rabbi asked.

"In two days," the prime minister answered. "A day in New York, with our U.N. ambassador there, an interview with WABC-TV, which I expect to go national, and a visit to my old friend Rabbi Samson at the Jewish Outreach and Learning Organization. Then the Washington stop and finally cross-country to Los Angeles for a Jewish Federation fundraising gala. Some federation leaders pleaded with me not to come—some were afraid they could never manage security. Others were afraid an appearance by an Israeli prime minister 'at this time might prove divisive'—with emphasis on divisive—'within the community.' I told them not to worry; we and the L.A. police department would take care of security, and as for 'divisiveness,' Jewish history's full of it, and somehow, we overcome."

"Greater New York, Washington, D.C. and L.A.," the rabbi mused. "More than three million Jews there, almost 20 percent of all of us in the world. A lot of them probably don't see the inside of a synagogue more than a couple times a year, let alone know any Hebrew. Nevertheless, a great many have Israel in their hearts and Judaism somewhere deep in their souls. So, you must go, and speak forcefully, regardless of who currently holds what office."

"Yes," said the prime minister. "Think what we could do with ten percent of them."

"You know, I'll be arriving in the U.S. about the time you depart," Rabbi Yehezkieli said.

"What for?"

"A series of lectures, and the English publication of my new book," the rabbi replied, without a trace of pride that might be expected from one who already had made the best-seller list, if briefly, three years earlier. That book was *From Torah to Today: Words That Matter*. About it the Jewish reviewer for *The Washington Post* had written, "If you think 'ethical monotheism' is a thing, you'll probably like Rabbi Yehezkieli's greeting card-style theology."

"What's the new book about?" the prime minister asked.

"The mystical meaning of the difference between genuine and false prophets and how that relates to our day," the rabbi said, smiling a little.

"Soon to be a major motion picture," the prime minister laughed.

Chapter Four:
702 C.E., Aures Mountains

She was tired, exhausted really. Hers had been a long war, extending across more than two decades and much of North Africa, and it was only part of a half-century struggle. She had fought not just bravely but brilliantly, first as an aide-de-camp to her uncle, the great Berber chieftain Kusaila, then as one his fierce bodyguards. He soon promoted her to field officer, and after he died—some said of wounds, others of a spell—she took his place as leader.

A woman warrior in an army of men was virtually unprecedented. There had been, of course, the biblical Dvorah, who held the same stature as male Judges like Samson and Gideon, but almost no others. As its leader, unthinkable among the Berbers, the multifarious tribes who referred to themselves as Imazighen. Except for a personality like hers. But now all her victories over nearly twenty years and all those of the Jewish Berber Jarawa tribe and their allies for thirty years before that were coming to naught. Three columns from the biggest invading Arab army yet seen in the Maghreb pushed up valleys of the Aures, trapping her and her men between them and steep mountain peaks.

Her birth name was Dihya, "the beautiful gazelle" in the tongue of the Jarawa and fitting for a princess of the ruling clan. The Jarawa were descendants of the 100,000 Jews deported from Judea, according Josephus Flavius, the Jewish general turned Roman commander and later historian, at the end of the First Roman-Jewish War in 73 C.E. Most were transported as slaves to Rome. But nearly 30,000 went to Carthage. Nearly all the deportees, both to Rome and Carthage, were men, Zealots who had fought as soldiers in the war against Titus and his legions. Though slaves, they nevertheless needed to find wives, and this they did among Berber women. As Zealots, they meant to perpetuate the Jewish people and, if not immediately, eventually restore their destroyed Jewish kingdom. Their descendants were joined after 135 C.E. by 10,000 survivors of the Second Roman War. That was the six-year struggle by a small people against the ancient world's superpower, in which the Jews—led by Shimon ben Kosiba, better known as bar-Kochba, son of the star—first retook the Galilee and pushed the Legionnaires from Jerusalem.

Rabbi Akiva, the greatest sage of the time, declared of bar-Kochba that "a star shall shoot forth from Jacob." This Torah citation, of Numbers 24:17, virtually anointed bar-Kochba as messiah. But the early Christians refused to join his revolt against Rome, as that would have made one messianic figure too many. Rome, facing the most threatening rebellion yet, reinforced Vespasian's army with legions from throughout the empire. It finally prevailed and a bloodbath ensued. Emperor Hadrian determined to face no more Jewish rebellions, in fact, to face no more Jews. Hundreds of thousands were slaughtered, tens of thousands deported in slavery to presumed assimilation and disappearance. Hadrian ordered Jerusalem plowed over, and, after minting coins reading "Judaea Capta," Judea Conquered, he attempted to erase even the memory of Jews and their land. He decreed the place renamed "Syria-Palestina" after the long-vanished Greek Philistines.

But the former Zealot fighters deported to Carthage did not assimilate and did not disappear. As their masters dispersed them into the countryside beyond the city, these defeated and enslaved soldiers, stubborn Jews that they were, sought wives. So, at least by tribal tradition, the Jarawa came to be.

Although reports trickled in of warfare to the east, Dihya, daughter of Tabat, a chief among the Jarawa, grew up in a world of prosperity and peace. She had an affinity for animals, able to communicate with them yet barely speaking a word, and learned to ride well. Curiously, Dihya also had an affinity for bow and arrow, not to mention swords. Though most young Berber girls were not likely to come into contact with such weapons, the princesses could ask for and receive them, and instruction as well. Tabat smiled on his military-minded daughter. If he had a son, a male heir as vigorous as she, it would have been well. But he had Dihya, and that, it seemed to him, was even better.

Chapter 4

The beautiful gazelle's world changed when the Arab armies appeared. By then a young woman with long black hair, large black eyes and who stood taller than most men, Dihya acquired a new name. Not only taller than all but a few of the males around her, she also was fiercer, and more far-seeing. Dihya became known throughout the region as al-Kahina—the Sorceress, the name bestowed in hatred by her Arab enemies, adopted in pride by her followers.

"Sorceress," her father scoffed. "This 'al-Kahina' is an Arabic corruption of the Hebrew, ha-Kohenet, the daughter of the Cohen. My lovely child is a descendant of the family of high priests who long ago served in the Temples in Jerusalem."

"The priests? Are you sure," her uncle Kusaila smiled. "I rather think, as many say, that Dihya comes, like yourself, from the line of kings in Jerusalem."

Princess of priests or of kings, she featured in stories the Jarawa told to illustrate Dihya's—or al-Kahina's—unflinching will. One concerned a distant cousin, the leader of a small tribal clan. He proposed marriage, several times. Al-Kahina, who had known him in childhood, refused each time. She had formed an opinion of him as short, soft, and stupid, a boy who would never be a man.

Eventually, the rejected suitor began raiding the Jarawa. Thievery followed thievery. "For the good of our people," al-Kahina said, and acquiesced. Then, the night of their wedding, she found that the short, soft, stupid child had grown to be a short, almost threateningly muscular, stupid man. In the bridal tent they fought, two determined people wrestling with each other. They grappled, sweated, fell and, grunting, rose to fight on. Tabat forcibly dispersed the crowd that had gathered outside the tent. Finally victorious, her cousin proudly, one might say haughtily consummated their union. The new groom then fell asleep. At which point al-Kahina took a mallet and drove a spike through his skull. Had she known she had been impregnated and would bear a son, her only child, the beautiful gazelle would not have acted otherwise. As it was, that night after wrapping her late husband's remains in a small carpet that she had never cared for, the sorceress received a vision. In it she was forced to hand her son to another.

As head of the Barghawata Berber confederacy, with his powerful Jarawa at its core, Kusaila won many victories against the Arab armies trying to carry their newfounded religion of Islam westward from Egypt after 680 C.E. His successes, first in guerrilla ambushes, then in open battles against generals sent by the Umayyad caliphs, swelled Kusaila's forces with Visigoths from Spain, Romans, black Numidians, Christians, Vandals from the German territories by way of Rome and other pagans. The Arabs might have swept through the rotting Persian and Byzantine empires in the Middle East and eastern Mediterranean, but facing the Berbers and their diverse allies in the Maghreb—the Byzantines' semi-autonomous Exarchate of Africa—every advance seemed to be followed by a retreat. This went on for decades.

That is, until 697 C.E. when General Hassan ibn Numan led 45,000 veteran soldiers, a force of size and training unseen in North Africa until then, against Carthage. Rebuilt and repopulated after the Roman conquest in 146 B.C.E., the prosperous, cosmopolitan city served as capital of the exarchate, Byzantium's religious and political district in the Maghreb.

"The Arabs will be here in three days," Hasdurbal III stated, his matter-of-fact, almost laconic tone revealing little emotion. "We know what they've done to those who have resisted them, resisted and refused their 'offer' to convert. Fighters, traders, farmers, men, women, the old, the young, they make no distinction."

"Yes," said his brother, Hamilcar the Younger. "But they won't find us here. The Byzantine navy—at least what's left of it—arrives tomorrow. Everyone is organized according to plan; we will take the entire population and all the gold, silver, ivory and other valuables we can carry to Sicily. Only the soldiers will stay to fight."

"We'll see how long it takes ibn Numan to digest his empty victory," Hasdrubal said. "With luck, he and his frustrated army will die of thirst in the desert."

General Hassan ibn Numan was too smart and too patient to waste his men in a pointless siege of a fortified city empty of every prize but with a determined fighting force awaiting him. He understood Hasdrubal's tactics. After surveying Carthage's three defensive rings, personally inspecting the city's water sources and examining the port facilities, he withdrew. Early the next year the Byzantine navy returned in triumph, carrying the Carthaginians home.

For nearly a year, the repopulated city thrived. A mood of nearly delirious happiness settled over Carthage. Trade across the Mediterranean, that vast water-borne market place, had never been better, the entertainment in the city's amphitheater never brighter, even the good weather, it was said, was a gift from well-disposed gods. The Arabs, it was believed, had retreated all the way to Egypt, harried by Berber ambushes. Having learned their lesson, having been outsmarted by Hasdrubal and his people, the Jarawa prominent among them, ibn Numan's army would not be back soon, if ever. Only Hasdrubal III and his brother, Hamilcar the Younger, felt uneasy.

"What did she say?" Hasdrubal asked his brother, referring to the most prominent woman in Carthage and its environs, a woman both he and his brother Hamilcar longed for but could not possesses.

"Al-Kahina says that indeed, General Hassan is coming, that his force is even larger than before, and we will not be able to hold the city," Hamilcar responded.

"How does she know this? Another of her damned dreams or visions or whatever she calls them?"

"A vision. It came to her at noon, in daylight, not a dream. That what she says, anyway."

"She would be tiresome, that woman, were she not so uncanny. Were she not so strong, so beautiful," Hasdrubal mused.

"That's the problem, isn't it?" his brother answered. "If only we knew her to be wrong once in a while, knew one of her pronouncements to have been mistaken."

"What was she doing when you spoke with her?" Hasdrubal asked.

"Does it matter? She was talking with a falcon perched on her shoulder."

"Talking with a falcon!?" Hasdrubal exploded. "What did this bird, her familiar, say to his sorceress?"

"It was not a conversation I could hear," Hamilcar said. "There were no words, hardly any sounds except for an occasional cry from the falcon. But looking at them, and I approached quite closely before they deigned to notice me, and then both at the same time, I could tell they were communicating."

For a commander of audacity when called for, of restraint, when necessary, of creativity always, Hasdrubal III felt exasperated, maddeningly so.

"Well, she is going to be wrong this time! I, Hasdrubal, descendant of Hannibal Barca himself, will prove her so!"

His brother shook his head. "I doubt it. They call her The Sorceress, but she is something else…"

"What else!?" Hasdrubal interrupted.

"A prophetess," Hamilcar replied.

"You only talk like that because you love her, and unrequited love is the worst. The heart clouds the mind," Hasdrubal declared.

"You should know as well as I," his brother said.

"Don't be ridiculous. I have wives enough without her, as if she could ever be a wife," Hasdrubal said.

"With a wife like that, a man would need no other," his brother responded.

"With her as a wife, a man could imagine no other," Hasdrubal said, almost in a whisper. Then, louder, "call in the commanders. We must plan for ibn Numan."

The plan succeeded, for a while. Night sorties from the city hit selected points of the besieging army. Greek fire catapulted into tents of Arab officers, the chemical incendiaries quickly burning the shelters and all within. And raids by Jarawa horsemen on the rear of ibn Numan's forces disrupted supply lines.

The Arab general expected this from the defenders. It could detain but not deter him. Using his overwhelming numbers he soon severed Carthage's connection to its port and cut off its main water sources. And he methodically undermined its ringed fortifications.

Fierce resistance from the Carthaginians inflicted many losses on the Arabs. This only served to enrage ibn Numan. When his troops finally broke through the innermost defensive ring, he gave the order for which history still remembers him: Massacre all the inhabitants and demolish all of Carthage.

But the order was not quite fulfilled. With Hasdrubal dead and Hamilcar captured, al-Kahina led the remaining Jarawa. Still a sizeable and organized force, the tribesmen retreated in good order to the city of el Djem. El Djem was no Carthage, but then Carthage was no more. Its destruction by ibn Numan had sent shockwaves across the Maghreb. Would the Arabs impose themselves on all the peoples of the region?

Al-Kahina did not intend to find out. In 699 C.E. her Jarawa and their remaining non-Jewish Berber allies fortified the old Roman amphitheater at el Djem's center. It served as a refuge and hub from which she led guerrilla attacks on ibn Numan's forces. Her success drew survivors from the Byzantine Exarchate's army and Visigoth tribes to her side. When the Arab general sent a larger force against her early in 702 C.E., she defeated it in open battle, using a battleplan recalled from Alexander the Great: Feint to the left and while holding the center, roll up the enemy's right, weakened as it would be by the adversary's move to reinforce his left.

"That's it!" ibn Numan stormed upon receiving word of the defeat. "We are going to find this witch, this so-called sorceress, pin her against the mountains and let her prophesy her own death!"

"I've already sent a detachment to find her in the Aures," said Mahmoud Ali, one of his most reliable captains. "It has not yet returned."

"And it won't. A single detachment against al-Kahina is doomed. If necessary, we will divide the army into enough columns to move through every valley, choke off every hiding place until the Jarawa and its allies, and its leader this, this … woman! are destroyed!" General Hassan ibn Numan spat those final words.

That last open-field victory had been months ago. The weight of the Arab army pressed al-Kahina's guerrillas into ever smaller, less effective raids. The final battle would come within the week. Three falcons circled her tent one night as the sun set, its usually orange rays against a pale blue sky, warm and reassuring, now turned blood red against a sky oddly green-gray. She saw the light as a last harsh gasp of day.

Each falcon landed in turn on the broad gold wristband above her right hand. Their news was as al-Kahina expected. Three big Arab columns, each nearly ten thousand men, had converged deep into the valley where she had sought refuge. Combined, they would push al-Kahina and her remaining Jarawa and their last allies, some local Christians and a few Visigoths, no more than five thousand total, against cliffs at the valley's head. The Romans, Nubians, and others who had retreated with her to el Djem had melted away long since.

Her falcons imparted one piece of intelligence she had not foreseen. A messenger would come from ibn Hassan under a flag of truce. Thirty years of stories, twenty years of experience, told her to expect nothing from an Arab truce offer.

Meanwhile, one more thing remained to be accomplished. "Lunja," she said softly, "ask Usaden to bring Yedder to me. I must tell them something."

If al-Kahina had been a queen, and these last caves, crags and precipices to which she and her force had been driven a castle, then Lunja would have been one of her ladies-in-waiting. As it was, the raven-haired girl just now passing through puberty reminded al-Kahina of herself when she still answered to Dihya. And her name, Lunja, would have been appropriate at court, meaning "fairy princess" as it did.

Yedder was al-Kahina's son, now twelve years old and, his mother thought with the merest sentiment she allowed herself, quite the self-possessed little man. That was fortunate, since he and Usaden would need all the self-possession they could muster. Usaden was, well, just who was he? al-Kahina asked herself as she had more than once. Start with the mystery of his name. Usaden was Berber, of course, but vague, a place name referring to an unknown location. The name also was masculine but with no one single attribute attached to it.

Very like the man himself, al-Kahina thought. A quite tangible mystery. He seemed to appear out the Jarawa forces soon after Yedder's birth. He informed the new mother that her fatherless child would need a male guide, and that the son of al-Kahina would need a bodyguard as well. Usaden was persuasive without being overbearing. About thirty years old, powerfully built, he strangely enough also could read and write, and promised to teach the boy, which he did. They became nearly inseparable, for which al-Kahina was glad. Had she not been burdened by leadership, by battle, she might well have taken a personal interest in this Usaden herself. But that was impossible under the circumstances. So, she told herself, several times.

"Yedder, please listen to me. I know you are a smart, brave boy. I want you to go with Usaden tomorrow at dawn. You and he will take the foot trail north over the mountains to Hadrumete on the coast. Then go by ship to Sicily and the port of Syracuse. There are Berber there and they have a synagogue. Ask for 'the Jewish steps,' because the synagogue is deep underground, down three flights of steep steps, carved out of the rock long ago so the Romans could not find it. There you will learn what you need to know, and meet people you need to meet. Do you understand me?"

With both arms tight around his mother's waist, tears in his eyes, the boy looked up at her and nodded. "Yes," he said.

She smiled, bent and kissed him. Not for nothing had she named him Yedder, which among the Jarawa meant "he will be alive," and symbolized the immortality of an unconquerable soul. Usaden bowed, straightened and said, "Your son will live his name."

The following morning, Yedder and Usaden already well on their way, al-Kahina received a delegation from ibn Numan under a flag of truce. "We have a message for you from the general," the chief envoy said.

"Well, what is it?"

"He will grant you and your followers a complete amnesty, provided only that you pledge allegiance to the Caliphate and convert to Islam."

"I am sure he imagines that is generous," al-Kahina said. "But tell him this is my reply: I shall die in the religion I was born into, free on free land."

The envoy did not bow but turned, signaled to the rest of the delegation, and rode back down the mountainside.

Calling Lunja to her side, al-Kahina said, "Tell Captain Wararni to report to me. We have much to prepare." As soon as the girl had gone, al-Kahina entered her tent, pulled the flap closed, and slumped on some cushions. She was more than exhausted, she was drained. But tomorrow would be another day. Unlikely better, but at least another. Probably the last one. When Captain Wararni found her, al-Kahina was honing her sword against a small block of novaculite.

Chapter Five:
New York City, The Present

"Is diaspora over?" Joshua Golden angrily asked the question many Jews still would not permit themselves to formulate. "There's an antisemitic outrage every week—every day if you read the Jewish press," he was saying. "Jew-haters rioted in Montreal last night, smashing windows in a Jewish neighborhood, setting cars on fire, marching in the streets and giving the stiff-armed Nazi salute."

"The Canadian government says it is outraged," Rabbi Samson said. "Not so much that *keffiyeh*-wearing neo-Nazis went on a rampage but that it took city police half an hour to respond. Apparently, after being alerted repeatedly by Jewish community leaders that something was up, the police commissioner left for a vacation."

"I don't know about Canada," Joshua Golden said. "I'm told it's a foreign country. But here in New York City certainly, not all assaults are reported. The police, politicians and news media recognize that the perpetrators often come from other minority groups—African Americans, Muslim Americans, sometimes Hispanics—and often downplay those that are reported. Right and wrong is one thing, self-interest in the face of voting blocs bigger and angrier than the Jews is something else again."

"Not a pretty picture, but one that reinforces your question," Rabbi Samson replied. "The answer to the question 'is Diaspora over?' depends on the answer to another question, which is: 'Is America over?' By that I mean the America in which, after World War II, after the Holocaust, Jews convinced themselves that they were part of a generalized civic religion based on something they were pleased to hear called the Judeo-Christian ethic. An America in which a majority of Jews actually lived in the *goldene medinah*, the envisioned golden country their Yiddish-speaking parents and grandparents immigrated to. An America with a broad middle class, secularized but still culturally traditional.

"Is that American is dissolving?" he went on. "Is a nation undergirded by the Anglo-Protestant civic culture, a culture that had absorbed what it thought of as 'Old Testament' morality, becoming a multipolar, almost tribal confederation of identity groups with a shrinking middle class squeezed between elites and a struggling working class? And are the non-elites simultaneously dependent on and angry with the welfare state? Is much of the country dumbed-down and divided by social media, communications and entertainment media? Is it divided by the very schools it looks to for education but instead gets indoctrination into secular fundamentalism, this so-called woke progressivism? If it is, what happens to the Jews, the People of the Book and writers and readers of so many books?"

"Your 'questions' sound more rhetorical than interrogative," Joshua said. "Isn't a post-book culture in some way post-literary, or even pre-literary, pre-literate? Hence ever-expanding use of acronyms and emojis in texts messages instead of words, hieroglyphics in place of language?"

Rabbi Reuven Samson did not reply directly. Instead, he said, "Look, we have to recognize when the ground shifts beneath our feet. In 1960, American Jews totaled about six million or three percent of a population of 180 million. That overall population, whether church-going or not, remained largely influenced by an Anglo-Protestant public culture. In that culture the Jews were more or less tolerated almost as if we'd been another small Christian sect. Individual Jews could and did flourish in all walks of life.

"Now, still maybe about six million thanks mostly to immigrants from the former Soviet Union and, unfortunately, from the incessantly pressured Promised Land, American Jews are more like 1.8 percent of a much more culturally diverse population of around 340 million. Due both to shrinking demographics and a 'diversity, equity and inclusion' ideology that marginalizes us not as an exemplary minority but rather as 'white adjacent' and therefore part of a 'racist hegemony,' we find ourselves virtually re-ghettoized politically and intellectually. Diaspora Jews are disdained as 'privileged' for our very successes, rather than recognized as accomplished despite historic obstacles. So, hatred of the Jews, thinly veiled as anti-Zionism—hatred for Israel, the most successful of the scores of post-colonial states—again becomes commonplace."

Joshua interrupted. "I can agree with your general perspective, but suggest that America was culturally diverse even before the Revolution. '*E pluribus unum*' and all that. Your critique would be strengthened by describing our contemporary body politic as less integrated, less assimilated—less *unum*—with an elite that pretends to disdain integration and assimilation except, of course, in the Hamptons, Palm Beach, Martha's Vineyard, Napa Valley and so on."

"Point taken," the rabbi said. "Hence the rejection of the concept of nationhood and resultant angry division over control of national borders. So, the real question is not 'is Diaspora over?' but rather 'is the United States that fought for itself in World War II and the Cold War—and not coincidentally for freedom and democracy in general, as it did against Islamic medievalism after Sept. 11, 2001—over?' Is history's longest running, most successful and most prosperous experiment in self-government still able to rally and defend itself? Will it defeat Chinese communist imperialism, Russian reactionary imperialism, Islamic imperialism like that of Iran, or Iran's ambitions, and their surrogates and collaborators? Can it eradicate the internal rot spawned by an individualism that has degenerated into radical personal autonomy for instance, the 'right' of the mentally ill and drug addicted to live on the streets, the 'right' of physicians to refuse to treat 'Zionist' patients, of men to dominate women's sports? Can an America that threw off the obligations that come with rights—in Judaism we might say the commandments, the *mitzvot*, that come with free will—survive? If it isn't able to recognize and defend its core values, then the United States and the longest running, freest, most prosperous and socially equal Jewish diaspora both are over."

"A Jew was murdered in the diamond district today. In daylight," Joshua Golden said. "Beaten on the sidewalk by three strangers. But not a robbery. They didn't take anything."

"He 'looked like a Jew'—black suit, white shirt, black hat," the rabbi said. "Something a killing like that changes things. In addition to destroying his family and the families that might have issued from it, and affecting the hundreds who might have been touched by it, it changes the pace of our work."

"How so?"

"It adds urgency," Rabbi Samson said. What he did not say was that the murder might have been a case of mistaken identity. But whose identity? Rabbi Yehezkieli's, the scholar now visiting the city? His own?

Chapter Six:
Havana, Cuba, the Present

It was late Friday afternoon. A slender, teenaged boy leaned against the seawall. He was staring out over the pale blue water. Waves smashed against the old, dark barrier just hard enough to send spray up ten feet or so and misting his face. El Malecón was one of his favorite places, in fact, his only special place. A triangular bit of promenade jutted out from the broad walk along the curving, six-lane road that separated central Havana from the sea. The road carried what traffic there was. With the city at his back and the water stretching toward the horizon in front of him, David ben-Veniste could almost forget where he was, forget what his prospects were.

He stood about five feet, ten inches tall and at barely 160 pounds, looked perhaps a bit underfed. But then, so were many of his peers. Many, but not all. Some were children of party members. His thick, curly black hair set off bright, hazel-colored eyes. More than a few girls found him handsome; others thought him unapproachable, peculiar even.

David ben-Veniste was 18, just out of secondary school and uninterested in attending the university—to study what, for what purpose in this land of the never-ending, never fulfilled, always aging "Revolución!"? The Havana he knew, the Cuba he had never left, not even for a weekend, was threadbare, impoverished, monotonously uninteresting but not too exhausted to be unable to beat those who sang of "Vida y Libertad!" instead of "Patria o Muerte!" and jail the poets of truly free verse. And ben-Veniste was a poet of sorts, a singer with a sparkling untrained tenor but commanding a two-octave range and letting go free-flying lyrics. This afternoon the occasional pedestrian passing behind him might have heard, as the boy gazed out to sea, a pleasant, mid-tempo tune, sung softly almost to himself, the Hebrew sounding nearly Spanish:

> "*Ani ma'amin b'emunah shleimah b'viat hamashiach,*
> *V'af al pi sh'yitmameah, im kol zeh*
> *Achakeh lo bechol yom sheyavo.*"
> I believe with perfect faith in the coming of the Messiah,
> And though he tarry,
> I will wait daily for his coming.

Channah ben-Veniste had been lucky. A colleague at work had a cousin who lived in a village outside the capital. For a "relative's price," that is, well under black market rates, the colleague purchased a large bag of fresh vegetables. For a "colleague's price," likewise less than black or even gray market costs, she resold enough to ben-Veniste so that she, her son David and sixteen-year-old daughter Dinah would have a big green salad to go with their too-frequent pasta and tomato sauce dinner, accompanied by small, expensive wedges of hard cheese.

Agriculturally, Cuba was a land of plenty, Channah knew. But something stood between the fields and her table. It was the same thing that had stood between her earnings as a physician and the government when she was sent with scores of others to Venezuela for two years to support Caracas in its "Bolivarian Revolución," a revolution that had reduced middle class families to eating their pets. It was the party and the government, essentially the same thing. Leasing its doctors to other struggling leftist regimes as a show of solidarity, the health ministry confiscated most of their earnings to prop up the chronically depreciating peso—worth about three American cents—not that she could ever save enough to convert to dollars.

"Is that you, David?" she called as the apartment door opened.

"Who else?" her son answered.

Who else indeed? One of her colleagues at the clinic recently had begun working part-time as a prostitute to help keep her own family fed and clothed. Channah had not asked how she kept her home life and second job separate; not yet, anyway. Nearly desperate, she would not let herself feel compelled. But since her husband, Ricardo, an electrical engineer, had joined a group attempting to pilot a motorized raft to Florida, compulsion loomed everywhere. None of their relatives or friends had heard from any of the rafters, and they had set out weeks ago.

"Did you work this morning?" she asked her son.

"Of course. But there was little to do. I finished shelving the supplies the Americans brought with them yesterday, and the pharmacy had few customers today," he said.

"Maybe the people of Havana are too healthy to need medicine," she joked.

"Maybe the people of Havana can't afford even our discounted stuff. Or don't want it; some of what the Americans bring has expired."

"Perhaps," Channah said. Or perhaps, she thought, people are reluctant to show themselves at pharmacies the government regulates but nevertheless terms private. Even when one closed her apartment door behind her in Havana, nothing could be assumed to be private. And the government, with its "block leaders" in every apartment building, did not care for private activities.

"I shouldn't sound ungrateful," David was saying. "The Americans—they are mostly Jews from B'nai B'rith, able to come on U.S. 'humanitarian' visas to help the Jewish community. Technically they're not just tourists having a good time seeing the ancient Fords and Chevies creeping around our workers' paradise, enjoying cheap cigars and cheaper Cuban women."

His mother shuddered.

"They do bring needed things, like aspirin, allergy pills, antiseptic ointments, bandages of all sorts, blood pressure monitors, vitamins, even some prescription drugs," David went on. "But it's all just a drop in the bucket. What this island needs …" His voice trailed off. "What this island needs …" he started again. "Never mind. What's for dinner?"

"Pasta and tomato sauce, a nice baguette I found at the bakery where I only had to stand in line half an hour, cheese and a big green salad."

"Fresh?!" he asked, amazed.

"Absolutely," his mother said. "Now go downstairs to the Fernandez's and get your sister."

Fernandez, Hernandez, Rodriguez, Mendes and Franco. The five Jewish Spanish family names. Of course, since at least the Inquisition most people with those names were not Jewish. Not as far as they knew. But their ancestors had known, some of them anyway.

Dinah ben-Veniste had turned 16 the week before. She was smart—more academically-inclined than her brother—pretty, about five feet, five inches tall and already shapely, with black hair even thicker and curlier than her brother's. Her usually effervescent personality seemed subdued this Friday evening.

"Not pasta again?" she complained. "How long has it been since we had beef for Shabbat dinner—for any dinner? Or even chicken, and not just the backs or the wings, but the breast?" Her mother felt the questions as demands.

"I'm doing the best I ..." Channah began.

Dinah interrupted. "I'm sorry, mama. I know. It's just too hard around here sometimes, especially since dad died."

"We don't know he's dead!" her mother nearly shouted.

"Mama, he and the others left weeks ago. No one's heard from any of them since."

Channah dabbed at her eyes with a handkerchief.

"Maybe the Cuban navy caught them and they're in prison. Or maybe they drifted ashore somewhere where they've been unable to contact us. Some remote island or even the jungle in southern Mexico or Guatemala. Someplace like that," her brother said.

"Maybe," Dinah replied without conviction. "Come on, let's eat," trying to change the subject and sound a bit more upbeat.

"First the blessings," Channah said, stuffing the handkerchief in an apron pocket. "Dinah, you and I will light the candles, your brother will bless the wine and the bread, and then we'll eat."

After dinner Dinah kissed her mother, stuck her tongue out at her brother, and announced she and Angelina Fernandez were going to the new pizza parlor just off the Malecón.

"It's mostly for the Norteamericanos and the Europeans, with their money, but Angelina and I have enough to share a beer and get a slice of pizza each."

"A Coke," Channah corrected. "and I still don't like you going out on Shabbat."

"They will sell us what we want," Dinah announced imperiously. Then she laughed, went into her closet of a bedroom, kicked off her sneakers, donned a pair of high heels over her stretch jeans, and, when Channah's back was turned, wobbled out.

"Be home before 11," her mother called after her.

Dinah did not stop at Angelina Fernandez's apartment. She did stop downstairs at the building's entryway. Under the dim lightbulb—brownouts and even scheduled blackouts were becoming ever more frequent—over the grime-covered mailboxes, she opened her purse, withdrew a small tube and applied mascara, which she then heightened with eyeliner. Red lipstick and more than a dab of a cheaply-priced and poorly-formulated Chanel No. 5 knock-off. Then, after unbuttoning the top three buttons on her blouse with shaky fingers and feeling her stomach tighten with anxiety, she walked toward the pizza parlor.

It wasn't three blocks before a car, a hotel limousine, pulled to the curb near her. The back window rolled down. "Are you available?" It was a middle-aged man, balding, a little heavy, speaking American English.

"Depends," Dinah said.

"On one thousand pesos?" the man asked.

Forcing herself to sound assured, she merely laughed.

"Two thousand pesos?" the man persisted.

"Three thousand, no less," she said. He agreed and opened the car door. More than $120 U.S.; to her family, an unexpected bequest. She would decide later how to explain the money to her mother.

Dinah slid into the back seat alongside the man. She had never been this close to a foreigner, let alone with any man by herself. She tried to stop herself from thinking, from hearing her brain telling her this was all wrong. She caught the driver's eye and he quickly turned away. He had seen this before.

The American's shirt was half buttoned. His pale chest and puffy belly were thick with hair, much of it already white. But what really disgusted Dinah ben-Veniste was his presumptuousness; he had spread a big hotel beach towel across the backseat in preparation. She thought she knew what to expect—she had read, she had watched the illicit videos, like Angelina Fernandez, like so many of her friends. But actually touching this man, this coarse stranger, letting him touch her, and in what should have been the most intimate, pleasurable, even romantic ways, not the animalistic pawing he was giving her, repulsed Dinah. Only the thought of the money, of the 120 U.S. dollars she compelled him to agree on, kept her moving forward. Her mother, her family needed it, especially now with her father gone.

Then he unbuckled and unzipped his pants.

She had not expected him to be so big, yet so ridiculously pink and exposed, vulnerable looking. Dinah felt odd, emotionally confused. She didn't know if in the next moment she would scream or laugh.

"Suck it," he commanded, his voice suddenly high and squeaky.

She laughed, trying to make it sound like what she imaged would be the chuckle of a self-assured, worldly woman but really putting off the inevitable. Eager, the man reached behind her neck and forced her head down upon himself. Dinah almost retched, tears coming to her eyes. As she did his bidding, she felt his erection get even harder. So this is a man, she thought with peculiar compartmentalized clarity. Their brains must be so small. And this is disgusting. I am disgusting.

He thrust himself into her mouth over and over. Dinah found it difficult to breath and started gagging. Finally, with a moan, the man finished and withdrew.

All this time, the chauffer stared straight ahead, never glancing at them. He's a worse whore than I am, Dinah thought.

Still in the car, Dinah felt nothing but remorse and self-hate. What had she done? She looked at her dainty wristwatch, a gift from her father. "For your bat mitzvah, when you have it," he had said on her 12th birthday. Barely 20 minutes had passed. She felt filthy, inside and out.

He had wiped himself with an edge of the towel and zipped up his pants. "Here," he said, taking out his wallet. "Here's $50."

She grabbed his fleshy forearm and dug her fingernails in.

"Ow!" he screamed. He had not expected a fight. The man threw off her hand as the nail on her little finger snapped off. She felt pain, but her other four brightly polished, elongated nails had dug in. Blood trickled in four separate streaks from just below his elbow toward the wrist.

"We agreed on $120," she hissed. "Do you want me to report you to the *policía*, you rapist?" With that she grabbed the wallet from his hand, reached behind her for the door handle, and started to back out of the limousine. One heel caught, sending her flying backwards onto the sidewalk. The man's wallet went sailing, contents spilling everywhere. Frantically, Dinah grabbed two more $50 bills.

"Why, you thief!" he cried from the car. On the sidewalk she caught her breath and flung the wallet back at the car. The driver brought up the rear window.

"And I will tell them I am underage, too!" she shouted at the back of the limo as it receded toward the Havana Hilton, a holdover landmark, faded but still operating in this iteration thanks to reciprocity between the regime and German investors. A profit always could be made somewhere by someone, generally on the back of someone else.

Dinah straightened herself the best she could and hobbled toward home, hugging the walls along the way and praying no one she knew would see her. She felt dirty all right. But I am not a slut, she told herself. Never!

However, she was a liar, temporarily and of necessity, she conceded the next morning, still wrestling with her conscience. "David," she said to her brother, "you must do something for me, for our mama."

"What is it, sister dear?" he asked in his big-brotherish, self-mocking solicitude.

"Take this money," she said, handing him the $150 dollars, "and convert it to pesos at the pharmacy. Take your time, so it doesn't arouse suspicion. Then give the pesos back to me."

David stared at the three bills in disbelief. "What ... where did you get this?" he demanded, almost angrily.

"Last night Pilar Ortega and I met a gringo at the new pizza tavern ..."

"Pilar Ortega? I thought you said you were going with Angelina ..."

"I changed my mind. Pilar is more, more outgoing, you know..."

"Outgoing? You mean ignorant, no sense. She's beneath you!" David was practically shouting.

Softly, calmly, Dinah resumed. "Anyway, she and I watched this gringo getting drunk, talking loudly, flirting with the waitress. We decided to help him."

"Help him?" David was fuming.

"Yes. We bought him another drink. Then he bought us one. By then he was shaky. When he paid for the last round and the food, he dropped his wallet. I was flirting with him. He was distracted as well as drunk. That gave Pilar time to pick up his wallet. She lightened it a little before returning it. We helped him walk back part way to his hotel. He was *so* appreciative." Dinah forced herself to laugh.

"Which hotel?" David demanded. "I'm taking this money back!"

"And give it to whom? We never asked his name, and didn't give him our real ones. That money is like a gift from above, and you know mother needs it. We need it. After you've changed the dollars to pesos, I'm going to put them into her purse, a bit at a time. Her heart will be a little lighter, and she'll smile once in a while, like she used to. At least for a time. You know I'm right."

"I know you're right about mother and 'found' pesos," David growled at her, just before the electricity failed. In the darkness, he told her, "and I know you are wrong about yourself and Pilar and the dollars!"

Chapter Seven:
Cairo to Baghdad, 915 C.E.

It was early March, 915 C.E. Saadia ben Yosef, just arrived from his native Egypt, rested on the roof of his family's newly-acquired three-story home in Tiberias. The thick, nearly black volcanic rock walls of the building, common to the town's structures, helped keep it warm in winter, cool in summer. Nevertheless, he welcomed the gentle breeze blowing into town from the Golan Heights to the east and down across the nearly 10-mile width of Lake Kinneret, known to Christians as the Sea of Galilee. Saadia knew from his new neighbors that a month from now the rainy season would end and the long, stultifying summer would take hold.

But here under the shade of a palm-thatched lean-to, the young man sought respite. Already known among the Jews for his *Agron*, a Hebrew dictionary and perhaps the first Hebrew book of grammar, he had been forced to flee Egypt. His effective polemics against the Karaites, biblical exclusivists who opposed rabbinic Judaism with its Talmudic base, sparked such hostile reaction that a mob sacked his home in Fayyum. It destroyed many of his papers and threatened his life.

In Israel, Saadia nevertheless continued his defense of rabbinic Judaism. His sustained literary and spoken counter-attacks exposed Karaite spokesmen as being in over their heads in the war of ideas with Saadia. But it was another of his works, *The Book of Beliefs and Opinions*, that cemented his reputation as an authority on practice and faith. Perhaps the first comprehensive effort to argue that traditional Jewish beliefs and classical Greek philosophy, much admired by educated Arabs among whom so many Jews lived and whom upper class Jews imitated, need not be considered mutually exclusive.

In this Saadia, not yet 25 and already honored as *Rabbeinu Saadia* ("our Rabbi Saadia") opened a new struggle. In addition to defending rabbinic Judaism against Karaite subversion, he now attempted to tug members of the Jewish elite back from assimilation into an Arabic culture they found attractive and comfortable. That he wrote in a graceful Judeo-Arabic implicitly told readers that here was a man knowledgeable about the larger world but who, despite such understanding, upheld Judaism as not only their revealed religion but also the enlightened philosophical system by which they should live.

"Saadia," his wife called up to him, "there are two men downstairs who insist they must speak with you." The young man allowed himself a minute's reflection before rising. Her voice, he thought, always sounded like water bubbling from a small fountain—positive, joyful and elemental. He knew that Rebecca, just 19 and mother of their first child, their infant son, Dosa, was the physical presence, the material force, that made his mental work possible.

He met her on the landing. "They are strangers?"

"Yes," she said.

"What do they look like?"

"Young men. Their beards are full, completely black. And they look strong, healthy. I don't think they spend much time indoors with books."

Rebecca often urged him to get out more, walk more, breathe fresh air and rest his eyes. She was right, of course. But then, he could barely read enough to keep pace with his writing, and hardly write fast enough to harvest the thoughts of his fertile mind. And the Jews kept coming to him, in person and by letter, asking for answers about belief, decisions regarding practice, sometimes questions that bitterly divided communities and threatened their continuation. The work, his own and for the Jewish world in general, never ended.

"Did they say why they wanted to see me?"

"No, only that it was urgent."

"All right. Take Dosa, go into my study and bar the door. If you hear anything that doesn't sound right, go out the back window to your uncle's." With that he walked down to the entryway. Two tall, well-dressed strangers waited at the front door.

Chapter 7

"Gentlemen, come in and have a seat here," he said, gesturing to a small parlor nearby. When they were seated, he asked, "What can I do for you?"

"Please forgive our bluntness," said the slightly taller of the two visitors, "but it is what we can do for you."

"How do you mean?"

"Do you remember Zebulon Ben Bag?"

"How could anyone forget the old mystic of Fayyum?" Saadia replied, with a hint of a smile.

"Yes, the elderly eccentric," the tall man said. "Eccentric, but not mad. In fact, quite learned, a *tzaddik* and holy man."

"He still believes he is a descendant of Phannias ben Samuel, the last High Priest of the Second Temple? A direct descendant of Aaron, Moses' brother and the first Kohen haGadol?"

"He does," the other visitor broke in. "And he sent us to you, because he also believes you are in the line of *Mosiach*, that is, a descendant of King David."

Saadia smiled ruefully and said, "he did not invent the belief about himself. Others believed it of his father, and so the story, the tradition continues through him. But it cannot be confirmed. Phannias ben Samuel died in the Roman destruction of the Temple in 70 C.E."

"And a tradition says he fathered three sons, one of whom survived the Romans and himself had three sons," the second visitor continued. "Eventually, from one of those sons, came Zebulon Ben Bag."

"Another name for tradition is, sometimes, legend," Saadia answered. "Our traditions are handed forward, links a chain. But legends—who can determine the facts of their roots?" Saadia answered. "But yes, so Ben Bag's story says," Saadia conceded.

"More than that," the first visitor resumed. "Rav Zebulon believes that you are a descendant of King David and, especially after the Karaite mob attacked your home in Fayyum, in need of *shomrim*, watchmen. We are watchmen."

"The story about me also is an old one, a continuation of ancient family lore. But like Ben Bag's connection to Phannias ben Samuel, missing a link or two."

"That does not invalidate it," asserted the taller visitor.

"No, we cannot prove such a negative. But for this great claim, the family tradition does not confirm it either," Saadia said. "Anyway, suppose some Karaites are lurking about, just waiting to assault me or my family. What could you do about it?"

The taller man took his stout walking stick, one hand at each end, and snapped it in the middle with no apparent exertion.

"It is now almost three hundred years since your ancestor, Yosef Bustanai ben Hanania, left Aleppo for *eretz Yisrael*," he said. "Many believe he eventually settled here, in Tiberias, studied Torah and raised a family. He was your great-grandfather many times over. Our great-grandfathers many times over protected him. We will do the same for you and your family, including your son, Dosa."

"And your sons to come, *baruch Ha-Shem*," his partner added, invoking God's blessing.

Saadia started to object, but the second man hurried on. "We will not interfere with your work. In fact, you will hardly notice us. But we will be nearby, just in case."

"I cannot afford to pay you. How will you survive?" Saadia asked, beginning to feel nothing he could say or do would dissuade these men.

"*Shomrim* such as ourselves are provided for," the tall man said. "We have what is sufficient."

"Then I suppose old Zebulon Ben Bag knows what happened to the treasures of the Temple vaults and has keys to their storage places now," Saadia replied in what he intended as an aside.

Taken aback, the tall man merely said, "Yes."

****

The next few years were good ones, and they passed quickly. The Jews of Tiberias were pleased to support the young scholar, whose renown, like his family, continued to grow. Saadia was increasingly known as "the Crown of the Kinneret." Used with easy familiarity in Tiberias itself, the honorific became more formal, more authoritative the greater the distance at which it was applied. In fact, in the famed, renewed Babylonian

Talmudic academies of Pumbedita and Sura, word of the title caused a tremor of unease at the highest levels.

"A letter for you, my husband," Rebecca said, entering Saadia's study. It was shortly after Passover, 926 C.E. She strode in, carrying their new-born daughter D'vorah, the younger two of their three sons trailing behind. Dosa, the first-born, now seven, sat quietly near his father as Saadia stared at something he had been reading. Stared unhappily, Rebecca thought.

She watched him read the letter again and grimace as he finished. "What's wrong?" she asked.

"It's from ben Zakkai," he answered, shaking his head.

"David ben Zakkai, the Exilarch?"

"The same, unfortunately," he said.

"And what does the spiritual leader of all the Jews in exile want this time," she asked, with soft but unmistakable sarcasm.

"Only that I should confirm his righteousness."

"Just that, and in public, no doubt?"

"No doubt. It seems some of his and our fellow Jews in Babylonia have objected to more of the Exilarch's land deals, and they have taken him to court."

"But since he is the head of the community, he also is judge of his own case in court, is that it?"

"Yes," Saadia replied disconsolately. "His letter says he's asked two colleagues in Babylonia and me here in *eretz Yisrael* to attest to his incorruptibility."

"And you, my righteous husband, are not going to do it, are you?"

"Of course not," Saadia answered. "I fought his fight once before, and won ... "

"At no little cost," Rebecca reminded him.

"Yes, at no little cost. It was good we had Isaachar and Naftali around then to safeguard us against some of our co-religionists," he said, referring to the *shomrim*.

"Did you ever see men run faster than that bunch of would-be thugs than when Isaachar and Naftali got through with them?" she asked, laughing. "The way they swing, twirl and catch their big sticks is truly wonderful to behold."

A quarrel over the calendar between Babylonia and *eretz Yisrael*, between Exilarch David ben Zakkai and the Gaon of Israel Aharon ben Meir threatened to divide the Jewish world and weaken Jewish communities everywhere. The ruling Abbasid caliph, Abu al-Fadil Ja'far, known widely and often with trepidation as *al-Muqtadir*— "Mighty in God" or "the All-Authoritative One"—told ben Zakkai to get his people in order, or else. The or else being implied loss of the Exilarch's considerable authority, regained incrementally ever since the Muslim conquest of the Persians and Parthians, over the geographically extensive Jewish communities' internal matters.

Ben Zakkai had called on Saadia to wield his pen against ben Meir. He did so in a series of letters of escalating polemics. Tension between the two Jewish leaders and between their respective communities nearly reached the boiling point before Saadia's appeals to both custom and law shattered ben Meir's challenge. What had ben Meir's campaign been about? His attempt to re-assert *eretz Yisrael's* authority over the Babylonian academies by inaugurating an adjusted religious calendar that would have moved observance of Rosh Hashanah and Passover up by two days.

"Why not defend him now?" Rebecca asked.

"Because no man should judge his own case," Saadia said. "But also because this time I believe there's something wrong, that the Exilarch may not be the righteous party he asserts he is. Here, look at this …" he said, handing her a list in his own handwriting.

She read it quickly.

"It looks like an indictment of sorts," Rebecca said, looking up. "You've listed four land sales involving the Exilarch that his accusers have brought before the court. After the first one, you've written a few sentences saying the evidence presented does not prove criminal intent or result. After the second, you've written the word "ambiguous," and a note that neither the claim nor counter-claim are persuasive.

"But after the last two, you say: 'Requires additional independent investigation. Let a panel of three respected men be appointed, one by the

Exilarch, one by the plaintiffs and one separately by the community at large. Give the panel three months to review the evidence and take new testimony. It should then issue its report. Seems reasonable to me, my judicious husband. So reasonable that the Exilarch will be furious with you."

"Yes, he will be furious with me. Furious over my saying out loud what nearly all the Babylonian community can see—the case of the young widow next door to him, the young widow with three children, whose wealthy older husband died suddenly and whose lovely home the Exilarch would like to add to his own at little cost. And the case of the prosperous farmer at the edge of the city whose land borders a spring-fed stream that never runs dry and flows into the nearby Euphrates River. The prosperous farmer who fathered only daughters and who has been unable to work since a bull broke his legs at harvest time last fall. A stream and land the Exilarch would like to acquire at a distress sale price for his oldest son, a brawny lad with no head for study, no tongue for speech."

"As if the Exilarch, and nearly every other Jew did not know it is written: 'You must not mistreat any widow or orphan,'" Rebecca said. "'Do not take advantage of the widow or the fatherless. You must not exploit a widow or an orphan.' It's a Torah injunction!"

"The Torah can be inconvenient, can't it?" Saadia smiled. "As you periodically and inconveniently remind us. In every generation someone must."

"And in our generation, it seems to be you," Rebecca said. "So, what are we going to do?"

"I think we are going to have to relocate to Baghdad," Saadia replied. "That's where the evidence lies, where the Exilarch and his accusers live and where justice will have to be done."

Rebecca actually snorted. "Keep your friends close and your enemies closer, eh?"

"And Isaachar and Naftali even closer. They must come with us."

"Oh, they will. They're probably already packed."

****

Saadia was weary. Did he really have to listen to this argument, or better, pre-argument, again? It was late. They'd been over all this before, more than once. But his interlocutors would not finish, though they had chewed this subject to bare bone.

"Rav Saadia," pleaded Solomon ben Yehuda, "we must have an answer for the caliph, soon."

"Everything depends upon it," added his companion, Shmuel ben Yitzhaki, known behind his back as Shmuel HaShemen—Samuel the Sleek, or less politely, Samuel the Fat. Not for his girth, which was considerable, but rather his wealth. Ben Yitzhaki and ben Yehuda, the two richest men in the generally prosperous Jewish community, were court bankers to Caliph Abd al-Fadil Ja'far, *al-Muqtadir*. That meant that when the caliph needed money, which was not infrequently given declining Abbasid influence and growing pressure from the provinces, he sent for them. "Another loan, you understand. By no means a grant," the caliph's men promised him. These loans were understood, all right, by all parties to be long-term, low-interest and quite possibly no interest at all, repayment when and if convenient.

Such an arrangement was an implicit tax on the Jewish community and cost incurred for the ruler's protection, when he saw fit to extend it. The community being useful to him as both resource and buffer against other minorities, let alone as a shield of deflection against ever-present agitators among his own true believers, he typically saw fit to extend that protection. Fear that they might give offense, inadvertent if not intentional, or disappoint the caliph in some way caused Jewish leaders like ben Yitzhaki and ben Yehuda to pressure other authority figures like Saadia and even the Exilarch to do their bidding, and quickly. So, though it was almost midnight, they repeated themselves.

"This controversy involving the Exilarch and his purchases ..."

"His desired purchases," Saadia reminded them.

"His desired purchases," ben Yehuda conceded, "worries the palace. There is concern that unrest in our community might spark trouble by example among other groups. It's been dragging on for more than a year now—more than that, since before your arrival here. We understand from the court that the caliph's patience is gone. He wants it settled. Soon, if not immediately."

"So you've said," Saadia responded softly, tiredly. "All right. Let me sleep on it. And not one night, but two. Come back after morning prayers two days from now and I'll have an answer for you to convey to those who demand one. Now, gentlemen, it's nearly midnight. We must each go to his bed."

Ben Yitzhaki opened his mouth to speak again, but Saadia had turned and, shoulders slumped in tiredness, walked out of the room.

He, Rebecca and their children had been in Baghdad barely a year. Their new home still was not fully furnished or organized, not even with generous help from members of their latest community. There had been so much to do. He headed a yeshiva, spending hours in dialogue, teaching the brightest older scholars. He heard complaints from all sides to the controversy of the Exilarch's desired acquisitions. He responded to endless inquiries from far-flung Jewish communities over rituals and faith. And, of course, Saadia expounded the principles of his *Book of Beliefs and Opinions*—the work's growing influence caused him to be referred to as "our Jewish Aristotle," in admiration by followers, derision by opponents.

Precious little time was left for what he told himself was his most important responsibility, that of loving husband to Rebecca and affectionate father to their children. Had he not himself written in *Beliefs and Opinions* that the magnetism of loving attraction some followers of Plato insisted united two halves, two souls, into one whole, primarily among males was real enough but properly applied to relations between the sexes, particularly to that between husband and wife? "For this matter is good only with a man's wife whom he should love and who should love him for the settlement of the world," that is, for the raising of children and maintenance of humanity itself? Yet here he was, being called on to make a decision that potentially could put every Jew under the extensive rule of *al-Muqtadir* at risk. Months shy of his thirty-seventh birthday, Saadia felt wearied by the burden.

In *eretz Yisrael* he had been one of three *geonim*, one each from the trio of gaonic families there, the families that tradition held descended from King David himself. That tradition, plus erudition coupled with his singularly forceful personality, had made Saadia a natural leader. But here in Baghdad, he stood by custom at the edge of a circle formed by six other *geonim*, their aristocratic families—aristocratic in the sense of authority founded on ancient lines of religious leadership—one also claiming descent from the House of David. They long held sway. A newcomer, an outsider, was unlikely to reach their level of eminence.

Consider the opening processions for the schools and rabbinic courts, the *bet din*. They featured the Exilarch, the *geonim* trailing him and the academy heads, the *avot bet yeshivot*, following the *geonim*—all of them in their silver-trimmed robes (gold being reserved, of course, for the garments of the caliph's court). These parades were something to behold. And gossip over, as the community did for weeks after. Who followed whom and what each one wore. The robes, sashes and the procession itself recalled, and were meant to recall, the splendor of the independent courts of the last kings of Judea as far as *al Muqtadir* would allow a conquered but still proud subject people any such splendor.

What lightning bolt of a suggestion, what jolt of insight could he offer to solve the Exilarch's controversy that the community would accept and the caliph tolerate? Exhausted, Saadia fell into bed. But mental agitation meant he slept little.

Awake before sunrise, Saadia slipped quietly out of bed so as not to disturb Rebecca. He threw on a robe and went downstairs. In the kitchen he found bread from the day before. Saadia dipped it into olive oil, broke off a piece of hard cheese, sliced a ripe tomato and made breakfast. Unrested, uncertain, he was not really hungry but knew he could not sit through the long morning ahead on an empty stomach, especially not with the showdown that awaited him.

The ceremonial procession that preceded opening of the high *bet din* finally over, Saadia at last was able to take his seat among the other senior officials on a raised platform at the west end (facing Jerusalem) of the assembly hall. Oh, Lord, he thought, must these sessions always be so formal, so stiff? We could hear twice as many cases, bring twice as much justice— "Justice, justice thou shall pursue," instructed the Torah—but no, the officials needed and the spectators expected time-consuming pomp and circumstance signifying authority and judgment.

Chapter 7

The Exilarch himself opened the hearing. First, he offered the priestly blessing, the words God commanded Moses to instruct his brother Aaron, the first high priest, to say to the Israelites in the desert: "May the Lord bless you and watch over you. May the Lord cause His countenance to shine upon you and favor you. May the Lord raise His countenance toward you and grant you peace."

From the Exilarch's mouth the wonderful injunction sounded more like a proclamation attesting to his own leadership, Saadia thought. Then the head of the Sura academy—overtly courteous to Saadia, covertly implacably opposed to this Tiberias upstart—put forth some words of Torah instruction. Finally, the spectators growing restless, the Exilarach asked, "Saadia, may we have your report?" He managed to sound polite and authoritative simultaneously.

"Yes, your Eminence," Saadia answered, taking care to speak matter-of-factly, without emotion. Before reading from the papers in his hands, he glanced about the large, crowded hall. The caliphs' men, in their bulk and their royal robes, occupied the center of the first row of spectators' seats. The bankers Solomon ben Yehuda and Shmuel ben Yitzhaki flanked them on the right. Behind them, at one end of the second row, sat Rebecca, accompanied by a stern-faced Dosa, now nearly 10, and Rebecca's close friend Sarah bat Yaccobi. Those who came late stood along the walls. Appearing to lounge casually by an open window about halfway back were Isaachar and Naftali, short, stout poles concealed beneath their robes.

"The panel finds, in the matter of the sale of the widow Naomi bat Daniel's house, that the purchase price—compared to similarly situated properties throughout Baghdad—was unusually low. Naomi bat Daniel has sworn that although she was not threatened at any time, she felt compelled to sell as she did. Regardless, we find that, as it is said, 'Do not take advantage of the widow or the fatherless,' the purchase price must be tripled."

"Ooh!" spectators exclaimed, as if one.

"Quiet, please!" the Exilarch commanded.

Saadia resumed. "As to the case of the farm at the edge of the city, owned by the crippled Yonah ben Tzelopheha, who has no son: He must be allowed to retain possession, with the fields and cattle to be tended by hired men, until his daughters reach the age of maturity. Then they can decide whether or not to sell, and if so, for how much. By strange coincidence," and here Saadia paused for effect, "we have the Torah analogy if not exact precedence of the daughters of the nearly identically named Zelophehad. As it is written in Bamidbar—which the Greeks called the Book of Numbers—after their father died, leaving no male heirs, they demanded their inheritance. Moses inquired of the Lord, who declared, 'The daughters of Zelophehad speak correctly. You certainly must give them property as an inheritance among their father's brothers and transfer their father's inheritance to them.'"

This time, applause mingled with gasps at the panel's—at Saadia's—audacity in the face of the Exilarch's well-known desires, rippled through the hall. The clapping signified satisfaction. Many Jews of Baghdad, and some beyond, had come to feel that this Exilarch had stayed too long, grown too self-satisfied and that they would be better served with someone else in his chair. Someone who possessed a little of the divine quality that made Moses fit to speak with God: humility, genuine and thorough-going.

As for *al-Muqtadir's* advisors, small smiles of approval, not so much at the decisions themselves but rather because the long, unsettling matter finally had reached a resolution, crossed their faces. The applause halted and the smiles vanished as the Exilarch, red in the face, rose from his high seat at the center of the raised dais.

"I accept the ruling of this court," the Exilarch declared, angry but controlled. "I accept." He paused, made the slightest, stiff bow, then straightened.

"I also decree the following: Its business ended; this court is dissolved. Its presiding officer, its *rosh bet din*, Rabbi Saadia ben Yosef al-Fayyumi, is hereby instructed to return to his yeshiva and his teaching duties only. His correspondence with distant Diaspora communities will be taken up by Eitan ben Rogel, secretary of my court. And for the next five years, he will confine his writings to private work, not for publication."

Rebecca rose to her feet and, fists clenched, turned toward the Exilarch. Saadia, recognizing that defiant posture, managed to catch her eye just in time. No, he shook his head. No. Across the hall, jammed with agitated spectators, they locked eyes, two determined, principled people. Then Rebecca, silent, sat down, fists still clenched.

The assembly growing increasingly noisy, Isaachar and Naftali moved protectively toward Saadia. "Friends, friends!" he shouted. "Please, hear me!" Still rumbling, the crowd quieted somewhat.

"Fellow Jews," Saadia implored. "Be not dismayed!" His voice rose, turbulent emotions—usually held in check privately and always before publicly—showed plainly. "Several nights ago, members of our community—all of them leaders well known to you—visited me. Troubled by the unresolved tensions among the Jews of Baghdad and many places beyond, they urged me to take a hither-to inconceivable step. I resisted, both as a newcomer to this community and as a participant in these proceedings.

"But today I see that the proposal they made to me is necessary. Therefore—and with great thanks to David ben Zakkai for his long, very long and valuable service to all Jews as Exilarch—by the rabbinic and gaonic authority placed upon me, and which all know I did not seek, I propose the name of our next Exilarch. He is the learned, judicious, respected Meir ben HaCohen, head of the Pumbedita academy!"

Disbelief swept the hall. The caliph's advisors pushed their way out. Rebecca, pulling Dosa by the arm, attempted to reach Saadia, now flanked by his two guardians. People who had been watching through the open windows from outside tried to shove their way in while many inside forced their way out through the crowded doors.

Late that night, Saadia sat at home, Rebecca at his side. Four men he knew well, each one a senior teacher at one of the academies, stood near him. Isaachar and Naftali watched from the door.

"My husband, my husband," Rebecca asked. "What have you done? What will we do?"

Saadia did not answer immediately. Chin down, eyes closed, fingers tented, he might have been dozing. When he looked up and spoke, it was as if the exhaustion that weighed on him in the months before the court session had lifted. His voice firm, his eyes clear, he said, "Only what had to be done. Only what we must."

"Yes," said Meir ben-HaCohen, the man who, resistance passing through reluctance to resignation, had allowed Saadia to propose him as the new Exilarch that morning. "Don't think I don't appreciate the honor you bestowed upon me this day," HaCohen said, almost wryly. "But Saadia, how do you image we will carry out my appointment at your hand? Who is with us? It's not like David ben-Zakkai will hand me the keys to his kingdom tomorrow and quietly walk away into retirement."

"The majority, probably the great majority, of our brethren at court today approved of the verdicts. They know ben-Zakkai's character and his grasping at riches all these years. They will support us," Saadia answered.

"Saadia, dearest," Rebecca said tenderly, "community sentiment favoring your wise judgments is one thing. Your Hebrew dictionary, and your book of grammar—not to mention the compendium of rhymes for poets, let alone *The Book of Beliefs and Opinions*—all embraced throughout our Jewish communities. So, persons in the most far-flung of them write, imploring you to settle their disputes. But this respect for you and your work is not the same as solidarity in favor of your challenge to the Exilarch and his power. That requires each individual to go out on a limb, something most people avoid."

"As usual, Rebecca speaks wisely," HaCohen said. "We need time to consolidate support, and time is something we don't have."

"No, we don't," Rebecca interjected. "Did you see the faces of the caliph's men as they forced their way out after your announcement?" she asked her husband. "They were not happy fellows."

But nothing unusual happened the following two days. It was if a high flame under a cook pot had been lowered to a simmer. Nothing except the discovery of several men skulking near their home after nightfall one evening, men whom Isaachar and Naftali sent on their way with hard blows and harder kicks. However, daybreak the third morning proved Rebecca correct. The sun's rays barely had begun to peek over the city when the pounding began at their front door. Meir ben-HaCohen, who had come before daybreak to speak with Saadia, had just close the door behind him.

"Who is it?" Issachar demanded.

"You know damned well who it is," came a rough voice. "The caliph sent us. We bring his message for the great Saadia," the voice said sarcastically. "And you 'watchmen' can put aside your legendary clubs—as if they could impede all of us. We are not here to arrest your master, only to inform him of *al-Muqtadir's* pleasure."

"Go ahead," Saadia said, standing behind Isaachar and Naftali, "open the door."

As they did, six big men, scimitars at their belts, strode in, followed by two smaller individuals in royal robes, trailed finally by the two ubiquitous black crows of ill-omen, as Saadia thought of them, the bankers Solomon ben-Yehuda and Shmuel ben-Yitzhaki. Only ben-Yehuda and ben-Yitzhaki were smiling. Or, Saadia decided, smirking. One of the officials handed Saadia a small parchment scroll, tied by a purple ribbon and closed with red wax on which was imprinted the royal seal.

"Please read it aloud," the official said. "We are to tell the caliph that you have read and understood it."

Saying nothing, Saadia untied and unsealed the document, three pages in all, looked it over, and began to read aloud:

"My dear Saadia Gaon," it began, "though we have not met, your fame has reached me and I have read some of your works, most notably your *Book of Beliefs and Opinions*. There is much in it I find congenial, especially your appreciation of the old Greeks and your attempt to harmonize some of their teachings with your *Torah*. I'm not sure you will succeed in that, anymore that my court philosophers will do with the *Quran* and old Plato and Aristotle, but I believe the effort must be made to permit the broadest development of our thinking. Though I'm afraid some of my own scholars object and want to forbid such inquiries. It will be a shame, even a danger, if Islam chooses to proceed in that direction, closing itself off. Imagine if the backward Christians, in their dank European castles, begin reading the old masters in addition to listening to their priests deliver sermons in a Latin they can barely follow. In but a few generations, thus enlightened, they might burst forth across the world. But, superstitious lot, they won't.

"In any case, your own deep reasoning, expressed in such beautiful Judeo-Arabic, deserves attention. But I digress. As you must appreciate, your attempt to name a new Exilarch—utterly on your own presumed authority and outside the least consultation with the royal court—is completely impermissible. Even if I were to agree with your choice, and from what I'm told, your Meir ben HaCohen is a fine fellow, your method is unsanctioned and the result, division in a minority, *dhimmi* community unacceptable."

Dhimmis, as Jews and Christians in the caliph's world well understood, were protected monotheistic minorities. Protected so long as they paid the *jizya* tax, did not build or repair synagogues or churches without permission and certainly not construct them as tall as mosques. They were minority members whose testimony in court against a Muslim was non-dispositive, and whose orphaned children would be adopted by Muslim families and raised in that faith. With the possibility of that protection, the quite conditional tolerance extended to them a custom resting on the ruler's pleasure and the public's emotion, Jews and Christians as *dhimmis* lived always on a fault line.

"You will do the following, immediately: Follow the decree the Exilarch, Exilarch David ben-Zakki has made—return to your yeshiva and teaching duties. Cease any correspondence with distant Diaspora communities. And for the next five years, you will confine your writings to private work, not for publication. After five years, any work you wish to publish must be read and approved by me personally. Should you choose not to comply, you will be exiled, alone, to Basra for fifteen years."

After Saadia had finished reading the proclamation, the court official handed him a second parchment. "You must sign this," he said. "We are to return with it."

The second parchment said simply, "I, Saadia Gaon, hereby accept the gracious terms extended to me by His Excellency, Caliph Abd al-Fadil Ja'far."

Saadia glanced at Meir ben-HaCohen, then looked to Rebecca. Again, as in the tumult of the assembly hall, they held each other's gaze. Basra, that hot, humid, mud-walled excrescence of a city sat on the marsh flats at the mouth of the Shatt al-Arab, where the Tigris and Euphrates rivers, having merged, flowed into the Persian Gulf. Basra would have been nearly impossible even with his beloved Rebecca and the children. Without them, a living death. His face full of sorrow, Saadia Gaon signed.

To Dosa, his father suddenly looked aged. I will never let anyone do this to me, he promised his eleven-year-old self. I will have men about me, even bigger and stronger than Isaachar and Naftali, men like the caliph's with their scimitars, but more of them. Then the world will see what a Jew can do! At that, startling the adults standing just inside the front door, he turned and bolted upstairs, tears in his eyes.

Chapter Eight:
Pechora, 1944/New York City, 1969

It was Wednesday, July 2, 1969. A man who looked like he was in his mid-50s but in fact was observing—not celebrating, never celebrating—his 39th birthday that very day, stood outside Rosen's Delicatessen on the Lower East Side. He nerved himself to enter. This was difficult; the thought caused his gut to churn.

Get a grip, he told himself. You lived in the woods how long, three years? You killed how many men? Three you're sure of, three whose faces you saw close to your own and no doubt more at longer range. And after nearly a quarter of a century you can't walk into a delicatessen in New York City in broad daylight?

The door opened from the inside and two customers exited, a young man and woman. With them through the open door floated the aroma of fresh potato *knishes*. A busboy, white apron around his waist, bent to load the *knishes* into a glass case near the cash register. The delicious smell, an almost intoxicating reminder of the day his world shattered, filled Samuel Meyer's nostrils. His eyes closed and he staggered backwards. The young man grabbed his arm, holding him upright.

"You okay, buddy?" the man asked. The woman with him looked at Meyer with concern.

"Yes," Meyer said, not convincingly. Forcing firmness back into his legs, he repeated, stronger this time, "yes." Then, twenty-seven years to the day they murdered his brother and, having smashed her face bloody with a rifle butt, dragged his mother away forever, Zygmund Meirovich—now Samuel F. Meyer—willed himself to walk into Rosen's Delicatessen. It was a warm, sunny day. In front, on Second Avenue, a bored cop waved cars through the intersection while a man in a bucket lift worked on the mis-timing traffic light. …

...The potatoes already grated, his mother was frying minced onions. Eggs, black pepper and salt stood ready on the counter. "Go play," his mother said. "The *potatoniks* will be ready in half an hour. For your birthday." She managed a small smile, turning up the edges of her mouth. But her lips were still pursed. It had been two weeks since they had taken his father. Every morning, she walked into town to the police station, asking, imploring them to release her husband. He'd done nothing wrong, they knew that. We've lived here all our lives, never a complaint against us. And how many townspeople had jobs in his textile factory, one hundred, one hundred and twenty? All of them always fairly treated, never a strike at the factory. They knew that.

"I know," the sergeant told her every morning. "But everything is up to them now." Them—the Iron Guard who dominated this remote part of Romania, and the German Nazis who stood behind them. The sergeant was a nice man, from him never of mean word or rude look. Nice, but not strong. Not a good man, only nice. Long before noon she would walk home alone, wringing her hands as she went.

Back in the kitchen, she cooked. As if things were normal. She still had to feed the two boys, and herself. They had sent Basya, the youngest of their three children, to live with friends in Cluj. "Call her Bette," the letter of accompaniment said. "And enroll her in the Catholic school." The envelope was stuffed with Romanian *lei* notes with many zeroes printed on them, not that they bought much. Not that there was much to buy now, deep into the third year of the war, with Ion Antonescu's Iron Guard in power. After its coup against the neutral King Carol II the Guard had consolidated popularity by massacring hundreds of thousands of Jews in Bessarabia and elsewhere.

Zygmund, usually called Ziggy, loved his mother's *potatoniks*. Like crisp potato pancakes but bigger and thicker, *potatoniks* were both a staple and a treat. After his mother sent him out to play while she finished cooking, he watched. Barely fifty yards from their house, he inspected everything about him. Ziggy didn't really play among the trees, the vines and brambles, the tall grass. Instead, he observed, studied, moving as quietly as he could. Zygmund Meirovich liked to imagine he was a red Indian in the wilds of America, like the ones he saw in the movies shown in the theater off the little town's main square. The ones he saw before the war, when he had friends and could go to the movies with them.

Now he was sneaking through the trees, taking care not to startle the rabbits or birds. He could identify, thanks to the guidebook his father had bought him, now dogged-eared and worn, nearly all the bird species in the woods. He could creep close to rabbits and birds, but not the foxes, not yet. They watched Ziggy watching them. The foxes seemed to know more about the woods than he did. More about himself than he did about them.

To call it a woods was misleading. It stretched for dozens of miles from the lower slopes of the Carpathian Mountains, rolling thick and green across Romanian foothills and pouring onto the territories of the Ukrainians and Poles. The Ukrainians and Poles his parents disdained—"imbibing Jew-hatred in their mothers' milk," his father had said—almost as much as the Iron Guard. The great expanse of old hardwoods blanketed hundreds of square miles. The deeper one went, the more impenetrable it became. Even on foot one often was forced to progress through deep ravines along rocky streams, once in a while emerging into a small meadow. He knew there were bears, and wolves too, somewhere among the trees, though he seen only one bear, once, lumbering off far away. Never any wolves, at least not of the four-legged variety, not yet. The few roads through the forest were little traveled. Winding, one lane affairs, they connected the rare clumps of houses to the outside world.

Near a spring—he thought of it as his spring—Ziggy checked his rucksack, hidden in the hollowed trunk of an ancient tree. Yes, it was there, neatly packed and strapped shut. As always, he took inventory: A bag of walnuts, two candy bars, an extra pair of socks, shoe laces, box of matches, short hatchet, a few *lei* notes. Tucked through the straps, a small blanket. All there, he thought, and touched the pocketknife in his right front pocket. All there. From the first American western he had seen, he had begun collecting these necessities. "You never know, pardner," an actor had intoned when asked why he always carried two canteens instead of one. "You just never know."

Ziggy repacked his rucksack and stuffed it back into the tree trunk. Surely half an hour had passed. He imagined he could smell the *potatoniks*, though in reality he must have been too far from home for that.

Approaching the house, he was about to break from the woods when he saw them. Two police cars and a black van with a flashing blue light screeched to a halt in front. Ziggy flattened himself behind a thick old oak tree.

"No!" he heard his mother scream.

"Mama, mama!" his little brother cried.

Crouching, Ziggy peaked around the tree trunk. This is what he saw:

A big man, a big man in a police uniform, had one arm around his mother's waist. With his other hand he yanked her head back by her long, brown hair and dragged her out the front door of their house. "Mama!" his brother cried, clinging to her ankles. A second man, also big but not as large as the first, ripped his little brother from his mother's legs, shook him violently and flung him head-first into the stone wall by the door. His brother dropped to the ground, blood coming from his nose and mouth.

"Yitzy, Yitzy!" his mother screamed.

That was when a third man—there seemed to be at least nine or ten men at their door—slender, young-looking, in civilian clothes, a suit and tie, with a smart brown fedora on his head, took a rifle from one of the men in uniform and smashed it into his mother's face. One piercing sound came from her that cut into the forest, startling squirrels and causing birds to take flight. The men threw his mother into the van and drove away, but not before splashing their kitchen with gasoline and setting it ablaze.

Ziggy stared at his house, at his brother lying motionless beside the door, his head and neck making a strange angle with his shoulders, at the flames now licking the window frame. He imagined that twined with the gasoline fumes he smelled *potatoniks*. It was his birthday. ...

Samuel Meyer sat at the counter on the stool closest to the door. He kept himself there by sheer force of will. The delicatessen was about half-full. People ate with gusto—Rosen's was deservedly popular—and talked animatedly. Waitresses joked familiarly with customers. Samuel Meyer took in his surroundings and felt like an alien from another place, another time. Disassociation, that's what a psychologist once called it, he remembered.

"What'll it be?" the counterman asked.

Meyer shook his head, trying to clear his mind. The counterman looked impatient. Meyer finally said, "a potato knish and coffee, black." He could have ordered a pecan roll, glazed with cinnamon and sugar. In fact, that's what he wanted to do. It would have been easy. It would have been a lie.

"Sure thing," the counterman replied, keeping his eyes on the man at the stool without appearing to do so.

You're managing, Meyer told himself, finally feeling he was beginning to master the anxiety, when he heard a sound, a voice, an accent that threw him back into confusion. At the other end of the counter, eight or nine stools away, a waitress pretended to flirt with a customer.

"Max, you say that to all the girls," she told him.

"Sure, Rose, but to you, I mean it," he said.

"Tell me again," she teased.

"Okay, once more: two eggs, over easy, hash browns and coffee, with cream and sugar."

"I knew you really meant it," she laughed, turning to shout his order into the kitchen.

Underneath the waitress' English, American English that really was quite good, Meyer caught a familiar accent. He strained to hear her speak again, and he was certain. It was the accent of northwestern Romania, of the Jews of northwestern Romania. A hint of a lilt, a suppressed purr abruptly punctuated by guttural hard consonants. She looked to him to be about his age, his chronological age, not his experiential one. Maybe a little older, say 41 or 42. Pretty but not Hollywood. Nice figure, a little on the short side, bright demeanor. He studied her and felt his anxiety begin to wane. He had heard an accent like that in the woods. …

… "Ziggy, tonight you guard the camp."

"No, I want to come too," he protested.

"Look, your leg isn't quite healed. You won't be able to keep up. And anyway, you're perfect for guarding the camp. You don't just patrol, you observe. That makes you worth three or four other guards. You know we don't have three or four people to spare and you also know what I'm saying is true: You can react quicker, more successfully, to any intrusion than anyone else, myself included."

Ziggy took the compliment and hated it. The Commander was always right. Nearly. The Commander. That's what they called him and it fit, even though at 21 he was only a year or two older than most of the others. Strong, quick, smart, born to lead. They didn't even know his real name. Not that in this war, in this forest, it mattered.

"Plus, you'll have this," the Commander said, handing Ziggy his own sidearm, a heavy Luger automatic. Ziggy felt the weapon's heft, its solidity. The gun felt good in his hand. He felt good with the gun. The commander slung a rifle across his shoulder and left.

Journalists then and historians later would call them partisans. That made them sound official, organized, important. What they were at the beginning was a band of seventeen boys and girls the war transformed into a dozen men and women. Half of them were the remainder of a Scout troop that had been camping in the forest when the Iron Guard overthrew King Carol and, among other things, arrested their parents. Two had gone home to see what was happening, and never returned. Three more died of sickness, wounds or hunger before the Commander was able to negotiate a deal with the leader of a bigger, nearby communist underground unit. The Scouts, and the orphaned strays who managed to join them, would function as a screening squad, sometimes a rearguard, sometimes reconnaissance. In exchange, "The Children," as the Reds called them, received some food, a few weapons, a little ammunition and a bit of training, mostly in sabotage.

Katya was very good at sabotage. "Ziggy, my little man," Katya was saying, "keep the camp safe tonight, and when we return, I'll keep you warm." She smiled, squeezed his hand, and walked to the Commander.

Katya was only three or four years older than Ziggy, who now, in early March of 1944, was fourteen. But if the gap between a 14-year-old-boy and an 18-year-old woman was always pronounced, between Ziggy and Katya it yawned. Nearly three years in the forest, living on the edge—hiding, running, killing—had hardened him. But he was still, at barely five feet, four inches tall, a lean one hundred and twenty pounds—a boy who hardly needed to shave. Those same years had made Katya an auburn-haired, green eyed, slender goddess. She had been the Commander's, early on. Or rather, she had been with the Commander. But lately they were all business and nothing but business with each other. Something had changed, something no one else in the little band knew just quite what.

Not that Ziggy needed to know. Two or three times in the past few months, Katya had squeezed next to him in the middle of the night, unbuttoned his clothes, and begun to teach him some of the things adults kept hidden from children. Inflamed as he was, he saw that in some way she was only entertaining herself.

"You are to dynamite the little bridge just before the main entrance to Pechora," the leader of the communist commandos told the Commander. "The one over the South Bug River. It's the same assignment as the bridge you hit a month ago in Suceava. More or less. When the bridge blows, you children fall back. Already in position, we will ambush the Guard who come running to investigate."

"Why Pechora?" the Commander asked. "It's just another place where they kill Jews." So it was, one of more than 100 under direct control of the pro-Nazi regime. Pechora made no pretense about being a work camp or even a concentration camp. A sign near the main entrance advised all who entered, "Death camp." Not that it had gas chambers or crematoria like the industrialized, efficient murder centers of the Germans. No, in Pechora, once the private, gated estate of a Ukrainian noble family, later a tuberculosis sanitorium, they killed Jews the old-fashioned ways: exposure, disease and starvation, beating, stabbing, strangling. The unusually hardy, a small minority, could be thrown into the cold, dark, swift-flowing Bug River.

"Because," the commando chief told him, "we know the Romanians are wobbling. Many want to get free of the Germans, now that it begins to look like the tide may be turning. Killing more of them, disrupting their operations helps confuse those in charge and demoralize the others."

Late that night, Ziggy, aware with both the alertness of a watchman and on fire with the anticipation of a lover, heard the explosion, a far-off dull rumble that moved through the forest muted by distance and foliage. Then, he thought, gunfire, barely audible. After that, nothing. He waited through most of the night. No one returned. Not the Commander, not Katya, none of the others. Before daybreak he was picking his way carefully deeper into the woods, the Commander's pistol at his side. …

… The waitress' voice was not that of Katya. Of course not. But it was similar. He lingered. All the crippling unsteadiness he had felt outside the delicatessen had gone. Eventually, the waitress moved down the counter to him.

"Refill?" she asked, smiling. The single word flooded through his heart, leaving a warmth long absent.

"Yes," he said, smiling back.

Sam Meyer and Rose Bloom—that was the name she took for herself after arriving in America in 1946, sponsored by her remaining relative, a second cousin in Flatbush—were married the next summer. They would have two children, a daughter they named Sandra, and a son called Gerry—good, safe American names—before they told each other more than the barest details of their lives during the war, during the years of death.

Chapter Eight, (continued): New York City, the Present

For a man of the spirit, the rabbi tried to be as practical as possible. He did not think of the two aspects—the intangible and the tangible—as contradictory, but rather complementary, even if he couldn't explain exactly how and didn't want to. It wasn't necessary. To begin at the beginning, literally, the opening lines of Genesis and the Big Bang theory were two ways of describing the same thing:

"In the beginning, God created heaven and earth. And the earth was without form, and void; and darkness was upon the face of the deep. And the Spirit of God moved upon the face of the waters. And God said, Let there be light: and there was light."

The ancient Hebrew is actually more precise, Rabbi Samson thought. The earth was not just without form and void, with darkness across what was about to become the universe. Rather, existence itself was without form and void, chaotic— *"tovu v' vohu,"* until the spirit of God—of the Creator creating—moved across it. Big Bang-wise, about 14 billion years ago clouds of cosmic dust suddenly contracted into incredibly dense matter that then instantaneously exploded outward in an incomprehensible release of energy, creating countless stars— "Let there be light!"—planets and the matter and anti-matter of the universe.

Why? The rabbi liked to ask this of all-too-certain students. And Who created the cosmic dust, and What was there before that? he prodded them. Displaying brilliantly colored enlargements of pictures first from the Hubble and later the Webb space telescopes, he let them consider images made from light that had traveled uncounted miles across billions of years to show mammoth gas bubbles condensing into fiery suns as galaxies formed. Let there be light, indeed.

This happened by accident, randomly? he inquired. We are here, unplanned collections of billions of cells that evolved by billions of chance occurrences over millions of years, from one-celled creatures to human beings, occurrences that had to happen in just the right order, at the proper temperature, over a specific time span on a planet neither too large nor too small, neither too close nor too far from its sun, which itself had to be a specific size, and so on, so we would be able to discuss this question as if the answer didn't really matter? There's only one thing more difficult to believe than that God created the universe, he would remind them, and that is that He didn't, that the universe and everything within it is here, in all its overlapping intricacy and interdependence, from tiny to huge, brute force and filigreed beauty, by accident and empty randomness.

Rabbi Reuven Samson did not doubt that God gave the Torah, both the written and oral, to Moses at Mount Sinai. That is, the whole Five Books of Moses—Genesis, Exodus, Leviticus, Numbers and Deuteronomy—and what became the Mishnah and Gemara, the basis of the Talmud. A lot to remember, to be sure. But Moses, the humblest man of his day and therefore the greatest, had been up to it. Especially since he had forty days atop the peak hearing it directly from God.

Put it another way, the rabbi thought. In micro—even though Moses' experience was utterly macro—not quite a millennium after Moses, the Prophet Jeremiah stood in Jerusalem, in the king's court, no less. There he railed against the Jews' backsliding, their abandonment of their covenant with the Almighty. They were going to be punished, he warned, and Nebuchadnezzar and his Babylonians were on their way to do so. This was just after 605 B.C.E., when little Judea found itself squeezed among the Egyptian, Assyrian and Babylonian empires and no longer could play them against each other. Marching toward dominance, Nebuchadnezzar, having eradicated the Philistines in their five city-states, made King Jehoiakim in Jerusalem his servant. The book of Jeremiah notes that the prophet's spoken words were transcribed by his secretary, Baruch ben Neriah, chamberlain to the unfortunate Jehoiakim's completely cornered successor, King Zedekiah. In a cache of 200 clay bullae found in an antiquities dealer's shop in Jerusalem in 1975, 2,561 years after the

Babylonians destroyed the First Temple and led Jewish survivors into captivity in 586 B.C.E., was the bullae belonging to Baruch ben Neriah.

On the other hand, Rabbi Samson considered himself an exactist, not a literalist. He didn't think the 7,500-foot peak long called Jebel Musa by the Arabs in the southern Sinai Peninsula, with the Greek Orthodox monastery of St. Catherine's at its base, was the biblical Mt. Horeb, the mountain of God. For one thing, this Mt. Sinai was surrounded by other mountains, including at least one higher. There was no plain, no room around it for two or three million Israelites fleeing Egypt to have gathered, as described in Exodus, chapters 19 and 20. Or just 20,000 Israelite slaves who had taken the opportunity of a weak Egyptian regime to escape back to their brethren remaining in Canaan, as at least one modern critic insisted. Mt. Horeb must be somewhere else in Sinai, or, if not Sinai, then in northwest Saudi Arabia at one or the other of two more physically promising peaks. Perhaps the 8,500-foot prominence Arabs called "Mount Lawz," that the newly opening monarchy liked to show Western tourists. Not that the rabbi worried much about correcting Muslim and Greek Orthodox believers on that geographic point.

Rabbi Samson's immediate problem, the Jewish Organization for Learning and Outreach's problem, was what to do about Gerry Meyer? On the verge of what the rabbi feared might be an unhinged breakout, the man could do great damage. Yet was he just a man, or something more? Exactist over literalist didn't help him here. He need advice. He needed to see the *Chacham*.

Chapter Nine:
Smartest Man in Brooklyn, the Present

The *Chacham*, literally a wise or learned person, a genius even, could be found—when he wanted to be found—in a *shteibel* on a side street off Washington Avenue not far from the Brooklyn Botanic Garden and Mount Prospect Park. In a city the size of New York, thronged with the incessant comings and goings of eight million impossibly varied people, the *shteibel* seemed almost disconnected. It sat inconspicuously in a quiet block of three- and four-story brownstones whose value continued to increase even if their upkeep as rentals or the homes of no-longer-affluent owners, did not. Residents, most of them non-Jews and either students, young professionals or retirees, took little notice of worshippers at the *shteibel*. There were twenty-five or thirty men, dressed in black suits, white shirts and black fedoras, and the occasional women in long-sleeved, high-necked dresses with hems that reached to the ankles, who prayed three times a day in the little synagogue. A few small children sometimes played around the ankles of the adults. Its exterior marked only by a small Star of David above the frosted glass door set in a dark wooden frame and by the *mezuzah* on the upper right door post, the *shteibel* harkened back to countless such community prayer halls in pre-1939 eastern Europe. Many now could be found in the Jewish sections of Crown Heights and Williamsburg not far away.

The *Chacham* was not this *shteibel's* rabbi. For all anyone knew, he was not a rabbi at all. But he was a regular at the small prayer house, rarely missing one of the thrice-daily prayers—morning, late afternoon, and evening—except when he did not appear for weeks at a time. Acquainted with his comings and goings, none of the other regulars would have said they were close. Quite willing to engage in detailed discussions of matters of *halacha* (Jewish religious law) or textual interpretations, the *Chacham* diverted personal queries with pleasant generalities. How long he had been coming to the *shteibel*, no one could quite say, except that it must have been some time.

A black Chrysler 300 with tinted windows slowed and then stopped in front of the Franklin Avenue/Botanic Garden subway station. Three men exited and began walking briskly along Eastern Parkway. The Chrysler closely trailed them. The trio was composed of a taller-than-average, solidly-built man in front, a somewhat shorter, squared-shoulder fellow who dressed like a traditionalist Orthodox rabbi second, and a younger, more slender man who trailed closely behind. To anyone who ever spent nine weeks in advanced infantry training, they moved as—although did not resemble—a 10-man squad. Minus seven.

In a few blocks the three turned into a side street, going another block, then pivoting onto a second even smaller, quieter street. The man in the middle caught sight of the Star of David over a frosted glass door and started up the steps. Anyone watching would have been struck by his quickness.

Would he even recognize the *Chacham*? It had been several years since their last meeting, after all, and then the man's brown beard already revealed signs of gray, his once lithe frame showed a little bulk. The rabbi glanced around. One of his companions stood by a side door halfway back; the other stayed close to the street entrance. Morning *shacharit* prayers had not yet started. Several knots of black-suited men stood talking. At the back, just beyond a draped *mechitza* separating men's and women's sections, two women, one stylishly slender in a neck-to-ankle sheath dress, the other improbably thickset and draped in folds of fabric, silently leafed through prayer books.

There he was. If you knew who you were looking for, the *Chacham* stood out, unique, a man whose bearing bespoke authority. But if you didn't know who you wanted to find, he was practically invisible, one more anonymous person in a teeming megapolis and in this little place, just another Jew praying with his peers.

The rabbi picked a prayer book off the shelf just inside the door and then slid into an empty seat beside the *Chacham*. The other man nodded.

Thirty-five minutes later, *shachrit* completed, Rabbi Samson rose, turned to the *Chacham* and said, "Coffee?"

"Yes."

They walked in silence up Eastern Parkway, accompanied by the rabbi's two companions, until reaching a small café. "Wizzotsky's Original New Old World Tea Shop." The window sign continued in smaller letters, "Coffee Too. And Bagels. And Schmear. And Pastries." At bottom, in even smaller letters, "Under Rabbinic Supervision Since 5763 (2004). Closed Shabbat."

Seated, coffee cups before them, a pecan roll in front of the *Chacham*, a cherry Danish before the rabbi (he would eat only half, he told himself without the slightest conviction), they finally spoke to each other again. "You've come to see me about this Gerry Meyer, I imagine," said the *Chacham*. With only the slightest surprise, the rabbi replied, "Of course. The Organization does not know what to make of him."

"You mean, what to do about him."

"Yes."

The men were quiet, sipping their coffee, eating their pastries. Then the *Chacham* asked, "What do you think you should do about him?" He had learned, in his early years as a licensed clinical social worker and middle years as a nearly full-time financial advisor and part-time archaeologist, that it was better to induce the patient or client—to lead him or herself through the difficulty at hand rather than attempt to instruct the person as if from on high. Unlike most people, he also was comfortable with silence.

"Well, we've determined that he is indeed a descendant of the House of David. His parents' stories, survival during the Holocaust, are singular, almost radiantly so, even for such biographies. And we've watched him begin a return to Jewish practice and Jewish study. But it appears to be an idiosyncratic, even dangerous return," the rabbi said.

"Dangerous? How?" asked the *Chacham*, knowing perfectly well how. But as the Talmud says, the scholar learns from everyone. Especially perhaps, from other scholars, even from one's students.

"In little more than half a year, Gerry Meyer has gone from a middle-aged, mid-life crisis-beset real estate lawyer and private investment banker, divorced father of two, to an impatient *ba'al t'shuvah*, attending daily prayers and studying with a rabbi, yes, but also flashing a charismatic streak, speaking as well as studying. He already has attracted a small following of men and women. He's started a weekly podcast—anyone can do so, of course, and so many have—to which more than a thousand have subscribed. The *New York Jewish Week* interviewed him and the *Jewish Press* published his commentary on the tension between tradition and modernity," the rabbi said, referring to the secular-leaning *Jewish Week* and Orthodox-inclined *Jewish Press*, respectively.

"And the commentary?"

"It was conventional, acceptable—up to the last paragraph. At which point he concluded that not only would modernity have to incorporate active Jewish tradition for Western societies to survive, but also that Orthodoxy would have to accept much of modernity not only to hold the Jews but also attract more converts if Judaism was to endure as other than, and here I quote, 'a marginal, antique cult.'"

"The eternal false dichotomy," said the *Chacham*. "Not to mention the powerful current of 'saving remnant' belief and assertion. Accept which part of modernity, I wonder? Freedom of speech, religion, the press, markets, abortion on demand, obesity, gender confusion, decriminalization of crime? The buffet table of materialism is long and overflowing. Those poorly-grounded experience difficulty making choices …"

"Whoa," said the rabbi. "We're getting away from Gerry Meyer."

"Are we? I understand he recently bought a red sports car in which he's been seen with an attractive blonde who has a Jewish last name but not a Jewish mother."

How did this man know such things, so many immediately relevant things? Rabbi Samson wondered. What he responded with was, "You look quite tanned. Where have you been lately?"

"Florida, one of our Holy Land annexes," he said. "I participated in a panel at a conference of financial advisors."

"A panel on what, if I may ask?" Rabbi Samson queried.

"One of the perennial topics: 'Gold in Your Clients' 401Ks: Fundamental or Foolish?'"

"Well?"

"It's free advice you want? A little gold is never a bad thing. Too much can be a disaster. And silver's more volatile. Given the inevitable, but perhaps still distant, reliance on nuclear power, I might suggest a small buy of uranium mining and refining stocks. But speaking of King David—as we always are, one way or the other—I was also in Jerusalem. I was helping supervise this season's work at the Large Stone Structure."

The structure, the rabbi knew, had been excavated by the late Israeli archeologist Eilat Mazur and identified by her in 2005 as the best candidate for the long-sought ruins of King David's palace from roughly 1000 B.C.E. Among items found at the site three years later was the bulla of Gedaliah ben Pashur. The Prophet Jeremiah mentions Pashur in Chapter 38, verse 1. Turns out ben Pashur was one of the princes in King Zedekiah's court to warn Jeremiah, on pain of death, against any more gloom-and-doom prophesying. No more about the backsliding Israelites being conquered by Nebuchadnezzar's Babylonians, ben Pashur ordered Jeremiah. "Bad for public morale, get it? The king doesn't like it, see?" That was ben Pashur's message to Jeremiah, if not quite biblically transcribed in those words. The king, through his minions, was attempting to issue an order of censorship. The court, and the priesthood, correctly recognized Jeremiah as a chronic thorn in their sides. But they always underestimated the man. For did he not have God with him? In fact, was he not carrying out HaShem's orders and with His promise of protection? Ben Pashur knew just what God had told the prophet. Hell, most of Jerusalem knew:

"Before I formed you in the belly I knew you, and before you came from the womb, I sanctified you, and I ordained you to be a prophet unto the nations."

Jeremiah didn't want the job. Who would? Prophesying to the Jews was thankless, even dangerous work. To all the nations? Even worse.

So, he said, as he confessed in the first chapter of his book, "Oh, Lord God! I cannot speak for I am a child."

No dice, God had replied. "Say not, I am a child, for you will go to all that I send you, and whatever I command you, you shall speak." And by the way, the Almighty promised the unwilling prophet-to-be, "Be not afraid of their faces for I am with you to deliver you." Just in case Jeremiah did not comprehend the full scope of his mission—though it was quite likely he did and that's just why he resisted—God added, "See, I have set you over the nations and over the kingdoms, to root out and pull down, to destroy and pull down, and to build up and to plant." So, Jeremiah's message wouldn't be for the Israelites only, for the Judeans alone, but for all mankind. Almighty God commanded him so. God almighty, what an impossibly large job description.

Gedaliah ben Pashur knew all this because he himself had ordered confiscation of the very scroll written by that damned court turncoat, Baruch ben Nirah. The first scroll. He suspected, no, he knew that ben Nirah, loyal to Jeremiah almost like a dog to its master, already must have written another one. The man who ben Pashur told the king deserved to be executed possessed a fantastic memory. There wasn't a better scribe in Jerusalem. You had to give him that much. That and maybe a scorpion-filled pit next to the one he had ordered prepared for the prophet himself.

"Did you find anything interesting this season?" the rabbi asked.

"Interesting, of course. For example, ivory-handled eating utensils and the remains of exotic foods, suggesting that the Large Stone Structure was used by royalty, by the dynasty, for centuries after. But not earth-shaking."

"Where did you study archaeology, if I might ask?" the rabbi said.

The *Chacham* looked at him closely for a moment before saying, "University College London."

"One of the best schools of archaeology," the rabbi noted. "When did you find time?"

The Chacham did not answer. Finishing their coffee and pastries almost simultaneously, the men sat quietly, seeming to meditate, each in his own thoughts for a moment. Finally, the *Chacham* said, "So, what is JOLO going to do about Mr. Meyer?"

"For now, continued close observation. And additional attendance at his public events. Subtle guidance if possible." The rabbi stopped. He picked up his coffee, realized the cup was empty, and set it down again. For all his erudition, experience and insight, he sometimes felt condemned to pick his way through a maze dimly lit.

"We know," he resumed, "that Maimonides, in describing the attributes necessary for recognition of the *Mosiach*, wrote that 'if a king will arise from the House of David who diligently contemplates the Torah and observes its *mitzvot* as prescribed by the Written Law and the Oral Law as did David, his ancestor, and will compel all of Israel to walk in (the way of the Torah) and rectify the breaches in its observance, and fight the wars of God, we may, with assurance, consider him Moshiach.' If Gerry Meyer even begins to those do things, fine. Although how anyone 'compels all of Israel' to do anything, let alone every necessary thing, is a mystery to me. If he does not, red sports car and blonde companion notwithstanding, we will find other measures."

"No doubt. But listen, Reuven ben Shimson," the Chacham said, startling the rabbi by using his full Hebrew name, "don't wait too long. The more influential this Meyer fellow becomes, the harder it will be to erase his influence, if not the man himself." The two men waited for the check in silence. "We won't," the rabbi finally said as they parted.

Chapter Ten:
Mainz, 1096

"Like locusts they come up the Rhine Valley," Master David said. "Their sacred father, the pope has called them to free the Holy Land from rule by the infidels, the followers of Mohammed. Mounted on their battle horses, adorned in armor, wielding swords decorated with silver and gold, they rehearse by slaughtering the Jews of Christendom. We know too well what they did at Rouen, for example, and what they have done since, laying waste to cities, martyring the Lord's believers, and destroying what possessions of theirs they do not carry off. They proclaim a Holy Crusade, but they commit robbery, rape and murder. We have but one question of your Excellency: Can we count on your continued protection?"

The Archbishop of Mainz was a prince of the Church. An imposing figure of a man, he had been elevated to archbishop by Pope Gregory VII. In Mainz, he acted with both the formal, if grudging support of new Pope Urban II, a reformer like Gregory but without his predecessor's human touch, and the friendship of Henry IV, emperor of the Holy Roman Empire. Henry, Master David knew, demonstrated a tolerance if not friendship for Jews unusual among Europe's rulers. He also had benefitted from the support, financial and otherwise, of Mainz's previous Jewish leader, Kalonymus ben Meshullam. Ben Meshullam had been a blessing and a curse for the Mainz Jewish community. Unusually wealthy, he attracted attention and, sometimes, protection. Protection, however uncertain, was welcomed. Attention was not.

Archbishop Ruthard, in the manner of his political ally the emperor, had been a friend, protector even, of Mainz's Jews. Of all this, Master David was well aware. But now he stood before the archbishop and on behalf of the city's anxious Jewish community sought reassurance directly from him.

"My friend," the archbishop said warmly, though he remained seated, "you know I have spoken not only to but also for the Jews of Mainz ever since I came to this city several years ago. And when actions were required in addition to words, as when some itinerant preacher led a few of the townsfolk astray, I sent my palace guard to, shall we say, reprove them."

"I know, Your Excellency. The community knows, and we are endlessly grateful. But there has never been a murdering mass like this before in the Rhineland. You know the horrors that befell Rouen, and not only there. Although the Jews of that city had paid vast sums to the councilors and to the priests, and even purchased a fortified keep and tower, and services of an armed guard, they were martyred in their thousands—men, women, children and babes."

Were he not speaking to the archbishop, Master David would have sobbed, images of the atrocities wreaked upon his brethren in the northern city—rape, even of little girls, dismemberment, decapitation—unshakably before his eyes. What he wanted to add, would it not have been a harsh intrusion into a conversation both men sought to keep polite, Master David would have said, "Faced with an army of beasts in human form screaming for Jewish blood, the guard melted away." He knew the Jews, confronted by a demand to convert or die, donned what armor they could, grabbed swords, pikes, knives or even clubs and—amateurs at war—prepared to sanctify the Divine Name, *kiddush HaShem*, by their own deaths. Deaths at the hands of professional knights transformed by the pope's order to reclaim the Holy Land into religious fanatics and followed by a ravening mob of illiterate ... illiterate peasants!

"I know about Rouen," the archbishop said, almost curtly, as if he had heard Master David's thoughts. "Do you know about my colleagues the bishops of Speyer and Cologne? No sooner had riots against the Jews started in their cities than the bishops stopped them, executing the leaders and, as warning to others, commanding that their bodies be cut up and burned." His tone softening, Archbishop Ruthard added, "Master David, you can tell your people that if trouble comes to Mainz, they will find me like my friends in Speyer and Cologne, not like those who failed in their Christian duty in Rouen and a score of other cities."

After the Jew had gone, Archbishop Ruthard, erect on his throne-like chair until then, slumped. *I wonder*, he thought to himself. Not about his own position, but about that of the rest of his clerical associates in Mainz, and about the loyalty of his palace guard. Would it stand firm once the crusaders, already being described as a human version of the locust plague Yahweh brought upon the ancient Egyptians, darkened the Rhine River valley near Mainz as the insect host had darkened the Nile sky so long ago?

As he left the archbishop to report to the other Jewish community leaders of Mainz, Master David wondered too. But not for long. Three days later, the head of the Crusader column appeared before the city walls, armored knights on horseback, lances at rest, swords at their sides. The force drew near under colorful banners emblazoned with all sorts of devices—crucifixes of course, but also icons of medieval heraldry including eagles, lions, dragons, unicorns, angels and more. The procession could have been that of a chivalric parade except for what followed the thousands of horsemen. Tens of thousands of men, and some women too, on foot, a few leading donkeys pulling carts, most carrying sacks slung over one shoulder and usually bearing a staff or even a pike or an axe across the other.

Watching from the ramparts, Master David smelled the lumbering horde almost as soon as he saw it. Unwashed, yes; who bathed then except aristocrats before the occasional investiture or high coronation and the Jews, who weekly immersed themselves in the *mikveh*, the ritual bath fed with "living waters" from the nearest spring or stream, just before the Sabbath? But more than merely unwashed, the approaching mob—swollen now with thousands of barefoot peasants and landless wanderers not only from France and the lower Rheinish provinces but from as far off as England and Sweden—was excited. For the first time in their tedious, exhausting lives, there were not only religiously virtuous acts to be performed—forcibly converting or killing the devilish Jews—but also the certainty of additional riches taken from those of the Christ-killers in their path. These Jews were to be robbed, raped, tortured and killed in sport so great it made them forget mere bear-baiting and wolf-sacking. And outside of their own tightly-circumscribed farms and villages, unidentifiable in their uncountable numbers, beyond the reach of local magistrates, they moved heedless of even imperial edicts and church-issued prohibitions against harming Jews. Their leaders, Peter the Hermit, William the Carpenter, Drogo of Nesle, the venom-spitting monk Gottschalk and, of course, the great Jew-hater Count Emicho were present, inspiring them, inciting them.

Three knights drew up to the main city gate. They threw back the face-coverings on their helmets. The horseman in the middle spoke. Looking up to the guards in their small turrets flanking the gate, he said loudly, but with no particular urgency, "We come in the fellowship of our Lord, Jesus Christ! We come by order of His Eminence, Pope Gregory. On the great Crusade to reclaim the Holy Land from the infidel Mohammedans, we are in need of your hospitality this night."

"We will tell the prince of this city, the archbishop, of your request," said the captain of the guard."

The knight laughed, a grating sound without mirth. "Tell your prince, an archbishop," he thundered, "that Sir Geoffrey of Saint Denis, liberator of the Rhineland, by the grace of God Himself empowered to liberate Jerusalem, does not make requests." He enunciated "archbishop" as if the word left a sour taste on his tongue.

Master David was not the only interested civilian watching from the city walls. The archbishop, in the cassock of a simple monk, shielded by several of his palace guard, also now dressed in plain clerical robes, peered intently at this Sir Geoffrey. They knew of him, of course. Coarse, crude, strong, remorseless. And possessed of just enough cunning to have enlarged his originally small, impoverished holding of Saint Denis into an area as extensive as a county, and one with the profitable market town that gave its name to the territory. Sir Geoffrey, accustomed to getting his way on a small scale, now led one column of the First Crusade, fired with ambition to get his way on a grand, perhaps eventually kingly scale.

Hurriedly returning to his palace, the archbishop held council with his bishops and officers of his guard.

"Do we have enough men to deny the Crusaders admittance and keep the gates closed?" he asked.

"For a day. Or two at most," said the guard general. "If we fight, we will suffer losses. With the knights are skilled archers. They can keep us pinned down as they batter the outer gate until it sunders. We could then fight them at close quarters between the outer and inner gate. We would inflict many casualties. But sooner or later they will overwhelm us through sheer numbers and then breach the inner gate, and Mainz will be defenseless before them. And, though they've shown they need little pretext, once inside and enraged at having been opposed, they likely will begin their customary slaughter."

"So, if we offer rich provisions from the city to them outside the walls while denying admittance, might that avail us?" the archbishop asked. But he already knew the answer. Geoffrey of Saint Denis had spurned such proposals from lower valley localities. In fact, their proffer—provisions but not admittance—only had incensed him, spurring him to greater pillage and rapine.

"Inform Sir Geoffrey that he and his commanders are to be my guests at a grand banquet in his honor tonight at sundown. We will open the gates and escort him to the assembly hall ourselves," the archbishop told the captain of the guards.

"Is there time to arrange such a feast?" the guard general asked, confused. "Are we going to poison them?"

"A divine thought," the archbishop said. "Except that Sir Geoffrey travels with a taster. He's already lost two of them, I understand. No, we will fashion a real meal for him."

The archbishop, still in a monk's cassock, had yet another question. "The water tunnel is still open, Isn't it?"

"Yes, as you instructed."

"And the horses just outside?"

"Yes."

"All right. We will cross the Rhine to Wiesbaden, then move southeast toward Vienna. It will be a long journey, so bring as many provisions as you can. Oh, and one more thing. Send a man to Master David, head of the Jews. Tell him, in my name, to take his family and flee to Vienna, not stopping in Wiesbaden."

Master David heard the messenger in silence. When the man finished, Master David responded only by saying "thank you" and sending him on his way with a gold coin for his trouble. He then stood in front of his house, calm, even stoic. He was not surprised. Finally, his thoughts and sight elsewhere, he turned his back on the unusually silent street and reentered his home.

The messenger, however, did not immediately depart. Lingering near a window of the Jew's house, he turned the coin over in his palm. He realized more, perhaps much more could be made from the Jews' distress. Wasn't that always the case? There were others, he had heard, who would pay fine sums for information about Master David and his family. Especially interested, so he knew from gossip at the archbishop's palace, were the Disciples of the Chalice. An order of military monks, so it was said. Not only did they persevere in searching for pieces of the One True Cross, but also in recovering the lost holy Chalice, the one used by Jesus Christ himself to serve wine to his disciples at the Last Supper. And, a few people insisted, in making sure no Jewish messiah, no false pretender to the throne of King David—now severed from the Jews by the Lord Himself for their stiff-necked refusal to acknowledge his Son as messiah-savior-redeemer—ever arose. But how to contact them, if they were present in Mainz, if in fact they even existed?

****

"No, Miriam. You must go. You must take the children and go. Now!" Master David, both anguished and agitated, actually raised his voice to his wife. Neither of them could have recalled when he ever had done that before. "And I must stay. I am too recognizable in this city to make good an escape, and if I tried would further endanger you and the children."

"Do you imagine we can make our way ourselves, alone, through this pestilential mob encircling Mainz? Even to entertain such an idea would be madness!" Now she raised her voice to him, a second breech in their lives as they had been until that moment.

"I imagine nothing," Master David replied, his voice softer than before. "I arranged for your passage the day after I first heard of these Crusaders, as they arrogantly call themselves. Take the children and go through the water tunnel to the river. At the second dock the boat of the trader Shimon Schiffenburger, the one they call Shimon the Red because of his beard, will be waiting. He will float you downriver in the opposite direction from these holy warriors and put you ashore at Cologne. There my brother, Jonathan, will meet you."

"I am not leaving you," she declared, wrapping her arms around him.

He kissed her, feeling the power of their love more strongly than at any previous time in their life together. And then Master David unwrapped her encircling hold. His hands still on Miriam's wrists, tears in his eyes, he spoke to his wife in a voice hardly more than a whisper. "HaShem has ordained this. We, Mainz, the Rhineland have come to the moment I must stay so you and the children may go, and live. We know who our son Amiram is—who he can become—through my own lineage, the famous double-edged sword. And we know how precious Esther and Rivka are, the women and mothers of Israel they are meant to be. You can save them now. I cannot."

Miriam stared into her husband's eyes with a look of turbulent emotions. Finally, she pulled her hands from his. "We will see each other again, my beloved," she promised. "In this world or *Olam ha-ba*, the next."

****

It was not quite sundown when Archbishop Ruthard and several of his senior prelates, accompanied by a small detachment of guards, exited Mainz's main city gate to escort Sir Geoffrey Saint-Denis and his senior commanders to a banquet in the palace's central assembly hall. The archbishop and his men were dressed in their finest clerical robes, the archbishop—his rank made clear by the golden, pointed mitre on his head, curved silver crozier staff in his hand—in the lead. The little column had gone no more than thirty or forty yards when mounted knights swarmed it from all sides. Riding leisurely up to join his men and their new captives came Sir Geoffrey.

"Ah, good evening, Your Excellency," he said self-indulgently. "Good of you to come visit us. And now, please be so good as to turn around and take us to your banquet. And ask your guards to leave the gates open so my army, my people, may follow. They too are hungry. Not to mention thirsty, and, of course, lonely from so long on the march."

"But I have food for only you and your senior commanders," the archbishop began to protest.

"Don't worry, Excellency. My troops are quite able to forage for themselves."

Barely an hour after sunset, in the darkening night, Master David watched from a third-floor window in his long, narrow house. At some distance, flames danced into the sky. He thought, though he could not be certain, that he heard shouts, and screams, coming to him on evening breezes.

Before going up to look, Master David had deposited as many of his holy books as possible beneath the stones of the kitchen floor, then swept over the hiding place to obscure its use. Their silver plate—candlesticks for Shabbat, serving platters, Elijah's goblet and the like—he left out. He doubted that would satisfy knights or more likely mob participants when they arrived to enrich themselves on their way to the Holy Land, but perhaps it would distract them. In any case, he had given most of the money in the house to Miriam, keeping just enough so that, with the silver plate, his imminent visitors just might be, if not satisfied, then delayed. He had closed his front door but not locked it. Master David wanted to hear their untroubled footsteps to try to determine how many he would face.

After looking from the third floor, Master David retreated to the narrow landing at the top of the stairs from the second level. In one hand he held a jar of ceremonial olive oil, which he proceeded to spill across the last steps up to the landing and on the landing itself. In the other he held a boning knife, about seven inches long, the one Miriam had used so often to prepare chicken, and once in a while beef, for Shabbat dinners. Master David was determined to give a good accounting of himself.

****

"Esther, Rivka, hurry!" Miriam urged her daughters on through the dark, narrow alleyways sloping ever downward toward the passage to the water tunnel, pulling her youngest, seven-year-old Amiram by the wrist. No one else seemed to be about. No lights shone from inside the shuttered windows, no sounds from those inside, if anyone remained there. Although, she wondered, almost amused, where could they have fled to? This was not the Jewish quarter and its inhabitants likely had not given much thought to the day they, too, would be forced to flee.

The passage she sought opened just to their left. But as she caught sight of it, a man stepped into her path from between two buildings ahead of her on the right. Big, broad, a little paunchy, he wore a knight's chain mail but no other armor over a long, leather apron like that of a carpenter, butcher or some other tradesman. Unlike any tradesman, he grasped a warrior's sword in his right hand.

"Mistress Miriam, is it?" he asked airily. "Good evening to you. I see you have your children—that would be Esther and Rivka, already handsome young ladies, and the precious Amiram, no doubt—with you. Going somewhere? And without Master David? That certainly won't do. Here, let us accompany you." As he spoke he stepped toward her, and she could hear at least two others approach from the rear, behind the children.

Miriam studied the man, studied his garments, rather. The apron, she saw, draped over his shoulders. Unlike the chain mail, it did not close at the sides. But the chain mail stopped short of his waist, as if hammered together for a shorter man, or this man himself when he had been a bit younger, a bit thinner. As he reached her he sheathed his sword to grab Amiram with one hand and take hold of her with the other. That was when Miriam thrust a short knife she had hidden in the folds of her garment between the front and back of the leather apron, up under the chain mail, just under his ribs. With all her strength, in a mother's fury, she drove it in to the handle and twisted. The big man screamed and, writhing, slumped to the bricks.

His companions, each of whom had gathered up one of the shouting, kicking girls—"the Sultan's procurers will pay nicely for fine such Jewesses as yourselves," one had said—stopped, momentarily unable to accept what had just happened. As they stood immobile, another group of men in cassocks but wielding swords, stepped into the passageway.

"Release them!" the guard general ordered. Deprived of their prey and taken by surprise, the remaining pair could not prevent themselves from being slain easily. Pulling down the cowl of his cassock, one of the men revealed his face to Miriam and smiled. Gently, he said, "this way." Since he once had visited their home, she recognized the archbishop immediately. He had not poisoned Sir Geoffrey, good idea though it had been, merely ensured he and his fellow banqueters now slept the sleep of the deeply intoxicated.

Chapter Eleven:
Key West, Florida, the Present

The synagogue, gleaming on this sun-washed, hurricane threatened speck at the southern end of Florida, was new. Pale blue trim on white stucco over concrete block, it stood several feet above the ground on a platform supported by sturdy-looking pilings. One hundred feet away the Caribbean Sea glimmered blue-green under a high, late spring sky. The structure itself included an office, library, two classrooms, a small kitchen and reception hall, and a sanctuary that could hold up to 120 worshippers, though it rarely hosted half that many except on Rosh Hashana and Yom Kippur. Then they crowded in, standing room only, 150 or so.

This outpost, a few blocks north of South and Whitehead streets, where America met the Caribbean, was, as JOLO Central in New York recognized, one of the quirkiest of the organization's more than 200 facilities around the world. As befit Key West's general population, the worshipers spanned the spectrum from secular to Orthodox; American, Israeli, Russian, South African, Cuban and Tunisian (the latter by way of France). They were male and female, heterosexual and homosexual, astoundingly rich and, quite frankly, poor who seemed to live off the sun. The young rabbi and *rebbetzin* in charge conducted adult education programs, Hebrew classes, Israeli folk dancing, challah baking and beef-and-bourbon cook-outs. And they made sure the helipad near the synagogue was kept clear of palm fronds, wandering sea turtles and wind-blown sand. It was always ready for JOLO's high-speed, low altitude helicopter, which among other assignments, regularly delivered kosher food from Miami or, if necessary, rushed congregants there for state-of-the-art medical treatment. It was known as a JOLO facility only to the rabbi, his wife and a few others. To the rest of Key West it was just a small, friendly synagogue.

This day, the chopper had just set down. As its rotors slowed, four men emerged, crouched beneath the beating blades. The first was Uri Stein, a little over medium height and not an ounce of fat, formerly an Israeli paratrooper, now head of the JOLO security team. Following quickly were Rabbi Reuven Samson; Dovid Fruchter, a chubby fellow whose expensive blue suit fit a little too snugly and who was the organization's chief financial officer; and a second security team member, a tall, spare man, formerly of the New York City Police Department, who this week was calling himself Murray Menschnikov.

Waiting to greet them, standing just off the pad, gripping his hand-woven Panama hat—no black fedoras for JOLO rabbis in Key West before November or after February—against the helicopter's backwash, stood Rabbi Jamie (Chaim with a semi-tropical accent) Berliner. Rabbi Berliner had his finger on the pulse of his community, or rather fingers on the community's varied pulses. Had he not been hosting the powers that be from headquarters this day, he would have been in khaki slacks and a tropical shirt, his black beard still filling in. Rabbi Berliner was all of thirty years old. He and his wife, Sarah—better known on Key West as Suki—had three children and were expecting their fourth.

As they shook hands, Rabbi Samson asked Rabbi Berliner, "are they here yet?"

"Oh yes, both of them," the younger man said. "They're so excited to meet with you a second time they can hardly contain themselves. Well, one of them anyway. Patrick actually spilled some of his tea while waiting—the Darjeeling he imports from West Bengal."

Rabbi Samson nodded sympathetically. To himself he thought, still importing? Good, that suggests he may be able to meet the request I need to make of him and Moshe. Patrick was, as the rabbi considered it, Moshe's partner. Not very likely the other way around.

JOLO Key West had been built with a multi-million-dollar donation from an Israeli-born doctor, 60-year-old heart researcher, Moshe Meital, and his husband, Patrick Jameson, an Iowa-born epidemiologist who ran a sizeable tea importing business on the side as what he called a hobby. When not at New York University's Grossman School of Medicine or the Cleveland Clinic, they worked remotely from their palm-shadowed Key

West Victorian. They attended synagogue only three times a year, once on Rosh Hashanah, once on Yom Kippur, and for the first Passover seder, but donated whatever and whenever needed. Odd, Rabbi Samson thought yet again. Odd, but dedicated in their way and reliably generous in their philanthropy.

After walking to a small but tastefully furnished meeting room in the headquarters, the four men and rabbi exchanged pleasantries with the two doctors who were waiting for them. Moshe Meital leaned back in one of the ergonomic, webbed-fabric chairs around Rabbi Berliner's conference table, and faced Rabbi Samson. "So, Rabbi, what can Patrick and I do for you?"

Patrick Jameson, having served everyone else the special Darjeeling tea, placed his own cup on the table and took his seat next to Moshe. A light yet unmistakable fragrance rose on wisps of vapor from the rich orange liquid. "Yes," said Patrick. "It's such a pleasure to see you again. How can we help the synagogue or your organization?"

Moshe Meital wore a starched white dress shirt over sharply creased gray slacks and polished black loafers. His large head was shaved and small black glasses perched on his nose. His appearance gave an impression of unrelenting competence. He could have been the chief executive officer of any successful corporation, Rabbi Samson thought. Close at his side, Patrick Jameson sat, leaning expectantly toward the visitor, his tropical shirt in Day-Glo colors half unbuttoned over white Levis and sandals, long light-brown hair curling up at the neck. He had the deep tan of one who played tennis outdoors, often.

"Is this one of your own teas?" Rabbi Samson asked him. "It's very good." The rabbi thought Jameson might be blushing under that tan of his.

"It is, rabbi, and I'm glad you like it," Jameson said. Rabbi Samson took another sip, slowly, looking as unobtrusively as possible at Meital and Rabbi Berliner over the edge of his cup. They eyed him intently.

"Gentlemen, as you no doubt assume, and correctly, we are here to ask your assistance again. Your backing of this *shul* building, in which we now sit comfortably, taking in the view of the beach and blue water just beyond, was unstinting. Without it, the Jewish presence and activity on Key West might be only a trace of what already has been accomplished, not to speak of what is to come. We all know that, with the blessings of *HaShem* and dedicated work of people such as Rabbi Berliner here and *Rebbetzin* Sarah, JOLO continues to expand. But the more we grow, the more we find we need to grow.

"So, I'm here today to tell you that the organization needs a second helicopter."

At this point, Meital interjected. "As I recall, Rabbi Samson, the one you arrived in today is only four years old ..."

"Five," the rabbi said, deftly interrupting. "And there's nothing wrong with it. It serves our needs well on the East Coast, especially in the Southeast. We're not talking about replacing it. We need, rather, to add a second to service far-flung organizational outposts throughout the Caribbean, Mexico and even Central America."

"Do you have a price estimate?" Meital asked.

"Yes," Rabbi Samson said. "We've located just the model we think we need, an almost new Bell 429 Global Ranger."

"I know that model," Meital replied. "New it runs at least $7 million. You said almost new ..."

"It's not quite two years old, and the owner, a large corporation, wants to move from the seven-passenger Bell to the 12-passengeer Sikorsky S-76-D. So, we can buy the Bell for a little under $6 million," Rabbi Samson explained.

"Not bad," Meital said. "The Bell is fast, agile and has advanced avionics. Based here," he continued, looking directly at the rabbi, "it could cover a lot the Caribbean and beyond."

"We're thinking of basing it in Mexico City. That's home to our largest operation in the Western hemisphere outside the United States. But though we can purchase it for $6 million or so, and even though it's nearly new, we will need to spend another $2 million or so for upgrades."

"What sort of upgrades?" Meital asked, his curiosity piqued.

"Stealth," answered the man who had been introduced as Murray Menschikov.

The others nodded silently, except for Patrick Jameson, who, jerking a hand to his face in surprise at the word "stealth," nearly knocked his teacup to the floor.

Chapter Twelve:
Jerusalem, 1099

"Yishai, what are you doing?"

"Nothing mother," Miriam Josephus Pelegos heard her son, now probably her only son, reply. Which was what she expected. When this difficult child, this boy whom she loved dearly and now more than ever before, said, "nothing mother," Miriam Josephus knew it could mean anything and sometimes nothing good.

"What, exactly?" she called through the open window. The family's little stone house, its three small rooms more than adequate ever since the Franks had come and built their siege towers. The Pelegos family's small structure, along with several dozen others, comprised the village of Shiloach. The community perched on a hillside above a narrow valley separating it from the southernmost walls of the great city. And from their windows they witnessed or heard the most incredible, the most horrifying events.

The Franks had come with their Teutonic, Venetian and Swabian allies, several thousand knights in armor, on horseback, banners flying, who had taken the cross. Promised by Pope Urban II plenary indulgence—remission of all penance for sin—in return for crusading, they wore large and colorful crosses on tunic-like vestments over their armor. Now they were gathered around the high walls of Jerusalem, along with what her neighbor Achmad claimed were "12,000-foot soldiers, maybe more," and it looked to Miriam like perhaps half that many common and, from the appearance and sound, unruly folk.

"Deus le volt!" they had cried, the day two months before when engineers completed construction of their siege towers. "God wills it!" Wills their personal redemption, the return of Christ's city and the rest of the Holy Land to Christendom from the hands of the infidel Musselman, and hastening of nothing less than the Second Coming. So Pope Urban had promised them.

This pope was a true believer but no fanatic. He operated as a practiced politician able to balance, much of the time, the rivalrous tribes, clans and dynasties, the counts and barons, and kings and queens of western and central Europe, not to mention scheming competitors within his own ecclesiastical realm. It helped greatly that his preaching, not only in his native and polished French but also smooth Italian and serviceable German, inspired most of his many and varied listeners.

It was then, Miriam realized, that worse than the encirclement of the city, worse than the depredations they had heard of as the Frankish army moved southward after its conquest of Antioch a year earlier, was what was to come. This even if Shiloach, removed from the city's bustle the way an eagle's eerie sits removed from the comings and goings of the forest floor far below, remained untouched. But it had not.

With terrible fascination, Miriam, her husband Simon Paul Pelegos, a big, strong, lazy man, and their four children, older son Gilead, older daughter Elizabeth, Yishai and daughter Eleanor stared as the Crusaders circled the city. Led by hundreds of priests preaching victory for their Lord, they marched with great solemnity. Musselman soldiers looking down scoffed and jeered, until the Franks rolled their siege towers to the walls. The men of Godfrey de Bouillon were first to breach the defenses. They were led also by Tancred, since Antioch styled by Pope Urban as regent of that city and Prince of the Galilee; Raymond de Saint-Gilles; and Robert de Normandy. The Crusader army, arrows flying, swords slashing, axes smashing flooded in behind them.

It had been four years since the pope had proclaimed the crusade. They had been long years in which battlefield victories had been followed by defeats, armies confronted by mountains and deserts, decimated by starvation and plague, and most dangerously, incessant bickering among commanders and rulers. But after a short, one-sided struggle, the holy city of Jerusalem was in their hands. The Musselman governor surrendered to Raymond at the Tower of David. Tancred promised protection for civilians in the al-Aqsa Mosque. Soldiers disobeyed. So did the commoners who accompanied them. The slaughter that followed lasted longer than the battle itself and when it was over, thousands of men, women and children—Muslims, Jews and Christians, not Christians like the Franks, but Byzantine like Miriam and Simon's people—lay slaughtered.

Among them, maybe, were Gilead and Elizabeth. Against their mother's command—their father was sleeping on the roof, as he often did after the midday meal—they had darted out of the house, down the hillside and across the little stream that issued from Shiloach Spring. "We want to get a better look!" her older son had shouted over his shoulder as they ran. That was the last Miriam had heard from, or seen of, her two oldest.

"Yishai," Miriam said again through the window, "shouldn't you be getting ready for vespers?" The boy was trying to skip smooth stones along the narrow stream at the foot of the hill, she knew. It was a recent, obsessive pastime. She tried to be patient with the boy, but with thoughts of, fears really about Gilead and Elizabeth always preying on her, patience with Yishai was proving difficult.

"I went to morning prayers," he protested. "I said the Prayer of the Publican, the Troparia, the Prayer of Saint Basil, even Psalm 50. Why do I have to go back to the church every night?"

This was getting to be an old story, Miriam thought, exasperated. Ever since the Crusaders took over, Gilead found reasons not to go to vespers. What was he avoiding?

"Day and night, morning and evening. Men pray both times," she replied, exasperated.

"Father doesn't. Often, he doesn't go either time," Yishai countered.

"He is a sandal-maker. He must work." Sometimes, Miriam thought. "Anyway, I'm talking to you, not your father."

Silence. A long silence.

"Mother, I will tell you," Yishai said, coming off the hill and walking into the house. She looked at him with fresh eyes. Barely twelve years old and he was growing fast, getting tall like his father.

"Tell me what?"

"I don't want to go to vespers so long as Father Theodokous leads them."

"Why not?"

"I don't like the way he looks at me," Yishai said flatly.

"What way?" Miriam asked. Her inquiry was sharp.

"Like a wolf looking at a sheep," her son responded, just as sharply.

"All right, then. Don't go."

Miriam knew that look. She had seen Achmad, him with the two wives and nine children already, eyeing Eleanor the same way. Suddenly she knew they had to do something few if any of their neighbors ever considered. Her little family had to leave Shiloach, leave the Crusader Kingdom of Jerusalem, if possible, the city's environs for sure. But where could they go? Constantinople perhaps. There were fellow Greek, not Roman Christians. But so far, such an implausible journey. Antioch maybe, closer but now Roman ruled. Acre, even closer, with Greek, Roman, Syriac, Armenian and other Christians, even still some Jews, traders and holy men said to be among them, and a few Musselmans. Yes, Acre. It would be better, safer, probably. And they no doubt needed sandal-makers in Acre too. She would inform Simon. He would protest, he would try to delay, but he would follower her. He always had.

Chapter Thirteen:
Narbonne, 1136

"So, Captain Priscus, what do you hear of your fleet?" The Hegemon of the principality spoke softly as he always did when conversing with Priscus V. But as the latter well knew—without question the leading Jewish *captain* of all the port's chief merchants—urgency underlay the Hegemon's civility. Fortunately, this day he truthfully could tell the ruler what he wanted to hear.

"My son Malachi, whom I sent eastward along the coast, sent word only this morning. The ships have been sighted off Toulon. With continuing fair weather, they should arrive tomorrow, or the day after at the latest. But Excellency," Priscus added modestly, "I have hardly a fleet: We are discussing only three ships."

The Hegemon of Narbonne allowed himself a pleasant little laugh. "Priscus, I know your ships well. Three in number, but carrying the riches of three times that many. Cargoes for which not just the archbishop but also ladies of the court, including of course my wife and daughter, and the many merchants glad to do business with you, all await expectantly."

Not to mention you yourself, Priscus thought. When the anticipation of the archbishop, Lady Elianna, or both turns to anxiety, they question you. And that interrupts your own calculation of the import fees I will be obliged to pay. Not that I mind, the fees are no more onerous that those in any other port city along the Christian shores of France or Italy and, in fact, less than some. Certainly, no more costly than in the Moorish ports of Spain. Yes, it must be acknowledged, life as a Jewish captain—in fact life as any of the more than 2,000 Jewish souls of Narbonne—was good. And, less than fifty years after the Crusade-inflicted horrors, quite likely to get even better.

Priscus V was not his real name, of course. It was an honorific of sorts, after Priscus II, III and IV, earlier merchants captains of Narbonne. Of sorts, since Priscus II, the richest man not just in the port but the entire principality, had been murdered as a result of a commercial dispute more than a century earlier. An ironic joke among the Narbonnese, the name Priscus originally referred to a local diplomat and failed early fifth century ruler who foolishly attempted to mediate with Attila the Hun. "Negotiate with whom and about what?!" the Hun had mocked him. That was just before he sliced off Priscus I's right ear and tossed it into the fire. Locals had applied the name Priscus serially ever since to men whose self-evaluation exceeded even their fortunes.

But Priscus V, Dovid ben Dovid ben Solomon at circumcision, wore the title lightly. Successful yet not arrogant, charity enabled by his wealth, he held the esteem of nearly all his co-religionists and a great many of his Christian neighbors as well. He spoke not only the French dialect distinct to the region and nearly incomprehensible to outsiders but also *Zarphatic*, the local Judeo-French, and *Shuadit*, Judeo-Provencal, as well as Italian. And, of course, he read Hebrew, the holy tongue, and could speak it passably if pressed.

Dovid ben Dovid ben Solomon's fortune, erudition, and extensive commercial, not to mention political contacts throughout the northern Mediterranean meant that the Hegemon, Viscount Don Aymeric IV, found him an invaluable source of information, if not consultation. Important as it was, though, the arrival of the captain's ships with their eagerly awaited cargo was not the main reason for the Hegemon's visit.

"There are rumors, Priscus," he said, "that French and Teutonic knights are planning once again to try to seize the Spanish port of Valencia from the Moors. What have you heard?"

Dovid ben Solomon suspected Don Aymeric was testing him, as he occasionally did, since the rumors were about an attempt on Alicante, not Valencia. "Excellency, perhaps your information is fresher than mine. But in any case, I have heard nothing substantive about Valencia, no movement of soldiers in that direction, no gathering of warships nearby. What whispers have reached me concern Alicante, but without hard facts about armies or navies on the move."

Don Aymeric was pleased to hear Priscus' rumors. They validated what had come to him. He smiled but did not laugh. "That is so frequently the way with talk about, or better from our knightly brothers: When they are not fighting, which often is the case, they issue idle chatter about fighting. Well, I expect to see you tomorrow or the day after, at the port to celebrate the arrival of your fleet." With that the Hegemon, his secretary, and three bodyguards, strode out.

Late the next afternoon, the sails of Priscus V's three ships indeed were sighted off the coast of Narbonne. As they made for the port their insignia, a golden lion rampant—the Lion of Judah—on each foresail, stood out. A cheer arose from the sizeable crowd, which included not only Viscount Don Aymeric and Lady Elianna, but also the archbishop himself.

"Congratulations on another successful voyage," Don Aymeric said.

"Thank you, Excellency," replied Dovid ben Solomon, anxious as always as the ships tied up, "but perhaps we should wait until we see the cargo unloaded before celebrating."

"You display the humility of Moses," the Hegemon said, "but judging by the happy faces of the seamen, you can safely indulge yourself in a little of the pride of your namesakes, David and Solomon."

Hurrying down the gangway, the captain of the first and largest of the vessels stopped before their owner. "We obtained everything on the order manifest, and a little more," he reported. "Goods were plentiful in both Latakia and Venice. Because of the plenty, prices were reasonable. We have spices—cumin, cinnamon and pepper mostly—silks, cotton, gold and silver jewelry, perfume, pottery and even bitumen."

"Excellent, excellent ..." Dovid ben Solomon was saying, when his younger son, Nachson, interrupted. "Father, may I leave now? I have an examination tomorrow and really need to continue my studies. Please?"

"Of course, Nachson. I'm glad you could spare the time to see *our* ships come in," he told his son, ever so slightly emphasizing the word "our." Unlike his older brother, this one—Nachson ben Dovid ben Solomon—his father observed, and not for the first time, had his head in his books. His brother Malachi loved the outdoors, loved riding and fishing. Competent in his Torah and Talmud studies, but no more, at sixteen calculations came to him easily and he already functioned as Dovid ben Solomon's righthand man. As for Nachson, at fourteen he thrived in the surprisingly active scholarly circle of Narbonne's small Jewish community. Mentioned several times in the Talmud, the sages of the port city's earlier days had been recognized by Abraham ibn Daud of Toledo, who had compared them to the exilarchs of Babylonia.

Even allowing for provincial exaggeration, the comparison was a deserved compliment and Dovid ben Solomon was pleased his son Nachson stood out as a student of exceptional promise. He just did not understand how the boy would make his way in the world beyond books. Leaving that concern, which was not yet a worry, for another day, the captain watched the last of the cargoes unloaded and transferred into his wharf-side warehouse. Arm around his wife Rivka—who had just come down to the port and whose hand held that of their young daughter Yehudit—he turned to walk uphill toward home. It was, he thought, a beautiful day to be alive and healthy in the bosom of his family in peaceful, prosperous Narbonne.

And such days would continue to roll out, as they had for several decades, until the sudden death of Don Aymeric a year later. Then the Count of Toulouse attacked the principality of Narbonne, sparking a century and a-half of tumult for the city and its Jews. But Nachson ben Dovid ben Solomon by that time would be far away, supported in Paris by his proud if ambivalent father, who prudently moved his import concern from Narbonne to Collioure. Collioure, smaller than Narbonne but a well-situated, cove-like port, lay to the southwest within sight of the Pyrenes. It was quiet, calm, good for trade and, most importantly, beyond the interest of the Count of Toulouse.

In Paris, young Nachson thrived. Immersed in studies at the yeshiva of Yom Tov, grandson of Rashi—Rabbi Shlomo Yitzhaki—the great Torah explicator, he felt happy, even blessed. And like Rashi, Nachson married at seventeen. Unlike Rashi, he fathered seven children, all sons. Five were Torah students, two of them great scholars. Late in life the pair would find themselves on opposites sides in the civil war that rent Western European Jewry. Not a clash of arms, but rather of opinions, bitter arguments between the followers of Maimonides, called by those few Churchmen who at the time understood the turmoil, "neo-Aristotelians," and their determined opponents, those labeled by the pro-Maimonides rabbis as "anti-rationalists." And when the inevitable riots occurred, first between followers of the contending rabbis, then—using the intra-Jewish unrest as pretext and opportunity—incursions by gentile mobs into the large Jewish quarter of Paris, the two sons disappeared. Some said Yakov ben Nachson ben Dovid and Yitzhak ben Nachson ben Dovid, and their wives and children, had been spirited away from the troubles to separate destinations, perhaps one to Greece, the other to Turkey, each by a few rugged-looking men. But no one was ever certain.

Chapter Fourteen:
New York City, the Present

'Why the hell did you let him go down into the subway?!" Rabbi Samson uncharacteristically exploded.

Once more Uri Stein, JOLO's security chief, explained. "Two of our best men flanked him, though, of course, he was not aware of that. And a third followed close behind. Rabbi Yehezkieli had a free hour or two and phoned his cousin in Brooklyn he wanted to meet. At his house, to see the grandchildren …"

"You didn't mention the point person. Where was he?" Rabbi Samson exerted himself to stick with the Talmudic teaching in *Pirke Avot*, "Ethics of the Fathers": *Who is the strong man? He who controls his emotions.* The rabbi managed, but only with difficulty.

"Point woman," Uri Stein corrected. "Sheila Kochavi. On the subway platform, an old women fainted in front of her. She stopped to help. Instinctively. And that's when four men rushed the rabbi, trying to push him in front of the train. We took care of three of them—broke bones, cracked skulls—but the fourth managed to slam the rabbi down. Sheila—she'd left the old woman, if that's what she was, almost immediately when the attack began—grabbed him and got him up just ahead of the train. But he struck his head in the fall. He's in Mount Sinai. One our people is on his care team and two are outside his room."

"Prognosis?" barked Rabbi Sampson.

"Concussion. Still unconscious," Stein said. "But the doctors think he'll come around." Stein, well aware of the same *Pirke Avot* instruction about the supreme virtue of controlling one's emotions, strove to sound even-keeled. Nevertheless, his mind raced. How had they let this happen? And to Rabbi Yehezkieli, a light on the Torah and thereby onto the world in this generation even had he not been a messianic candidate. Which he was. And distracted by one of the most ancient dodges, the old person suddenly in distress, temporarily distracting those nearby from the real action. Once more he reproached himself, as if that helped.

"... and I trained her myself," Rabbi Sampson was saying. "We've done well, in this generation and the previous one. After the *Shoah*, I mean. Not a single candidate harmed. But now this ..."

It was Stein's turn to interrupt. "We cannot train the next Sheila to kick the next fallen *zaken* to the side as we run by," he said, using the Hebrew word for elderly person. "Whether we're protecting a prospective messiah or not."

" 'If you're planting a tree and are told *Mosiach* has arrived, finish planting the tree before you go to greet him,'" Rabbi Sampson quoted, half musing to himself. "I know. I know. Nevertheless ..."

"Yes, nevertheless the attack strongly suggests that the Knights of the Chalice still pursue us, after all these centuries," Stein finished.

"Or *al-Jaysh ha-Ain Jalut*," Rabbi Sampson added.

"Them too," Stein conceded.

By the mid-twentieth century, Stein's predecessors had become convinced that the shadowy Knights of the Chalice, sometimes considered as more rumor than fact, no longer existed. If they ever actually had, with their purported mission of making sure no Jewish messiah arose to challenge Christian belief in Jesus. Either way, Nazis, Communists and Arab-Islamic movements seemed to have done much of the work of the Knights of the Chalice and *al-Jaysh ha-Ain Jalut* for them. But if the rise of the reborn Jewish state of Israel stimulated a post-Holocaust resurgence of Jew-hatred, politely referred to as antisemitism as if to spare the rawest feelings of Jews and possible guilty consciences of non-Jews, perhaps the Knights, too, had reemerged from the mists of history. Mistrust and verify, Stein thought.

That went for *al-Jaysh ha-Ain Jalut* as well, he reflected. Named to recall the 1260 battle between the Mamluk army of Egypt and Mongol forces of Il-Khan Hulagu, grandson of Genghis Khan, this army was a relative newcomer to the anti-*Mosiach* threats. Stein could not trace its origins, or rather reports of them, before 1529 and Sulieman the Magnificent's failed siege of Vienna. That signaled the end of Islamic imperialist expansion in Europe, at least until the great Muslim migrations of the late twentieth and early twenty-first centuries. These waves carried with them Islamic triumphalists who considered their predecessors' defeat more than 400 years earlier merely unfinished business. They were incited, not infrequently, by imams financed first by Saudi Arabia, later by Qatar, Turkey and Iran. Thanks to social media, these preachers' influence extended far beyond the walls of their *mashjids* in London, Paris and Berlin.

After Vienna, some of the more fanatical Muslim sects had cast about for those first to blame and second to defeat. The more numerous Christians having finally withstood their advance, such true believers looked to the Jews. "First the Saturday people, then the Sunday people!" It was an old/new battle-cry. With their infidel insistence that something more was to come beyond Mohammed and the Quran—the Final Revelation—the *bani Isra'il* or children of Israel topped their usual suspects list.

In the two years leading to the Battle of Ain Jalut—the spring of Goliath, located in the southern Galilee—Mongol forces intending to expand Genghis' empire from Central Asia throughout the Middle East and beyond already had conquered Baghdad and Damascus. In Baghdad they put to death the last of the Abbasid caliphs and stacked their victims' skulls in pyramids of ten thousand each. Damascus fell the next year. The Mongol army then reached the Mediterranean Sea and turned southeastward. Mamluks, non-Arab slave soldiers and mercenaries who served Egypt for three centuries beginning around 900 C.E., before rising to control both it and Syria for another 300 years, met them at Ain Jalut. There the Mamluks achieved what the Arabs alone could not, a decisive victory. They turned back the Mongols, saving Egypt and perhaps Islam itself. *Al-Jaysh al-Ain Galut* cloaked itself in the afterglow of such a world-historic accomplishment. To Stein the name seemed grandiose, almost humorous in the way of juvenile braggadocio, like the Shi'ite Muslim fanatics in Beirut in the 1980s who called themselves "The Oppressed of the Earth." Juvenile, except for the deadly seriousness and relentless dedication of its members, kidnapping, torturing and murdering the occasional Westerner. Then, fueled by Iran, they transformed into

Hezbollah, the Party of God, fanatically committed to torturing the world into *submission*, into their one, true Islam.

So, who exactly was it who had tried to murder Rabbi Yehezkieli?

Probably not the agitators and the fashion-followers who, bedecked in their *keffiyehs*, now stood on the sidewalk below his hospital room shouting, "Rabbi, rabbi you can't hide! We charge you with genocide!" and "Hey, hey, ho, ho! The bearded Jew has got to go!" Leave it to *The New York Times*, which reported Rabbi Yehezkieli's hospitalization down to his room number, to serve as an intelligence source for every inquiring Jew-hater, Stein thought. He at first had considered such campus trend followers and hangers-on more as irritants than threats, more mindlessly theatrical than militantly effective. They had not seemed to be as trained or determined as the actual attackers. But how much training did it take to rush an old man on a subway platform? A few texts and WhatsApp messages—after years of indoctrination by teachers and professors—and the attack was ready to be organized.

The mostly white, mostly young and heavily female group waved professionally-printed placards reading "No sympathy for the occupation! No aid for the occupier!" and "Globalize the Intifada!" as they screamed up toward the rabbi's window. The two chant leaders, each with a megaphone, were women, their hair covered by *keffiyehs*, their faces obscured by surgical masks. Like Ku Klux Klan hoods, Stein had thought the first time he watched them.

It bothered him that the police had made no move to quiet the Jew-hating drones, let alone shoo them away. But that was politics in the polyglot city, he reflected, especially as the *glot* that prayed in Hebrew declined in comparison to the *poly* that cursed in countless other tongues grew. However, the telling detail that caught his eye was the line at the bottom right of the placards, in small but legible type: Printed by Democratic Socialists of Bronx, N.Y. for Progressive Humanity Foundation, Brussels, European Union.

****

A surprise awaited Joshua Golden as he entered a small meeting room on the second floor of Hamilton Hall on Columbia University's

Morningside Heights campus to defend his dissertation. A puzzling surprise. On his way into the building, Joshua had passed William Ordway Partridge's dramatic statue of Alexander Hamilton right in front. Hamilton was an alum, having attended when Columbia was known as King's College. Entering the building and looking at the stained-glass lobby windows depicting Sophocles and Virgil, Joshua felt a surge of excitement. These symbols of classical learning with a particularly American slant seemed to welcome him into a world of philosophical inquiry he had rigorously prepared himself to join. The windows, almost exact copies of the originals smashed by Hamas idolizers in their April 2024 building takeover, turned the sunlight golden.

So, who was the middle-aged woman with the broad metallic green streak in her otherwise brown hair sitting at the table with Professors Edelvitch, Haynes, Murray and Silverglade? Where was Professor Lazio, the fifth and final member of his oral exam defense committee?

"Good morning, Joshua," said Professor Edelvitch, smiling. "Please be seated." Edelvitch chaired the committee and knew Joshua well, having served as his principal dissertation advisor. "You know Professors Haynes, Murray and Silverglade, of course. I'm afraid Professor Lazio had to be excused. Replaced, in fact—another gastric flare-up, unfortunately, and though he's been released from the hospital, he'll be confined at home from some time. But we have, in his stead, Professor Sybil Rothgott-Marquand from Barnard College-Columbia. She was assigned to us by the Barnard degree review committee. You may be familiar with her groundbreaking work in critical gender theory and her recent, much commented on monograph, 'Late Classical Greek Thought, Queer Centered.'"

If Joshua had ever heard of Rothgott-Marquand it could only have been in passing, and he was pretty sure Professor Edelvitch never had held a copy of "Late Classical Greek Thought, Queer Centered." Nevertheless, he smiled and said, "I'm pleased to meet you. I must confess, however, that my concentration on natural law and the individual as sovereign has left me little time, so far at least, for other lines of philosophical research." Professor Rothgott-Marquand stared at him, her face an unreadable mask.

Then she looked down and scribbled something on a note pad. Joshua felt a pang of unease.

"Since Professor Rothgott-Marquand is the newest member of our committee, so as not to influence her by questions from more senior members, we will begin with her. You have had time to read Mr. Golden's dissertation, I take it?"

"Yes, I have," Rothgott-Marquand said, her voice flat and, Joshua thought, harshly nasal. Judging by that accent, Joshua thought, probably from somewhere along the Great Lakes, west of Cleveland, east of Chicago.

"You are a lecturer here at Columbia, correct?" she stated more than asked.

"Senior lecturer, actually," Joshua said, forcing himself to sound pleasant. She had to have known that from reading the biographical summary that went with his dissertation.

"Well," Rothgott-Marquand continued, "Mr. Golden, you've written more than 200 pages on the origins of natural law theory"—here she snapped a pen on her copy of his dissertation—"and not cited a single woman as a major influence. Please enlighten the committee as to the reason for this glaring omission."

"Three hundred and five pages, exclusive of end notes and bibliography," Joshua said testily. "I cited about two dozen individuals as major contributors to the Anglo-American concept of natural law and others who had some noteworthy if relatively minor influence. That none of them happened to be women reflects more the times in which natural law theory developed, times in which the opportunities of women for higher education and participation in philosophical speculation and debate were, as we know well, virtually non-existent, don't you think?"

"I think that, if indeed such unjustifiable exclusion was the case, you might have considered reframing your research toward a more acceptable end, say examining the distortions of natural law theory imposed by toxic masculinity in the bubble of hetero-normativity."

"I'm not sure I follow you, Professor Rothgott-Marquand," Joshua replied, struggling to sound equanimous rather than peevish. "My research dealt with the times, the relevant individuals and their work as they were, not as we might wish they had been. To do otherwise could have meant straying from fact-based conclusions toward inconclusive opinions. I should note that my advisor, Professor Edelvitch here, and the other committee members, including Dr. Lazio, approved the topic without qualification."

"All men." Professor Rothgott-Marquand's expression, if mask-like before, now was drawn. It broadcast anger. "Mr. Golden, don't you think that decisions of what is 'relevant,' of what is "fact' and 'opinion,' are often used to maintain structures of privilege by a white patriarchy?"

Joshua did not need Rachel's finely-tuned social oscilloscope to recognize Rothgott-Marquand's agitation. Her head seemed to vibrate from side to side. Her large, thin hoop earrings shook.

Chairman Edelvtich struggled to regain control of the examination. "Colleagues, friends," he said softly, "let us focus first on Mr. Golden's central contention, that James Wilson, sometimes called the 'Forgotten Founder,' advanced a distinctive perspective of natural law and made it part of American constitutional theory. Let me turn the questioning now to Professor Murray. Professor Rothgott-Marquand, I will return to you in the second round."

"No need," she declared, noisily gathering her papers, standing and—to the extent possible in her pink Croc platform mules—stomping out.

****

"Why so downcast?" Rachel asked him at dinner that night. "What happened at your dissertation defense?"

"I got four positive votes. Enthusiastic positive votes."

"Isn't that good? What happened with the fifth member?" Rachel asked.

"She stormed out. It was quite dramatic, actually. Should have been on video; would have gone viral."

"Stormed out?" Rachel was bewildered.

"Absolutely. She confirmed that I was a male chauvinist pig, me, James Wilson, and the whole lot of the natural law crowd. As well as, by implication, assumptions about the individual and government embedded in our Constitution. Not to mention the other members of the review committee. None of us worth another minute of her time or thought."

"So, you still got four-to-nothing approval," Rachel said.

"Dissertation endorsement requires assent from all five committee members," Joshua said. "It's got to be five-to-nothing, or it's nothing."

"What are you going to do?" she asked, worried.

"If I can't have a rerun, when Professor Lazio's able, I'm going to ask Professor Edelvitch for a new committee."

"But won't that be like starting over. Don't the committee members have to get to know you beforehand?"

"Ordinarily," Joshua said. "But what happened this morning was hardly ordinary."

Neither was what happened next. Two days later *The Columbia Spectator*, the student newspaper, carried a page-one article headlined "Feminist Prof. Quashes Ph.D. for Male Supremacy Apologist." The story read, Joshua thought, like it had been dictated to the three reporters whose bylines it carried, as if leaked by Rothgott-Marquand just after she slammed the door on her way out of the review committee. None of the three had bothered to contact him. A day later a virtual rewrite of *The Spectator* article landed in *The New York Times* at the bottom of page A-8. This time a reporter had called him.

"What is your response to Professor Rottgott-Marquand's charges," she asked.

"Well," Joshua replied, considering his words carefully, "however contemporary they might be, what I understand of her objections—she barely mentioned any elements of my dissertation at the review committee—ignores the reality of eighteenth-century society and the philosophical currents influencing natural law theory then."

"But we live in the twenty-first century," the reporter said. "Are you calling her objections anachronistic?"

"Aren't some discoveries in chemistry in the eighteenth century relevant today? So might be the building blocks that underlie American social thought in the twenty-first century."

"The eighteenth century was the 1700s, right?" asked the reporter.

"Right," said Joshua, suddenly tired.

"Now, who was this James Wilson you wrote about? Did he enslave people?"

"Wilson was respected by most of the other Founders and influenced them as well. He was the only man to sign the Declaration of Independence, the Constitution and serve on the Supreme Court. He played a primary role in achieving both a unitary presidency—instead of three people trying to share chief executive responsibilities—and the Electoral College, helping ensure that smaller states would join the proposed federal union. So that Southern states also would join, this also involved the three-fifths compromise Wilson proposed regarding counting slaves for voting purposes for president.

"Wilson had studied thinkers like David Hume and Adam Smith at university in Scotland and brought Scottish Enlightenment ideas with him as an immigrant. Some of those natural law ideas, I argue, were and are key to American concepts of individual rights and the balance of freedom and social responsibility. Natural law and natural rights theory holds that law properly grows from morality—that an elevating moral sense precedes genuine law and law-making. In other words, that to serve human beings and be humane, law must reflect morality.

"And yes, Wilson owned a household slave named Thomas Purcell. He eventually freed Purcell after his wife persuaded him. His wife's name was Hannah Gray."

"Would you repeat that about the Electoral College and three-fifths compromised. I want to make sure I get it exactly."

"Three-fifths compromise. You can Google it, of course," Joshua said.

"I know, but I want to get it in your own words," the reporter said.

"My own words," Joshua repeated to himself. After this, the audience for those words is going to be quite small.

About that, he would prove to be wrong, not that he or Rachel would be entirely pleased.

****

The review committee had met on Monday, *The Spectator* article appeared that Wednesday, *The Times* story on Thursday. Friday morning Joshua slumped in his chair across from Professor Edelvitch.

"Been a hell of week, hasn't it?" Edelvitch said.

"You can say that again," Joshua replied.

"Look, I know you're discouraged. Who would not be, by such an unfair and unforeseen turn of events? But I think we can sort things out and retrieve progress toward your doctorate."

"How?" Joshua asked, feeling the merest spark of hope.

"Basically," Edelvitch said, "we just reconstitute your review committee and schedule another oral defense."

"How long would that take?"

"No more than two semesters, I should think," Edelvitch said.

Another year, at least, Joshua thought. Probably more, given typically slow-moving, self-referential and consensus-based faculty politics. The spark flickered out.

"Meanwhile," Edelvitch was saying, "I've taken the liberty of recommending your dissertation for publication."

The spark flickered anew. "By Columbia University Press?"

"No, not in the current brouhaha," Edelvitch said. "Approval by the Press' own review board would be uncertain, stacked as it is with faculty more likely to be inclined to Professor Rothgott-Marquand's views than ours. And in any case, that could take who knows how long. To strike while the iron's hot, so to speak, I called an old friend at Touro University Press, Daniel Pearlstein. I told him about you and your work. He'd read *The Times'* article, of course …"

"Of course," Joshua said. "Who in our world hasn't?"

"… and he seemed quite interested. He wants to meet you. Say next Monday?"

After Joshua Golden left his office, Professor Edelvitch immediately called a cell phone number in Brooklyn. "Did I catch you at a bad time?" he asked.

"No," answered the man at the other end, "just sitting in the Jacuzzi after my workout."

"Still three times a week?" the professor asked.

"Down to twice," the other confessed. "So much to do. But I'm able to get weight-work in twice a week also. Keeps the blood flowing, a necessity for Talmud study."

"You've seen *The Times'* story? A flaming leftist sabotaged Joshua Golden's dissertation defense. You had asked me to keep you posted."

"Yes, thanks," the other man said. "How is he doing? No doubt a bitter disappointment for him. But one door closes and another door opens."

"That's in the Talmud?"

"No doubt," said the fellow the professor regarded as the smartest man in Brooklyn. "Rav Alexander Graham Bell."

Outside Professor Edelvitch's office, Joshua's own cell phone rang. He glanced at the number. Area code 740, somewhere in Ohio. "Verified," his screen told him. He didn't answer. Probably spam, Joshua thought. If it was legitimate, whoever was calling could leave a message.

At lunch later at nearby Hamilton's Deli—the chili con carne was excellent, as usual—Joshua listened to his voice mail. One new message.

"Is this Joshua Golden? This is Dean Donald O'Brien from the Franciscan University of Steubenville. Steubenville, Ohio. I read about you online today in *The Chronicle of Higher Education*. I'd like to talk to you about an opening we have in our political science department. It's to teach a course on American social thought at the time of the Revolution and another on natural law philosophy, its moral-religious basis and how it fits—and what opposes it—in society today. This is a tenure-track position, and you would complete your dissertation here, of course. My number is 740 555-1212. I look forward to speaking with you."

Where the hell was Steubenville, Ohio, Joshua wondered? "To save this message, press nine," his phone reminded him. "To delete it, press seven." He pressed nine.

Chapter Fifteen: Barcelona, Spain, 1263

It had been a hard day. Another hard day, thought Rabbi Moses ben Nachman, the most renowned sage of Girona's small but esteemed Jewish community. One could hardly image the vehemence with which the Jews of Spain insisted on conducting their internal disputes. As if they were not, as often the case in *galut*, in exile, a minority simultaneously small but prominent, influential but vulnerable. No, the various factions insisted on pursuing their grudges and debates as if the fate of all Spain hung on which rabbi and his followers had the final word in the argument between the rationalists and anti-rationalists, between the traditionalists and the mystics. They went at each other verbally and emotionally, as if the increasingly powerful and increasingly fundamentalist Christian kingdoms of Castile and Aragon, of the somewhat more tolerant Valencia and his own Catalonia, as well as the shrinking but still resistant Moorish lands of Andalucia centered on Granada, were irrelevant to their own lives.

He threw his embroidered cloak across a hook on the door and slumped at his table, one end piled high with books and papers. Somehow, he thought ruefully, it fell to him, as always, to mediate and moderate. He must prevent the Jewish communities' quarrels from spilling outside their vibrant if constricted quarters and perhaps giving the gentiles a pretext for yet another "intervention." Still, no one else was better placed then he to do so. Rabbi Moses ben Nachman, known far beyond Girona as simply Nachmanides or, among Jews as the Ramban, stood almost equal to Rabbi Moses ben Maimon of a century earlier. His embroidered cloak, a gift from King James I himself, attested to that fact.

Maimonides, widely known among Jews as the Rambam, had been court physician, theologian and author of *The Guide for the Perplexed* and the *Mishneh Torah*, among other works. The first sought to show instances of harmony between the thought of Aristotle and rabbinic Judaism, adducing rational explanations for Torah accounts. The latter was a heroic and enduringly influential effort at codifying rabbinic law. Of the Rambam—Rabbi Moses ben Maimon—the Jews said, "from Moses to Moses there was no one like Moses."

Of Ramban, the Jews of Spain and southern France said something to the effect of "let Rabbi Moses ben Nachman settle it." With the implication, it seemed to the Ramban that he must decide in every side's favor without alienating any of them. Which was virtually impossible, given the rationalists' drift from the received and to-be-respected wisdom of prior generations. Or, no less important, he mused, giving offense to the gentiles. No easy matter when attempting to adjudicate opposing claims like the charged question now before him: "Do Psalm 79 and Jeremiah 10 apply to all gentiles, only to non-monotheistic pagans or specifically to nations that warred with the Jewish people?" The sources cited called on God "to pour out Your wrath on the nations that know Thee not." Impolitic, to put it mildly. Inflammatory was more like it. Devoutly to be desired in at least a few cases.

The Ramban looked out the window. In the middle distance below, he saw the double-arched aqueduct constructed by the Romans more than a millennium earlier. It soared improbably nearly 100 feet into the sky and still brought water to Girona, perched on its high hills. The structure never ceased to remind him of the creative might and brutality of Rome. On one hand, the Romans commanded respect. Their language—still the basis for the Spanish spoken all around him, as well as Italian, French and even the semi-civilized English—their institutions, including both the Senate and their military legions, and their engineering, witnessed daily by Girona's aqueduct, declared greatness. Yet their behaviors—the slave foundation of the empire, the savage entertainments in the Colosseum, the two-dimensionality of their pantheon and the sexual perversity of the ruling classes—invalidated any claim to moral or ethical example.

The empire had conquered and later destroyed rebellious little Judea, slaughtering hundreds of thousands of Jews and exiling hundreds of thousands more. Yet its power withered and the empire fragmented long ago while he and his fractious Jews were still here. The same, of course, could be said about the Jews and the pharaohs of Egypt, kings of Assyria, the Babylonians, Seleucids, and currently, the last of the Crusaders, now retreating before the Mohammedans to their last Holy Land stronghold of Acre. This odd, perhaps even threatening survival was, Nachmanides suspected, one more reason gentiles feared and hated his Jews: all history's other powers rose and fell, but the Jews alone remained.

Whatever the deeper problems, maintaining the present perilous, anxiety-ridden equilibrium had fallen to him. A man of many parts, like Maimonides before him he was a physician, theologian, and Torah commentator. Nachmanides also was, unlike the Rambam, a kabbalist with deep knowledge of Jewish mysticism. Though he himself inclined toward the anti-rationalists and toward the mystics, by personality Nachmanides opted for conciliation when possible, and for moderation. He was a good listener. That made even those he eventually decided against feel they had been heard. Perfectly willing and able to criticize the revered Rashi's Torah commentary, the Ramban sought to protect his Jewish community—or more precisely communities—by bringing them together.

No other Jew in Spain at the time could attempt to perform such communal balancing acts, the Ramban knew. As for handling this latest challenge, not even his respected colleague Rabbenu Jonah Gerondi would be able. Not the challenge of deciding the proper interpretation of Psalm 79 and Jeremiah 10, but of responding to the invitation—command really—from the king.

King James I of Aragon, known throughout the Iberian Peninsula as The Conqueror, had extended Aragonese power south through Valencia. Over his nearly unprecedented reign of 62 years, and in conjunction with a contemporary, King Ferdinand III of Castile, he continued the Reconquista of the Spanish kingdoms from the Moors. James' Most Christian knights periodically pushed the Muslims back toward the Mediterranean, reversing the latter's earlier occupation of nearly all Spain and Portugal, shrinking their fabled Islamic Andalusia in the process.

So, when the Ramban received an invitation from James, he recognized it not only as an honor, which to a certain extent it was, but also as an order. "My Dear Rabbi Nachmanides," it began, "as you know, some men of influence in the Church and at court have made certain claims against the Jews of my realm. To be precise, against the holy books of your people. You also know, from our long and amiable friendship, my respect for you and the people of your community loyal to myself and Aragon. Therefore, it is my wish that you dispute those claims against their advocate, Paulus Christiani, at my palace in Barcelona this July 20 in the year of Our Lord Jesus Christ 1263. My Confessor, Raymond de Penforte, who is Friar Christiani's Superior, will make all necessary arrangements, including providing for your journey from Girona to the palace and return. Your King, James."

Christiani! Nachmanides looked for the divine spark in every individual. It was an obligation. If the Almighty had fashioned each human being in His image—a literal impossibility, since God Himself was incorporeal, but rather a spiritual necessity, implanting a soul in every person to enable elevation of human over animal—then the disgust he felt at reading that name was inexcusable. It was itself a sin. But what was Pablo Christiani if not someone who willfully had chosen to trample on his own God-given Jewish soul? It would have been one thing to be called to dispute de Penforte, head of Christiani's Dominican order. One might say de Penforte came by his anti-Judaism honestly, the Ramban thought with bitter humor. But Christiani? Not just a convert from Judaism, but a renegade apostate, aggressively baiting his former co-religionists and inciting hostility against them. Did not the Torah itself, for example the Prophet Micah, warn that "a son dishonors his father, a daughter rises up against her mother, a daughter-in-law against her mother-in-law—a man's enemies are the members of his own household." Christiani was such a dishonoring enemy.

An accompanying paper, signed by the Dominican Master-General himself, outlined the subject of the Disputation. That is, it listed Friar Christiani's indictments against Judaism to be argued:

"That, based on the Talmud itself:

"One, the Messiah already has appeared, which the Sages of the Talmud hinted they knew;

"Two, He was both human and divine, and;

"Three, He died to cleanse humanity of its sins."

Nachmanides shook his head. Any learned Jew could refute such assertions, if the rules of the disputation permitted refutation. A big if. In such staged debates—show trials actually, of Judaism that already had taken place in Europe—fair rules rarely had been the case, the Ramban knew. But, considering his relationship with the king, a possibility. At least, he would proceed as if it were a possibility. Pressing a blank page against the table, he began to write:

"My Most Revered Sovereign, thank you for your gracious invitation to the palace in Barcelona on July 20. I am gratified at the opportunity of seeing you again and will be pleased to fulfill your Highness' bidding.

"Since I am familiar with the efforts, largely unsuccessful, of the former Saul ben Nehemiah, now known as Paulus Christiani, to convert the Jews of Provence by sermonizing in synagogues and distorting the plain meaning and long-established interpretations of our holy books, I will gladly take the opportunity you afford me to reply. Cognizant as always of your equanimity and concern for all your subjects, whether Christian, Jewish or even Moor, let me assume that I will perform the command of my sovereign the King if you will grant me permission to speak as I wish. I must note that in his letter to me that accompanied your invitation, Master-General de Penforte wants to impose the condition that I can speak freely 'so long as you do not make insults.'

"I intend to speak, as always, in a decent manner. De Pentforte informs me that he, Raymond Martini, Arnold de Segarra and the general of the Franciscans in Spain, Peter de Janua will join Friar Christiani, but that I alone will speak for the Jews and our religion. I am quite willing to do so as long as I can say all that I desire about the matter under debate, just as I expect them to say all they desire. I will speak, as you have invited me, and speak of my own free will."

The King's reply, when it came, was simple. And irresistible. "We will welcome you to our palace on July 20."

****

The Royal Palace, Barcelona

Paulus Christiani began the debate first. "Your Highness, Gentlemen and Ladies of Court, and my colleagues, we see that the Sages of the

Talmud, in more than one of their Midrash stories, in more than one of their Aggadic tales, even in accepting the Torah examples of angels among men, speak of God sending otherwise incorporeal beings to do his bidding on Earth. And if angels who appeared as men, then why not a messiah in the flesh, The Messiah—Jesus Christ Himself? Fully human, and as the Son of God, fully divine?

"Not only did the rabbis of old believe it possible, we see that they understood it was necessary. Otherwise, their Talmudic laws would fail. Otherwise, in the Torah itself, Moses could not have heard God speak from the burning bush. Otherwise, Balaam's donkey would not have seen the angel with his sword, barring the way. His beast of burden saw what Balaam the great prophet and sorcerer of Midian, hired by Balak, King of Moab, to curse and destroy the Israelites coming from Egypt, did not. Balaam would have cursed the Israelites instead of blessing them but for God speaking through him. And the Holy One began this transformation by first causing Balaam's donkey—who never spoke before or after—to rebuke him.

"The Sages may not have said so explicitly, but the import that angels move among men and animals as God wills is in their words implicitly. And," Christiani closed his summation, "for all the greatness of Moses which we recognize, for all the insight of the Old Testament prophets who constantly were tasked with warning the Israelites against their backsliding from the word of the Almighty, not to mention for all the accursed influence of Muhammed, who blasphemously claimed direct communication from Heaven, only the willfully self-blinded refuse to see in Christ Jesus the Messiah. Had the stiff-necked Pharisees of old publicly acknowledged what they admitted privately, that the Messiah had come, mankind could have avoided our long purgatory awaiting His Second Coming!"

Paulus Christiani was a handsome man, his thick black hair pulled back, his dark eyes flashing. He stood taller than most other men in the royal chamber that day. Except, of course, King James I himself. And the contentious Jew, the angular, sharp-faced Nachmanides. Several ladies of the court tossed their nosegays at Christiani's feet. In approval or adoration?

It was July 31, the fourth and final day of the Great Disputation. As Nachmanides recalled in his journal, "Christiani said to me, among other things: 'Your Sages have said about the Messiah that He is more honored than angels, and this is impossible unless it refers to Jesus, for He was both Messiah and God Himself!' Then he asserted to those present that 'in your—meaning my—Aggadah it is said, 'My Servant shall be exalted and lifted up and shall be very high'—this is Isaiah 52:13. And it means exalted above Abraham, lifted up higher than Moses, and higher than the ministering angels. It can refer only to Our Lord Jesus Christ!'

"And Paulus finished thusly: 'Only He cleanses our sins, only He grants us eternal life after death! Does the Bible not record that Jesus told His disciple John that 'I am the way, and the truth, and the life; no one comes to the Father but through Me?'" Having thunderously delivered his last sentences, Christiani took his seat with a self-satisfied air. As he did so, Raymond Martini, Arnold de Segarra and Peter de Janua nodded approvingly at him.

But de Penforte did not. Rather, the Ramban saw him glance at the king and frown. Well, he might, Nachmanides thought as he rose to face the tribunal. Dramatic style Christiani had. That's why he insisted on sermonizing, without rebuttal, in the synagogues of Provence. And his rhetorical flare, his Jewish audiences knew, rested on more than theological arguments. On his behalf, local nobles and clergy held both carrots and sticks. Among them, tax remission for converts, expulsion for community leaders who clung to their old beliefs. Expulsions or potentially worse. They were aware of the fate of the Jews in southern Italy. In the Kingdom of Naples, the ancient Jewish communities that had taken root not long after the Roman expulsion from Judea more than 1,200 years before were no more. Those who had failed to convert, who felt rooted in the land of their birth, those who remained after orders of expulsion—they were slaughtered, at least 10,000 of them.

"Your Most Gracious Highness, honored members of this tribunal, ladies and gentlemen of court: You have heard, over four days now, the arguments of my opponent and myself, so I will be brief in my conclusion," said the Ramban. "He has style, I will acknowledge. Perhaps a surfeit of style. But of substance, I'm afraid, when it comes to Judaism and our holy books, not enough. Not nearly enough."

At this, several members of the audience gasped. Christiani started to rise from his chair. De Pentforte raised his hand peremptorily and the chamber quieted.

"My opponent," the rabbi continued, maintaining his practice of not referring to Christiani by name, "confuses rather than clarifies the Talmud for you. The Talmud is not one book but several dozen, essentially commentary on specific topics in the Torah. That is, on the Five Books of Moses, the Prophets, and the Writings—books like Kings, Chronicles, Psalms and Proverbs. What you may refer to as the Old Testament. But remember, for us Jews, it is not Old but eternal. As you quote the one you refer to as Jesus to have said, 'I tell you truly, until heaven and earth pass away, not a single jot, not a stroke of a pen, will disappear from the Law until everything is accomplished. …'

"Here my opponent strays." Nachmanides saw Christiani shift almost imperceptibly in his chair. "Yes, much of the Talmud interprets and comments on the Torah to establish the laws of Judaism. But recall, the Torah is written in Hebrew, in which words rest on three-letter roots, all consonants. Context, study and familiarity permit the reader to know which vowels belong where, bringing the three-letter roots with particular prefixes and suffixes as necessary to life as quite specific words and then phrases. So, interpretation and commentary are required. Learned interpretation.

"In addition, the Midrash and Aggadah that my opponent referred to, stand separately from the Talmud. They contain much that is not primarily about legal decisions on religious or theological matters. Folklore, for instance. Discussion of ethics—which though based on the Sages' thoughts and debates, are not legal rulings. Even legends. Of these often helpful but not obligatory words, as it is said, 'if anybody believes it—all well and good; while if anyone does not believe it, no harm is done.'

"As for my opponent's claim that our Sages have said about *Mosiach* that He is more honored than angels, and this is impossible unless it refers to Jesus, the Sages say this about all noteworthy righteous people. For example, 'greater are the righteous than all the ministering angels,' as in the Talmud, Tractate Sanhedrin.

"Then my opponent asserted to those present that 'in your—meaning my—Aggadah it is said, "My Servant shall be exalted and lifted up and shall be very high"—this is Isaiah 52:13. And it means exalted above Abraham, lifted up higher than Moses, and higher than the ministering angels. He says 'it can refer only to Our Lord Jesus Christ!'

"But to the contrary: our *Mosiach* will do more than even Abraham, Moses or all the ministering angels. Since 'his heart will be filled with the ways of the Lord,' as Chronicles II tells us, he will come and command the Pope and all the kings and peoples, as Moses did to the wicked Pharaoh of Egypt, 'let my people go that they may serve me,' as in Exodus. But whereas Moses spoke only to Pharaoh and performed God's signs and wonders only in Egypt, *Mosiach* will speak to all Europe which, if it does not obey, HaShem will smite the entire continent with his signs and wonders."

At this, Ramban would write in his journal, "Fray Paul was silent."

Nachmanides saw Martini glance quizzically at Arnold de Segarra. Good, he thought, they are beginning to wonder if not doubt. And, he reminded himself, I have not insulted anyone. Not yet, at least.

"Of course, the Almighty has sent angels among men. The Torah notes many such instances, including the three angels who Abraham hosted not long after his circumcision and the two angels who rescued Lot and his family from Sodom just before God destroyed it." But, here Nachmanides turned slowly to glance around the chamber at the assembled clergy, nobles and their ladies, and finally look directly at the King, "none of these supernatural beings lived their lives among humans. Each and every one appeared briefly for a divinely-assigned task and once that task was accomplished, vanished from this world.

"In any case, in Judaism, a divine being cannot be the Messiah. The Jewish *Mosiach* must be a human being, a direct descendant of King David, and one who will restore the house of David and sit on the throne in Jerusalem. And one whose sons will do so after him. I have never heard nor read that in your religion of Christianity, the figure of Jesus was to be such a person and do such a thing."

The chamber now buzzed with agitation, some of it whispered, some louder. This time it was King James I himself who signaled for quiet. "I mean to disquiet no one," the Ramban went on, not quite truthfully, since he hoped to disquiet Christiani greatly, "when I note also that, though my opponent speaks of the one he calls Christ Jesus as the Redeemer of Israel and Salvation of the world, he should remember that in his prior belief the Redeemer was God Himself. As for salvation, we pray three times daily—just as he once did—to that self-same God in words that also clarify the role of King David's descendants:

"'Speedily cause the scion of David Your servant to flourish, and increase his power by Your salvation, for we hope for Your salvation all day. Blessed are You, Lord, who causes the power of salvation to flourish.'

"Your Highness, my lords and ladies, honored Churchmen," Nachmanides continued, "I am not here to refute Christianity. It is your religion and I could not have it otherwise. I am here to refute the one who now calls himself Paulus. He may say what he will, but perhaps he should not presume to tell Jews he speaks for them and for Judaism while telling you he speaks for Christianity.

"If the rabbis of the Talmud truly believed that the messiah my worthy opponent speaks of had come, they would not have bothered to hint about it, they would have converted to Christianity as Saul ben Nehemiah, who stands before us today as Paulus Christiani, did. But they did not. Rather, they continued living as Jews.

"Further, I say this not as an insult but simply as an observation each of you may test according to your own knowledge, given that the Jewish *Mosiach*, this descendant of King David and heir to his throne, is to herald the coming of the kingdom of God on earth: If a Jewish messiah already has appeared, and a mighty empire—Rome—adopted his beliefs, why did it crumble? Now, the worshippers of Muhammad have more dominion than you. And likewise, our Prophet Isaiah says of the time to come, 'Nation shall not lift sword against nation, neither shall they learn war any more.' Yet from the days of Jesus until now the whole world has been filled with violence and pillage.

"As to the point of the footsteps of *Mosiach* and kingdom of God on earth, all of us here know that Christians, moreover, shed more blood than other nations; and how hard it would be for you, your Majesty, if these knights of yours were not to learn war anymore.

"Now, in your New Testament are many good sayings and beliefs about how men are to live together in peace, in charity and hope. Some, I think you might find come directly from the Torah. Some do not. But that is not what I was summoned here to dispute. I was requested to debate my opponent's assertion that his messiah is my *Mosiach*. That is what I honestly have tried to do, and no more."

Nachmanides had barely finished this last sentence when Christiani and Peter de Janua were out of their seats, shouting something he could not be sure of in the general uproar now filling the chamber, but which might have been "heretic!" and "blasphemer!" King James I stood and signaled the captain of the guards. The palace guards made a show of unsheathing their swords.

"This disputation is recessed," the king declared. "I will consult with my Confessor, Major-General de Penforte, and inform you regarding its resumption."

That evening a deputation of Barcelona's Jewish community leaders stormed into the Ramban's temporary quarters in the city. "Did we not beg you to withdraw from this abomination after the first day?" they demanded of him. "Did we not warn you of the possible, no, of the likely consequences if you won, if you so clearly defeated the cursed Paulus? Now the city talks of nothing else, and how the arrogant Ramban must be humbled, how the insufferable Jews must be put in our place."

"I was commanded by the king to appear and participate. You wish I would have bitten my tongue and submitted to Paulus' lies?" Nachmanides challenged them. "That would have benefited you? No, it would have increased the pressure—pressure the king himself has deflected—to convert. The king recessed the proceedings. Unless I am mistaken, he and de Penforte will send Paulus back to Provence and in time today's emotions will calm."

"You can't believe that," asserted Yonathan Hezekiah ben Franco.

"I believe the king announced a recess to cover the fact that Paulus had been exposed. I don't believe the disputation ever will resume. But you're right in one respect: For me personally, this controversy will not blow over. I attracted the lightening. Meantime, I advise each of you to look to your own interests, your own families. Maybe you can stay in Barcelona."

The next day, August 1, the king called Ramban to the palace. "Never has an unjust cause been so nobly defended," he said. Then he handed Nachmanides a bag holding 300 gold coins. That Shabbat, Ramban attended Barcelona's Sinagoga Major, one of the oldest synagogues in Europe. A conversionist sermon was to be preached, but instead something unheard of in all Europe happened. King James I attended and addressed the congregation. He spoke of Aragon as a home to all its people—Christians, Moors and Jews.

Nonetheless, not even the monarch could contain the furies unleashed by Nachmanides' victory over Christiani. Instead of abating, they grew more intense. Days later, Ramban left Barcelona. By the end of the month, the king ordered portions of the Talmud Christiani and his superiors found offensive to be excised. Still, the reaction did not end.

In 1265, the Dominicans of Aragon persuaded Pope Clement IV to order the collection of all Jewish texts in the kingdom. They were to be examined by the Dominicans and Franciscans, under the supervision of Paulus Christiani himself. In this reaction to the Great Disputation was laid one basis for the Inquisition's prosecutions of suspected Judaizers.

In 1267, Nachmanides, who had journeyed back to Girona, departed Spain altogether for *eretz Yisrael*. But not before delivering one last talk to his fellow Jews in the city that had been, until the Great Disputation with its pyrrhic victory, his city and congenial to his work.

"How do we know that King Solomon in fact did write the Book of Ecclesiastes?" Ramban asked his audience in the Sinagoga de Girona. Several hundred Jews crammed the small building. The structure, already several centuries old, with its gray stone roof gracefully arched over a reddish flagstone floor, marked the center of El Call, Girona's small but densely populated Jewish quarter.

"We know," Nachmanides was saying, "because of course that is what our tradition tells us. But it also is what the book itself says, and in its first line."

"Why is he talking about Ecclesiastes?" Malkah bat Romani whispered to her friend Ora bat Toledano. "The priests are burning our holy books …"

"Yes, and the most bloodthirsty among them, like Christiani, will want to burn us next," Ora hissed back.

"Line one, verse one states openly that Ecclesiastes is 'the words of Koheleth, the son of David, king in Jerusalem,'" Ramban said. "Koheleth can be read as Preacher, but the identity of this preacher is plain: He was the son of David and king in Jerusalem. Now, we know David had several sons, but only one, Solomon, was king in Jerusalem."

"What has this to do with us today in Spain, in these terrible times?" Malkah bat Romani demanded of Ora bat Toledano.

"If anyone knows, it is Ramban himself—and he better explain it soon!"

Which he did, after a fashion. "Some rabbis wanted to exclude Ecclesiastes from the Torah. Koheleth, that is, Solomon's assertion that 'vanity of vanities, all is vanity' struck them as dangerous cynicism that might undermine faith. But a deeper reading of the book and an understanding of biblical Hebrew discloses that by 'vanities' Solomon meant transient, insubstantial. A better translation would have been mist, that is, ultimately man's temporal affairs are as mist to the eternity of the universe. …"

"'Mist!?' Perhaps, as some say, his dangerous victory over Christiani has unbalanced the Ramban as it has threatened us," Malkah whispered a little loudly.

"Shh! Shh!" their neighbors hissed at her and Ora.

"… but not meaningless," Nachmanides continued. "'One generation passes away and another generation comes; But the earth abides forever,' Solomon continued. Even more, later in his book he famously tells us that 'to everything there is a season, and a time to every purpose under the heaven: A time to be born, and a time to die; A time to plant, and a time to reap; A time to kill, and time to heal; A time to break down, and a time to build up …'

"We live in a time in which some seek to break us down, even to kill us. So, with the wisdom of Koheleth, we must plant and reap, we must build up, and—when necessary—defend ourselves. If we cannot do these things where we are, we must find the place where we can."

What turned out to be Nachmanides' farewell address to the Jews of Spain left many of his immediate listeners disappointed at first, even disgruntled. Until they learned that shortly thereafter, he had taken ship for *eretz Yisrael*.

"I understood him all along," Malkah bat Romani was telling Ora bat Toledano some days later. "He meant that according to the wisdom of Solomon, it is time for all of us Jews to return to our land and there build up."

"You did?" Ora scoffed. "It didn't sound like it at the time. In any case, we can't all leave, certainly not at once. If we do, my husband says, the Catholics will not buy our homes, our shops, even the *sinagoga, mikvah* and other community property for what they are worth, or maybe not buy them at all, just take what they want. And they do want El Call, occupying the center of Girona as it does."

Nachmanides, his heart heavy at having to depart Spain for his own safety but his mind focused on what must be done in the future, soon found that he had exchanged one set of difficulties for another. In Jerusalem he encountered a battered, dispirited community. In his new neighborhood, he could not always gather even enough Jewish men for a *minyan* of ten, the ritual prayer quorum. Yet he wrote to the Jews of Spain that the city was "where the Temple Mount is great and holy," and from where "the world was set firm and whence the foundations and boundaries of the earth first branched out." The land was everlastingly sanctified and longed for the Jewish people's return to lift it from its current degradation, he said. Only they could make it bloom again. Three hundred rabbis from throughout Western Europe would follow him. But not enough Jews would follow them. Not then.

Chapter Sixteen:
New York City, the Present

"How is he, doctor?" Rebbetzin P'nina Yehezkieli asked. She had been sitting at her husband's bedside in Mount Sinai Hospital for three days now, ever since arriving from Jerusalem. She clasped her hands; the lines at the corners of her mouth furrowed deeper.

"Better, I'm happy to say. His vital signs are good and have been stable for thirty-six hours. The bleeding in his brain not only stopped but basically has been reabsorbed. That doesn't always happen. But it means we're able to bring him out of his induced coma."

P'nina Yehezkielii hands fell on her lap. "But what about damage?" she asked.

"It's too early to be certain, but I'm optimistic," the physician said. "I've seen other cases like your husband's make a complete recovery. And he seems otherwise to be in good health, strong enough to recover. Now, why don't you go downstairs to the cafeteria and get something to eat? You've been sitting here for hours. There's a kosher section. I eat there myself," he smiled.

She was in the elevator on the way down and so did not hear when the demonstrators far below her husband's window took up their latest chant: "Rabbi, rabbi, Israel lied! It kills kids for genocide!" and "Intifada Revolution. We demand the Final Solution!" They had materialized almost immediately after the ambulance carrying Rabbi Aaron Yehezkieli arrived at the hospital's emergency entrance. Nearly one hundred of them, self-propagating via social media, their leaders trained by Students for the Liberation of Palestine and American Sons of Ramallah Society. They must work in shifts, the doctor thought, since they were almost always there, chanting robotically, blocking the sidewalk.

The American Sons of Ramallah Society, Rabbi Yehezkieli's doctor knew, derived from Egypt's Muslim Brotherhood. The century-old Brotherhood was the mothership of Sunni Islamist triumphalist movements throughout the Middle East and beyond, most notably al-Qaeda, ISIS and, through its Palestinian affiliate, Hamas. Uri Stein, when establishing the rabbi's security cordon, had told him so. The doctor peered down at the mini-mob, confined to the sidewalk by police, including a few on horseback. Most of the demonstrators' heads were covered by *keffiyehs* and surgical masks. By their behavior they mimicked little Hitler *Jugend* or Stalinist *Komsomol* members, he thought. Or a combination of the two.

The doctor pressed a button on his watch and spoke. "The rebbetzin is on her way down. Keep an eye on her."

In the cafeteria, P'nina Yehezkieli slid her tray up to the cashier. The sight, and smell of food had overwhelmed her. She could not remember when she had eaten last. A cup of soup, half a sandwich, a bag of potato chips—wonderful American potato chips, such an indulgence, not the Israeli Styrofoam-like confections—and a cup of coffee filled her tray. She paid, walked to a table, put her tray down and sat. Then, folding her arms next to the tray, she put her head in the crook of an elbow and promptly fell asleep. From two tables over, a young man watched her. He smiled to himself. The woman was a saint, and if she wanted to sleep, he would make sure she was not interrupted.

Friday night services had just ended at the Jewish Revival Institute. That was what Gerry Meyer called his new operation, now nearly five months old. "A store-front facility," *The New York Daily News* referred to it in a few paragraphs of its standing "Around Town" column. "But this is not your cookie-cutter little *shtiebel* in Crown Heights or Boro Park," the reporter noted. "At the Jewish Revival Institute you won't find a wrinkled old rabbi with an untrimmed beard *davening* along with twenty or thirty followers in a dimly lit hole in the wall.

"Instead, you'll walk into a repurposed Duane Reid pharmacy, the bright space divided into three rooms. The first is a sanctuary complete with an *aron kodesh* (Torah ark for those of you who've forgotten your bar or bat mitzvah lessons) complete with two Holocaust Torahs retrieved from a warehouse in Poznan, Poland where they'd been found a few years ago, miraculously well-preserved, and one hundred or so chairs. Next comes a reception area for luncheons or events and finally a small office/library. That's where the brains behind the JRI, Gerry Meyer often can be found. The one-time golden boy of real estate law and finance holds classes, calls would-be donors, pays bills, writes sermons or tapes podcasts. And not infrequently lately, gives interviews."

Another Friday night service—Gerry Meyer did not think he or JRI were ready yet to hold regular Saturday morning Shabbat services, complete with Torah reading. The operation, he had to admit, was still a little catch-as-catch-can, too much a one-person show, ragged at the edges. His current reading, for example, included Abraham Cohen's *Everyman's Talmud*—a classic first published in 1949 but nevertheless only an introduction to the subject—former Israeli Chief Rabbi David Lau's commentary on *Pirke Avot*, Ethics of the Fathers—and the new *Idiot's Guide to Rashi*, which, no idiot, Meyer was finding slow going. What's bothering Rashi? —the medieval Rabbi Shlomo Yitzhaki of first Troyes, France and later Worms, Germany—had sparked discussion and debates among Jews ever since his death in 1105. The sage himself both asked and answered such questions, always attempting to explicate potentially unclear Torah passages by revealing their plain, primary meaning.

What Gerry Meyer found more fascinating, more to the point, or to his own point anyway, was the legend that long held Rashi to have been a thirty-third generation descendant of Yohanan haSandler. Yohanan was a fourth-generation descendant of Gamliel the Elder, chief judge of the Sanhedrin in the first century C.E. And Gamliel, of course, was a descendant of King David. So, legend held, and Gerry Meyer found that holding congenial. He began to find it pleasant to wonder if he himself perhaps was a descendant of Rashi's. Had not his mother often said, 'Gerry, you come from a long, long line of sages. So why do you act like a juvenile delinquent?"

In any case, he thought of JRI and himself as primed, but not quite ready for prime time. Hence, no complete Shabbat morning services. Not quite yet, anyway. Getting there was necessary, he told himself again, what with largely ineffectual competition from the fragmented local Jewish establishments, with their reactionary social-cultural attitudes—still imagining they were living in the mid-20th century American golden diaspora—and their time-wasting bureaucracies. And fighting resurgent antisemitism? The more money they threw at the danger, the worse it got. They were no help to him and his Jews. That's how he was coming to think of JRI regulars, as his Jews.

Anyway, JRI's attraction—his attraction for the now one-hundred-plus people who showed up regularly each week—was definitely not that of an ordinary synagogue or rabbi. Though he closely followed the ritual and prayer book of Conservative Judaism—Conservative Judaism as it had been practiced a generation earlier, when in equalitarian fashion women could be called to the *bimah* for the honor of reading a blessing during the Torah service but same-sex weddings still were prohibited. Gerry Meyer did not set himself up as a congregational rabbi. After all, he had not been ordained and had no plans to put himself through the long period of study and examination required.

What he was doing, in the same manner as he had strategized some of the city's leading property firms' mergers and acquisitions a decade earlier, was building a brand more and more people would want to follow, participate and invest in. He was the face of the brand but not the thing, the product, itself. No, that was Jewish Revival, he told himself, always with capital letters. That he had been called to lead the revival he told no one, no one except his psychiatrist. The question bothering him, or one of them anyway, was could she be trusted?

Activities—he was not ready yet to call them services—started promptly at 8 p.m. each Friday. They finished an hour and fifteen minutes later, more or less, depending on how enthusiastically the participants—Gerry Meyer still hesitated to think of them as congregants—sang the hymns *Lecha Dodi* and *Yigdal*, and how often they interrupted to ask questions. Then came *Oneg* in the reception area. A social cap to the activities themselves, *Oneg* featured coffee and tea, cookies, cakes and conversation.

As the gathering broke up around ten, he stood at the front door and bid farewell to each as he or she left. "Wonderful sermon," Simon Peltz told him, grasping his hand and shaking it vigorously. "I especially liked your emphasis on the fact that we don't just sing 'We shall overcome someday' but that we are destined to overcome in the time of *Mosiach*, which God-willing will be soon. I never got that inspiration in my old *shul*," Peltz was saying.

"Thank you, thank you so much," Gerry Meyer said, feeling moved but not necessarily modest.

As Peltz and most of the others drifted off into the evening, Meyer retreated to his office/library. There he found seventeen or eighteen of his hardcore regulars waiting. The Stalwarts, he thought of them, again with a capital letter. Most had been with him from the beginning. They were, he understood, followers. His followers.

Meyer sat behind his desk and scanned the room.

"All right," he said. "It's time, past time, someone, anybody, freed Rabbi Yehezkieli. Freed him from that incessant, intolerable verbal torment. Since no one else has run off the little Amalekites under his window," Meyer told them, referring to the ancient tribe who for no reason but gleeful hatred had attacked the Israelites on their way out of Egypt, and whose descendants arose as foretold to war against the Jews in each generation, "we will.

"Yoni, tomorrow night, after Shabbat, when the police take their horses back to the stables, you'll walk by close to those temporary barriers they've set up. Then, pull this pin and just toss this little cannister—it's a tear gas grenade—as far as you can into the clump of … of Nazis in blue jeans, that's what they are, carrying their placards— 'Go Back to Poland!' Toss the tear gas and keep walking. With the demonstrators and police distracted, Mona here," said Gerry Meyer, pointing at a spiked-haired middle-aged woman in coveralls and work boots, "will lead the charge across the street.

"Remember to rub the backs of your hands, necks and exposed areas of your face with Vaseline and tie damp bandanas across your nose and mouth. That should protect you against any police tear gas or pepper spray from the punks long enough to swing those bats that were donated to us. And remember to get the bicycle helmets and put them on just as soon as Yoni's grenade goes off. The helmets and baseball bats will be in the bushes beside the sidewalk in front of the Church of Our Lady of Perpetual

Care." Gerry Meyer laughed. "Perpetual care, that's what we're gonna give 'em! Swing hard, follow through like I showed you, and aim at joints—elbows, knees, hips. We don't want to knock anyone's head off. Not tonight anyway. Get a few good, hard swings in, then drop your bats and scatter. And don't forget to tear off the latex gloves. No fingerprints, please.

"Now, it's possible one or two of you might get arrested. If so, be polite. You can give the police your name and address. But you don't have to answer any questions beyond that. Just say you're waiting to talk to your lawyer. And I have a good one on retainer. A very good one. Sometimes the governor calls him herself. So, if any of you are picked up, you'll be out in no time."

Later, alone in his office, Gerry Meyer leaned back in his chair, hands clasped behind his head. He had to start small, he realized, but his ambitions were large. In his effort to give himself at least a basic grounding for his mission, he had been reading a lot, religion, ritual, history. One fascinating thing he learned had nothing to do with theology or synagogue, at least not on the surface. But it was timely. He found that in the late 1930s New York City Judge Nathan D. Perlman, a former congressman, had grown alarmed at the rise of the pro-Nazi German-American Bund on the East Coast and the Silver Legion in the Midwest. Each of these organizations counted several tens of thousands of members and held large rallies at which they spewed antisemitic, pro-Hitler vitriol. They became increasingly brazen as no one held them to account.

So, Gerry Meyer discovered, Perlman called on an acquaintance, though by no means a colleague, named Meyer Lansky. Lansky was basically the Mafia's chief financial officer, the man who more than any other put together the mob's long-lasting Five Families system in New York and its even more notorious Murder, Inc. affiliate. Lansky in turn contacted Bugsy Siegel, the homicidal Abe "Kid Twist" Reles, Abner "Longie" Zwillman and, in Chicago, Al Capone's associate Jake "Greasy Thumb" Guzik. Perlman's request to Lansky ran along the lines of "do whatever you want to these Nazi bastards, just don't kill anybody." And that was what the Jewish toughs recruited by the gangsters did, breaking up meetings and causing more than a little confusion and paranoia among

Bund members and Silver Legionnaires until Pearl Harbor deflated their momentum and brought scrutiny by police and courts.

Until he had come across accounts of Jewish gangsters versus American Nazis, Meyer had been fuming. The city's Jewish Community Relations Council issued anguished and, he thought, frankly embarrassing pleas for the public to respect Rabbi Yehezkieli's privacy. City council members made anodyne statements against "hate" and could not condemn antisemitism without adding "and also Islamophobia," as if the latter actually threatened the growing numbers of Muslims in their wards. In reality, flash mobs of social media connected Israel-haters and Jew-haters—it was nearly impossible to tell the difference—now frequently gathered intimidatingly outside the homes of well-known donors to Jewish causes, occasionally blocked congregants from entering synagogues on Saturday morning and, in ones, twos and threes, assaulted Jews on city streets. Long disturbed by this trend, Gerry Meyer now had a plan for countering it. Like the Jewish gangsters before him, he opted for direct action and found at least a few Jews eager to carry it out.

Two hours had passed by the time P'nina Yehezkieli returned to her husband's room. When she awoke in the hospital cafeteria, she found her soup lukewarm, her coffee cold. Nevertheless, in less than ten minutes she finished the soup, the half sandwich, and all the chips and coffee.

As she walked through the door of her husband's room, she let out a little exclamation. "Oh!" P'nina breathed. Rabbi Aaron Yehezkieli was sitting upright in his hospital bed, talking with the doctor. The physician was holding up three fingers on one hand.

"How many this time?" the doctor asked.

"Three," Aaron Yehezkieli said.

"And now?"

"Two."

"Very good." Catching sight of P'nina, the doctor put a finger to his lips. About to hurry over to Aaron and embrace him, she stopped and stood silently.

"Why, hello," the doctor said pleasantly. "Look who's here."

Aaron turned and stared. "Hello," he said.

"Is that all you've got to say, rabbi?" the doctor asked softly.

Looking at P'nina quizzically, Aaron Yehezkieli added, "I'm glad to see someone other than the doctor here, though he is a nice enough fellow. You look familiar. I feel I should know you. What's your name?"

Suddenly, all three of them turned toward the window. They had heard an explosion on the street below, followed by pandemonium. A small, well-deserved riot had broken out.

****

Two days after, during morning rush hour, a half-dozen men entered a crowded subway car at the Nevins Street subway station in Brooklyn, four stops on the Red Line 2 train from Wall Street in lower Manhattan. They were dressed in black fatigue pants and leather jackets, with black-and-grey keffiyehs wound around their heads, obscuring the lower part of their faces. Only their eyes showed above their scarves and below the brims of pulled down navy blue New York Yankees baseball caps. Though it was a warm day, all wore gloves.

As the train pulled out of the station, they positioned themselves in pairs at each of the three now closed doors. From their backpacks they pulled short, thick metal rods, at which point the car grew completely quiet.

"Good," said the leader, standing by the middle door. "Now that we have your attention: Zionists, identify yourselves! The next station will be your last chance to get out!" At first, no one stirred. Good," barked the leader. "No Zionists, we're clear." Some passengers cheered.

For a long moment, silence inside the subway car somehow suppressed the sound of the train clattering through its tunnel. Then a tall, slender man rose. Elderly, he had been sitting only a few paces from the leader.

"If by Zionist you mean Jew, a Jew proud of his heritage, his religion and his people, then I am a Zionist."

Witnesses would tell police later that the one they called the leader made a sound something between a growl and a shout. Taking one long stride toward the old man—a witness described the movement as almost ballet-like in its athletic fluidity—he smashed his iron bar onto the man's kneecap. The man screamed and collapsed. His face was ashen as he writhed on the floor. At that moment the train halted at the Hoyt Street Station, the doors opened and the six attackers leaped out. Only then did two other riders move to help the Jew on the floor.

A week later Rabbi Reuven Samson stared across his desk at the man called Murray Menschnikov. The latter thought the rabbi looked unusually careworn, melancholy even. "You have to ask for my resignation, I know," Menschnikov said. "You have it."

"I wish there was an alternative," Rabbi Samson said, sounding tired.

"There is none," Menschnikov replied. "JOLO cannot risk the stain that would come if it were discovered and made public that Hubert, Gal and I took revenge on the subway thugs."

"It cannot. But the organization can ill afford to lose you. Any of you, especially now," the rabbi said. "Who else could have identified and tracked them as quickly as you three?"

"Anyone, anyone who remembered that intelligence gathering starts with networking. Data mining, data analysis, of course. But connections with others in the field, individuals and agencies gives one perspective, leads, sometimes even classified information. And, occasionally, access to surveillance cameras, which are virtually everywhere in the city these days. And once in a while, to vocal pattern analyses."

"Amazing," Rabbi Samson said softly.

"But who else would have acted without discipline, outside the chain of command, so peremptorily?" Menshnikov continued.

"Yes, giving them what they gave their victim," Rabbi Samson said with the slightest of smiles.

Menshnikov rose to leave. "Sit down," the rabbi ordered. "I haven't accepted your resignation or dismissed you, not quite yet."

Surprised, the younger man complied. "When you leave this room, you will be severed from the organization. Hubert and Gal also. Officially. But before then, one more assignment. Or rather, request, since you will no longer be part of us. Not formally, not in any established chain of command. Consider it an urgent request. Until you hear otherwise from me ... or my successor ... the three of you, with you as leader, are to recruit a few others of like mind and ability. You'll form a small strike force. This force will deal anonymously, surreptitiously, with enemies of JOLO, as you have just done with the subway criminals. Revenge, justice really, measure for measure. No more, no less, always covert.

"I'm going to give you a number to call. Memorize it and call tonight at eight o'clock. The woman who answers will have seen to it that an account has been opened in your name—your newest name—to fund the activities of your group. Once you leave here today there must be no further direct contact between you and me, between this new force and JOLO. My secretary has your new identification documents. They already are on file with the relevant local, state and national agencies. Don't worry. You're still forty-three years old."

The rabbi closed his eyes and leaned back in his chair. Murray Menschnikov said nothing. Finally, the rabbi spoke again.

"I've long wondered if, after the Holocaust, after World War II, Jews had—on their own—scoured Europe and the rest of the world, tracking down former Nazis and their collaborators and killing them then and there. The Israelis did some of that, of course, the Eichmann capture and trial the most noteworthy. But not many such cases, not enough. Would large-scale retaliation have had a more widespread and lasting effect in countering antisemitism than the occasional war crimes trials, than—as they came later—the Holocaust memorials, Holocaust studies and governmental proclamations of 'Never Again!'? It became easy to do justice for dead Jews. Doing justice for living Jews, on the other hand, is always a troublesome matter."

"The Prophet Micah told us to 'do justly, love mercy and walk humbly with God,' and in that order," Menshnikov said. "Justice, mercy, humility. Some consider that a summation of Jewish ethics."

"Yes," the rabbi said, "and I am sure you and your force will act justly and remain humble. As for mercy, you will judge."

The two men were quiet for a moment. Then the rabbi spoke again. "These demonstrations outside Rabbi Yehezkieli's hospital; the subway thugs; closure of Jewish Studies departments at Columbia, Harvard and Penn; arson at the Holocaust Memorial Museum in Washington, beatings of Jews browsing an 'Anarchists for Palestine' book fair in North Carolina, destruction of a Jewish cemetery in Cincinnati, a hotel in Denver refusing Israeli guests. Murder on the sidewalk in Washington in front of the

Capital Jewish Museum. One might conclude these are the birth pangs of *Mosiach*, the last days of diaspora and exile. The Vilna Gaon said all the days of exile are like the duration of a pregnancy and the final stage is comparable to the difficult pangs immediately prior to birth."

"We're enduring the pains, all right," Menshnikov replied, "and that's without mentioning the several thousand deaths in Israel from war with Turkey and the condemnations of Israel by spineless European leaders and co-opted international courts for having the *chutzpah* to fight back, and the weak knees of more than a few American politicians, including some Jewish ones."

"We're not here to discuss the former Senate majority leader," Rabbi Samson said, the old twinkle back in his eyes, "but we can be certain, as certain as possible that the moment of birth is imminent. As Isaiah says, in Chapter Sixty-six, verse nine, 'Will I bring on labor and not open the womb?'" Shifting gears, he added, "you can expect that I will follow your activities to the best of my ability, with admiration. But that's all."

Rabbi Samson rose and reached across his desk to shake the other man's hand. "Good bye, Benjamin Ross. *B'atslacha*," he said. Good luck.

"*Baruch HaShem,*" replied the man now to be known as Benjamin Ross, the only child of Russian Jews named Rosen who immigrated to Chicago. He was, the man would explain, when necessary, a mostly absentee owner of a dry-goods business on Chicago's North Shore. Business was good, Baruch HaShem.

Chapter Seventeen:

Speyer, Holy Roman Empire (Germany), 1352

"Most distasteful," said the bishop.

"Most," agreed the prince.

Then both men laughed. Life did have its pleasant moments, even now, the horrors of the Black Death having barely abated. Nearly half the city's population and a third in the outlying towns and villages were gone. The survivors, those outside the cathedral precincts and palace grounds, were listless, traumatized. In the countryside, too few able-bodied peasants remained to plant a full crop. Potential famine loomed after the fall harvest. Just as bad if not worse, the non-agricultural economy had fallen to ruins. Quite simply, hardly anyone was left to tax.

But it was late spring now, the weather finally agreeable, many of the two men's closest associates had survived the great plague, and food stores still were plentiful, for them at least. Bishop Jerome and Prince Ludwig sipped their wine. In the prince's comfortable private reception room—smaller and better furnished than the austere public "throne room"—the pair appeared well-satisfied with life and their status in it. Nevertheless, a difficulty confronted them.

"We are going to have to invite the Jews back," the bishop said. "I don't see any way around it."

"Neither do I," agreed the prince.

"Distasteful," the bishop said again.

"Extremely," agreed the prince.

"So, there will have to be conditions," said the bishop.

"Of course," responded the prince. "Serious conditions."

This time the two laughed even longer.

So it was that a few weeks later, the town council of Speyer recorded the following decree:

"In agreement with His Eminence, Bishop Jerome, and His Excellency, Prince Ludwig, We the Burghers of our City of Speyer, do hereby declare and ordain:

"One, the eternal ban of the Jews of Speyer, decreed in the Year of Our Lord 1348, as punishment of their venomous role in causing and spreading, in conjunction with Satan Himself, the Black Death, is hereby lifted;

"Two, said Jews, many of whom fled to the outermost villages of this principality rather than face the righteous wrath of their Most Christian Neighbors, are invited to return to the City of Speyer promptly;

"Three, the Jews of Speyer will be afforded the gracious protection of Prince Ludwig for a period of seven years. This protection may be lifted on two-weeks' notice;

"Four, the Jews will retain their status under His Royal Highness, Emperor Charles IV. That is, they remain 'serfs of the imperial exchequer'; and

"Five, privileged to receive this kindness by the Holy Roman Empire, the Jews who will dwell with us in Speyer, henceforth and forever, shall belong to us and to our city and shall be ours in respect of body and property."

In Landshut, a hamlet dusty in summer, muddy in winter and at all seasons some distance from Speyer with its cathedral spires and palace walls, nearly twenty men, most of them bearded, all wearing close-fitting caps, had gathered in a small house. More accurately, a large hut. "What does this decree mean?" demanded one of the younger men.

"It means, Gershon ben David," said the apparent leader of the group, a fifty-year-old man who, with his gray beard and squinting, pale blue eyes, looked more like seventy, "they cannot do without us. They cannot do without our businesses, without our crafts especially glass-blowing, gold and silversmithing and without those of us they used to trust to manage their affairs."

"Or, as insatiable borrowers and infrequent re-payers, without our money-lending or without our taxes," interjected ben David.

"That goes without saying," the older man responded. "Only four years after massacring many of us, burning entire families at the stake in public spectacles, seizing the homes and businesses they did not burn ..."

"Those we didn't burn ourselves first." It was ben David again.

"...they realize, at least their leaders realize, they cannot do without us."

"But only seven years protection? Revocable on two-weeks' notice?" Gershom ben David questioned.

"It was, my son," said the older man, Isaachar ben David, father of Gershom, "the best I could negotiate. When one has no soldiers and little gold, one must play a weak hand as skillfully as possible."

"It doesn't sound very skillful, father," the young ben David said.

"No? And if I told you the original terms included only three years protection and two days' notice of cancellation, do you imagine you could have done better?"

"Maybe not," the son conceded. "But we all know that those who were our envious neighbors in Speyer just four years ago and those who are the superstitious peasants outside city walls may take it into their heads again to riot, plunder, rape and murder ..."

"... To satisfy their greed while 'upholding the honor of their One True Church' against the Devil and his agents, that is, against us. 'Protection' will avail us nothing, just as in the past. And we also know that the prince and his bishop will lament such un-Christian behavior, after the fact," interjected another young man.

"What would you have us do, then?" asked Isaachar ben David. "Do we really have a choice, other than to risk it?"

"We do," his son Gershom declared. "We can join the migration of Jews from all around this part of Germany and go east, into the lands of the Slavs. Whatever is said about them—and I grant that little of it is complimentary—they are not said to be as rash, as murderous as these Germans."

"Yes, let us go east," agreed several of the younger men.

"Go then," said Isaachar ben David. He sounded not angry but tired. "Go to where you know not, places from which those who already left our neighboring communities have sent few descriptions and almost no invitations to join them. Here, at least, we have been granted the privilege to settle in new streets, not the ruins of our former Jewish quarter and allowed to establish our own guard patrols."

"Father," Gershom said, himself no longer angry but rather resigned. "I know you have tried, and I respect your desire to keep our remnant community together. But I also know that it cannot be done here. We will never have a place, a secure place among these people."

"And how do you know that, with such certainty?" challenged Noach ben Shlomo. Ben Shlomo, a glass-blower, long had served as Isaachar ben David's right-hand man, a secretary and administrator of sorts. Gershom eyed the other man. Once tall but now stooped, slender and hard-faced, it had been years since Gershom ben David had called the man "Uncle Noach." "Is it through that golden-haired *shiksha* you visit at night near the palace gate?" ben Shlomo demanded.

Suddenly red-faced, Gershom moved toward the older man.

"Gentlemen! Stop!" thundered Isaachar ben David, animated in a way he had not been previously that night. Others in the small group stirred but said nothing. After a moment or two, a more controlled but still furious Gershom, staring directly at Noach ben Shlomo, spoke in a cold, deep voice:

"Let me ask you a question, *Adon shel Dat*," said Gershom ben David, mockingly addressing ben Shlomo as Master of Knowledge. "These new streets we Jews will be allowed to inhabit, aren't they at the edge of Speyer, adjacent to the marsh, with its foul emanations? Won't they have a wall around them? And won't our own Jewish guards be required to make sure the gate is closed and locked at night, so we Jews are safely contained like cattle in a barn?"

The meeting did not end so much as crumble. Most of the older men went one way, most of the younger ones followed Gershom ben David in another.

About the same time that night, a young woman in Speyer prepared for bed. Not just any young woman, but the daughter of Prince Ludwig himself. Princess Wendelina looked at herself in the mirror as she combed her long blonde hair. She knew she was fortunate to possess a mirror. In fact, the princess, in virtually all things a sensible, intelligent young woman, mature at seventeen realized was that she was fortunate to be a princess, to live in a palace, to have maids to wait on her and a father who could protect her. From most things at least. The plague had taken her sister, one brother and, hardest to bear of all, her dear mother. But she herself had survived, healthy, vital and hopelessly in love with that strong, handsome Jew, Gershom.

It was worse than foolish, she knew. It was dangerous, dangerous for both of them. And even if they made good their escape to the east, which Gershom had been talking about for weeks, how would they then live but in poverty, ostracized by those around them—non-Jews like herself—always endangered? And how could she not continue praying to the Savior, Jesus Christ instead of that maddeningly intangible, frequently unresponsive God of the Jews?

Still, glancing into the mirror, she asked herself wistfully, "Am I not beautiful?

And still young? Should not youth and beauty embrace youth and the most handsome good looks, the most comforting voice?" "Oh yes, they should!" she told herself. As they already have and so ecstatically, she thought, patting her slightly rounded abdomen.

Such meetings and discussions as those that broke up in Landshut that night were being held in cities, towns and villages throughout the French and German-speaking lands. And time and again parts of the Jewish communities—and occasionally entire populations—gathered their possessions, what possessions they retained after the Black Death and subsequent robberies and massacres. By cattle cart or on foot they began the slow, harrowing trudge toward places they only had heard of. These were places with names like Poland, Lithuania and Russia, names without romance, with little inspiration but offering the merest hint that life for the Jews might be better there.

Chapter Eighteen:
New York City, the Present

It sounded like metal trash cans being knocked to the ground. Gerry Meyer released himself from Judith Krakower's embrace, rising from the supple body beneath him. The woman rarely missed a day in the fitness gym of the Marlene Meyerson Jewish Community Center at Amsterdam Avenue and 76th Street. A moment ago, they had been passionately entangled on his office couch. He had let ecstasy take him. It had been so long. He had felt the hot, unreasoning desire of a teenager and in sheer lust fulfilled it. It had been wonderous, until sounds of fighting exploded in the alley behind the Jewish Renewal Institute.

Pop. Pop-pop. They looked at each other in silence.

"Is that ...?" Krakower whispered, her eyes wide.

"Shh," Meyer ordered. He began pulling on his clothes.

He was about to punch 911 into his cell phone when they heard the sounds again.

Pop-pop! Pop-pop-pop. A second's quiet, then a final pop-pop-pop.

No need to call 911. From somewhere in the night, they heard sirens.

"Get dressed and straighten up as best you can," Gerry Meyer said. "Police will be here soon. We were working late reviewing JRI programs. Right?"

"Right," Judith Krakower replied, sounding not at all certain.

"I'm going outside to take a look," he said.

"Be careful!" she implored. Still naked, she embraced him. Feeling her body, simultaneously taut and tender against his, Gerry Meyer grew aroused again. Breaking free, determined to look outside, he thought to himself with what he knew was hubris, God knows I deserve her. And Lisa Lenkowitz too.

With sirens growing louder, he stepped into the alley. Two trash cans were lying on their sides. And next to them lay four men. Curiously, all wore black from head to toe. Three of them, in a rough semicircle, did not move. Gerry Meyer saw that irregular circles of blood had seeped onto the chests of each. Inside the little arc a fourth man—the only one with a beard—was still alive. Barely. It looked like he had been shot in the stomach. Meyer leaned over him and heard a reedy, fading *"Shema Yisrael, Adoni Elohaynu, Adoni Echad."* Then nothing. "Hear, Oh Israel—the Lord our God, the Lord is One." The most important of all the lines of all the Hebrew prayers. A declaration of unshakable faith as much as a prayer, it was not only on the lips of those at daily services but also on those of the dying from before the Romans and through and beyond the years of the Holocaust.

Squad cars began pulling up at the head of the alley. Gerry Meyer stood there, awaiting the police. Looking down at the four bodies he wondered: Who were these men? He did not wonder what they were doing there, though. That he understood. They were there because of him.

****

"First, they arranged to shove Rabbi Yehezkieli in front of a subway train, now they kill Chaim Fellner apparently attempting to snatch, or murder, this Gerry Meyer fellow. The attack on Rabbi Yehezkieli basically was a one-day news story, except for that mini-riot outside his hospital later, but this—with four dead, each suffering multiple bullet wounds—won't fade for a long time. *The Daily News* and *New York Post*, local TV and talk radio will keep it alive. The Internet will be alight with conspiracy theories, and one or more might actually touch on the truth, at least part of it.

"Who shot whom. Why? Who were they and who sent them? All that and more. Inquiring minds will want to know. NYPD will pursue this investigation with perhaps uncharacteristic diligence, we can be certain." Rabbi Samson was more upset than Uri Stein had ever seen him.

"That sort of attention, publicity, public curiosity, JOLO does not need, does not want, and must sidetrack to the extent possible."

Chapter 18

"Yes," said Uri Stein. "Yes." And only that. But Rabbi Samson was not finished.

"We know who shot the men who killed Chaim. Thank God that Feldman—his first name is Herschel, right? —managed to move from watching the front door and catch those in the alley. No one else needs to know. No one else must know!"

"They call him Harry, yes," Stein said.

"Yes? Is that all you can say?" Rabbi Samson asked, frostily. "I'm sorry," the rabbi added, almost immediately. "But we've been caught off-guard, or short-staffed, twice now. That cannot not continue. Our primary mission, for more than one thousand years, has been to protect the messianic candidates. Yet within a few days we've nearly experienced a double-failure in the most Jewishly populous city in the world. We must do better. Starting with getting that ben-Veniste boy out of Cuba. And constant protection of Professor Golden. Whether it's the Knights of the Chalice, Army of the Spring of Goliath—they call themselves *Jaysh ein-Galut*—or simply antisemites grown in today's hothouse of hatred, someone actively opposes us."

"And maybe there's someone on the inside, a leaker," Stein said.

Both men knew the stakes had been raised.

Chapter Nineteen:

Havana, Cuba, the Present

"Leave our apartment? Why?!" Dinah ben-Veniste was near tears. "What have we done wrong?"

"Why?" responded her mother, Channah. "Just look across the street." Through the window in the living room of their small apartment they could see a pile of rubble that until two days ago had been the front half of an old, three-story masonry apartment building nearly identical to their own. Four days earlier a torrential storm had moved through the city. Poorly maintained like so much of Cuba's infrastructure, Havana's storm sewers could not handle the runoff so water stood in the streets and saturated the ground.

Around noon the day after the storm, with a rumble like that of one more thunder-clap, one so close it followed the lightening instantaneously, the front of the building opposite them sheared off and slid down across the sidewalk and into the street. Three of the picturesque, pre-revolution museum pieces of Detroit-made automobile machinery Cubans kept running out of economic necessity lay smashed under large chunks of concrete, shards of glass and broken furniture. So too, it was assumed, did the bodies of three missing pensioners. Everyone else apparently had been out of the building, at work, school or waiting in line at the local bodega.

The building supervisor, whose repeated warnings about growing cracks in the foundation had gone unheeded, was smoking a cigar in the shade of a palm tree half a block away when disaster struck. "Now the bastards will believe me," he muttered out loud. "Not that it will matter. Not that they'll do anything."

Those in charge had done something though, and with alacrity. While rubble still blocked half the street, they found new residences for a party member and his family displaced by the collapse. That family, the Ortegas, was to move into the ben-Venistes' apartment next Monday.

"What have we done wrong?" David ben-Veniste mockingly repeated his sister's question. "Nothing," he said through clenched teeth, answering her. "Nothing, except to live on this hell hole of an island." The boy kept squeezing his hands into tight fists as he spoke. It appeared involuntary; he did not seem to realize what he was doing, but his mother, as a physician, noticed.

"Where are we supposed to live?" Dinah was crying now, her tears flowing freely.

Holding a piece of paper with an official seal at the top, Channah ben-Veniste read: "Familia ben-Veniste: By order of the municipality: You are to relocate temporarily to the apartment of the Fernandez family, on the second floor of the building in which you currently reside, not later than 31 July. Simon and Liora Fernandez have been instructed to provide you with a room. You will be relocated permanently when suitable accommodations become available, or until the damaged structure at 66 Calle Campanario is rebuilt.

"Authorized by M. Diaz, Supervisor, Residences and Hospitality.

"Approved by José de la Castro-Nueves, District Capitán, Democratic Workers Revolutionary Party."

"A room?! A single room—for the three of us?" Dinah shrieked. "As if Angelina's family has any extra space!"

"I will eat on the stairs and sleep on the roof," David said flatly, slamming their apartment door as he stalked off.

Channah ben-Veniste, who since the disappearance of her husband Ricardo had tried her best not to cry in front of the children, now wept openly.

It was mid-August and only two weeks into the ben-Veniste and Fernandez families' forced cohabitation. Though everyone concerned tried to make the new and claustrophobic arrangement work, the stifling closeness and lack of privacy meant tempers already grew short. David was at work one morning, stocking pharmacy shelves with the symbolic if well-meant little shipment of humanitarian supplies brought by the latest Norte Americano visitors from B'nai B'rith. The government long had authorized these humanitarian visits, as apart from tourism, from the land of Yankee imperialism. They encouraged those in Washington who wanted a "more open" policy toward Havana, and might eventually swing the door to larger-scale American assistance. At least some in the regime hoped so. As the group looked around the pharmacy, one man, a stocky, bearded fellow, said to him in a whisper, "It's time for you to leave Cuba."

Startled, not believing he had heard correctly, David stared at the man.

"I can take you and your family safely to Florida."

Now David gaped, open-mouthed. He glanced at the group's handler, who, entirely disinterested, had stepped out to smoke a cigarette while the visitors looked around at the mainly empty shelves. "It will not be as others have tried to flee," the man said. "We have special means for special cases."

"We?" David asked in disbelief, gesturing at the others with this man. They were gray-haired men and women, for the most part, amiable but none who impressed him as much out of the ordinary. One even used a walker.

"I am with this group but not of it," the stranger said. "You know of the first Soviet Jews who escaped Russia?"

David nodded. His parents had whispered about them.

"We did that."

"And you think my family's case is special?" the youth asked, terrified the handler or pharmacist would come over and ask what they were discussing.

"Your father's middle name is ben-David, is it not?"

"Yes," David replied, "but how did you know?"

"And so was your grandfather's, and great-grandfather's," the man said. "All the way back."

David put his hand on the counter to stop his sudden swaying.

"I will return with this group tomorrow," the man said. "Speak to your mother and sister. Be ready."

David had so much to say, to ask, but like Jacob wrestling with the angel, could manage only, "Who are you?"

Unlike the angel, a providential messenger in human form, this quite human man, black beard flecked with gray, shoulders broad, said only, "Stein. Uri Stein."

Late that evening the sea breeze blew in gently, steadily. Stars shone with unusual brilliance in the newly-darkened sky. A teenager softly strummed a battered, second-hand guitar and sang quietly to himself on the spit of land jutting into the harbor at the edge of the promenade bordering the Malecon. Sang in a language that was not Spanish, the words from an old folk hymn heard around campfires decades earlier on another continent, the singers then young men and women in shorts, loose shirts and work boots, some still in their teens, World War II-surplus Sten guns at their sides. Like those before him, but more softly, the teenager now sang: "*Heinei matovu mani'im, shevet achim gam yachad ...*" "How good it is to sit together with one's brothers." To passersby the musician appeared to be just one more young person taking advantage of a balmy night.

But David ben-Veniste was playing and singing almost by rote. Staring at the stars high in the northern sky, he continued debating with himself what to say to his mother and sister. Not what to say, but rather how to say it. How to convince them of what he had decided, that this Uri Stein was legitimate and not some party plant sent to entrap them in retaliation for his father's flight? How to convince them that his offer was genuine and that they had to act now?

He gazed again at stars he had studied for a long time. The young man, having found a dogged-eared old edition of *Astronomy for Beginners* in a party-approved used book store, pored over its pages. Unable to escape his oft-proclaimed island paradise in fact, he traveled the heavens in fantasy. A half-a-dozen times he had studied the stars from this very vantage point. There as always, due north and bright, flashed Polaris, the North Star. And not far off, north by northwest in the great orb of the heavens stood a companion, Perseus, nearly as bright. They seemed to beckon him. He must convince his mother and sister. But how? The answer, when it finally came, was simple. He would insist on the truth, truth they already knew, had known for a long time.

Chapter Twenty:
Lisbon, Portugal, 1492

"Name?"

"Nehto. Joao Nehto."

"Occupation?"

"Navigator's mate," said the man, who looked to be no more than 20 years old.

An ensign, barely eighteen or nineteen himself, added the name to his list and, hardly glancing at Nehto, gestured toward the gangway. "You may board."

Hoisting a heavily-laden sack across one shoulder, Joao Nehto, his face impassive, moved onto the ship. His countenance may have been expressionless but his heart raced. For one thing, he knew little about navigation and nothing beyond what he had read in the books he carried aboard in his sack. But the young man, literate in four languages—Spanish, Portuguese, Hebrew and Ladino, a mixture of the other three—was a quick study. More importantly, his name was not Nehto but Aaron ben-David ha-Ivri. Aaron, son of David the Hebrew. His family had fled Spain during the 30-day "grace period" Their Most Christian Majesties, Queen Isabella of Castile and King Ferdinand of Aragon had granted any Jews remaining in their newly-united Spanish kingdom. That realm now also included Leon, Valencia, Granada, Seville and Galicia, and all Jews within it must convert or flee before the Inquisition finished its work.

That work consisted primarily of obtaining confessions under torture to root out Marranos. These were Jews who had converted overtly to Christianity and newly-known as *conversos* while continuing to practice their banned religion covertly or who were suspected of doing so by their neighbors. The Tribunal of the Holy Office of the Inquisition conducted *auto-de-fe*, coerced ritual acts of faith amounting to public penance. These spectacles of religion and entertainment usually ended in confessions of heresy. Such admissions typically were followed by public execution. Marrano, by no coincidence at all, was a Spanish word meaning pig. Also targeted were the Judaizers. These persons in the Decree's words were those "wicked Christians" who by "continuing to have contact with the Jews, whom we thought in our graciousness as long ago as the year of Our Lord 1480 only to confine to their quarters in each of our several towns and cities where they enjoyed residency, have committed the sin of apostacy and abandoned the One True Church."

When his new ship set sail, it would mean he finally was free of the threat that enveloped every Jew or suspected Jew in Spain, a land that within memory of some of the oldest community members had been home and sweet at that. Most of the time. Fleeing across the border to Portugal seemed to be his family's only chance at refuge. In fact, after the Alhambra Decree of March 31, 1492, by which Their Majesties had given the Jews until July 31 to clear out of the Iberian Peninsula, Portugal would turn out to be another act, a particularly cruel one, in the family's long nightmare.

Soon after arrival, Portuguese officials—for whom the rapaciousness of the Inquisition in Spain served as example—separated the younger children, Adina, 15; Miriam, 12; and Ezekiel, 11, from their parents and himself. "There are many good families eager to raise them," the official in charge informed his mother and father. "You can rest easy now as their immortal souls will be saved."

"No!" screamed his mother, Batsheva. In a frenzy she grabbed Miriam and Saul by their arms.

"That will never do, I'm afraid," said the official in charge, one Pedro Andrade, sergeant commander of the royal customs at the village of Castro Marim. Aaron's father, David ha-Ivri, had bribed a Spanish bargeman to carry himself, his wife and the four children across the wide Guadiana River from the town of Ayamonte to Portuguese territory. They were to have shoved off shortly after midnight, but through one exasperating delay after another—a missing pole, a loose oar-lock, balky lantern—the bargeman, who despite the rather large bribe he received from David ha-Ivri never seemed to be in much of a hurry, did not put them ashore until just before sunrise. That was about the time Sergeant Commander Andrade

Chapter 20

routinely began collecting the Spanish Jews straggling into Portugal and attempting, however futilely, to find their bearings. Later he would just as routinely collect half the bribes his boatmen friends had accepted from their fleeing Jews. "Another few weeks of this blessed Inquisition," Andrade had informed his wife, Dona Rosa, "and we will be rich. There is no other way to say it."

"Then do not say it at all," replied his wife, crossing herself and thinking, as she must always, of their eight children. Dona Rosa Andrade had dreamed nearly the whole of her married life of having a maid. Dreamed of being able to live finally not as a woman harried with ceaseless domestic chores from dawn until dusk but as a lady, free to sit in shade during midday heat and relax with a cool drink. Could there be anything better?

"Then do not say it at all," she repeated. "Do not boast. We must not attract the evil eye," Dona Rosa Andrade instructed Pedro Andrade.

If hearing "no" from a man angered him, then coming from a woman, sometimes even his wife—especially from his wife—made Pedro Andrade furious. This woman is always telling me not to do something, he thought. Though sometimes she is right, he had to admit. Still, he did not like it. Not one bit.

In the Castro Marim central square later that morning, light from a still-rising sun glinted off dun-colored sandstone of the three-story town hall. The rays caught a thin stream of water gurgling up from a pedestal-shaped fountain that marked the middle of the plaza. Beyond, across the square from the town hall and still in shadow, stood a long, narrow church. Its high, small windows meant that even when large candles burned brightly only a dim, wavering light enveloped the nave.

This particular morning a crowd had gathered in the square. It surrounded a group of fifty or sixty people, young and old, male and female, Jews. They were pinned near the fountain by Sergeant Commander Andrade's customs officers, their swords drawn. In the group Batsheva ha-Ivri, face distorted in fear, still clutched her two youngest children. Officers attempted to pry Miriam and Ezekiel from her.

"No!" she screamed again, tears streaming down her cheeks. She squeezed the children so hard Miriam cried, *"Emma,* you're hurting me!"

David ha-Ivri, who was pressed against Aaron, attempted to reach his wife but an officer's sword stopped him.

"This woman carries on too much!" Sergeant Commander Andrade announced to the crowd. "The Jewess must be hiding valuables. Search her!"

The spectators, having assembled in expectation, based on previous experience, of just such an entertainment, pressed closer. Two officers gripped Batsheva tightly as two others ripped away her clothes. The crowd shouted in approval and pushed even nearer. Batsheva, in only her underskirt and trembling, attempted to cover herself with her arms.

"Where are your gold coins, your jewels!?" Andrade demanded.

"She has none, can't you see?" David ha-Ivri tried to shout. But constricted by fear and anger, his voice emitted only a high, thin complaint.

"I will see what she is hiding!" Andrade roared. And with that, thrusting his sword deep into her abdomen just above the navel, he used a two-handed grip to draw the blade upward to Batsheva's breast bone. Her anguished wail, more nearly a silent scream, was lost to the crowd's gleeful approbation. Intestines spilling onto stone pavement, what was left of Batsheva ha-Ivri collapsed in the square. Miriam fainted. Ezekiel ran shrieking into his father's arms.

"See what the Jewish bitch tried to conceal in her innards," the sergeant commander ordered his men, his sword pointing to Batsheva's torn and bloodied body. Customs officers struggled to control the crowd as it pressed in on the sacrifice. As they did so, Aaron ben-David ha-Ivri backed surreptitiously through the crowd. Escaping into a narrow street, he ran down the first alleyway he saw. Then turning into another he stumbled. A strong arm pulled him up by his collar.

"Keep running, south out of town," a voice hissed into his ear. "Don't look back until you gain the woods."

Aaron did as instructed. Finally, in the forest and out of breath, he leaned against a large tree trunk, panting. As he did so he made a vow:

"One day I will avenge you, my mother. I will kill them all, as many as I can reach."

****

"Name?" the young ensign asked the man in line behind Joao Nehto.

"Aboab de Aguilar," said the man. Dark-haired, dark-complected, a little shorter than average but stockier, he like Nehto and all the others waiting to board carried his sailor's bag over one shoulder.

"Occupation?"

"Abled-bodied seaman," said de Aguilar.

The ensign looked askance at him. More than one crypto-Jew had tried to join the crew by claiming to be something he was not.

Noting the officer's raised eyebrows, de Aguilar added "and sugar-maker." That was the truth, or at least part of it. The ensign's eyebrows remained raised. Both he and this fellow calling himself de Aguilar knew that some Sephardic Jews of Spain excelled in the semi-secret art of crystallizing sugar. They also knew that Spanish possessions in the Caribbean Sea included islands home to expansive sugar cane plantations, plantations whose vast acreages were virtually worthless unless the juice of the cane, which grew year-around in the steaming climate, demanding endless toil from the African slaves continually arriving, could be rendered into the "white gold" so desired in Europe. The cane had to be run properly through an inferno-like process of cutting, rolling, boiling, drying and molding into loaves. Improperly done and the desired pure white granular sugar might emerge dirty and brown, especially in the tropical humidity, and therefore worth less in European markets. Done right the plantations' white gold brought the yellow stuff that enriched planters, the factors who lent them money between bad harvests, ship owners and captains, warehouse proprietors, bakers, coffee shop keepers and impost collecting governments.

Both men also knew that many Portuguese ships, including those plying the Caribbean routes, were owned by *conversos* and included many such as crew and no doubt more than a few crypto-Jews as well.

"Seaman. And sugar-maker," the ensign inscribed on his list. "Board."

So it was that Aboab de Aguilar followed Joao Nehto onto a ship named, perhaps by coincidence, perhaps *b'sheret* (ordained by God), *The Queen Esther*. Also, not by coincidence but by assignment Aboab de Aguilar had been following and watching over Joao Nehto most of the younger man's life. His name really was Aboab de Aguilar, named after the great Portuguese poet and scientist, bestowed by the man's father Samuel de Aguilar. Before the Inquisition gained momentum, the Catholic convert Samuel de Aguilar went by the name Jonah ben-David Isaacson, attended synagogue and traded in sugar cane from Sicily.

Nehto's first three days aboard *The Queen Esther* passed without incident. On his watch he observed the chief navigator closely. He saw how the man handled his precious brass astrolabe and magnetic compass to determine latitude. The ship's hourglass, used in combination with its log—not the captain's record of the journey but a piece of wood attached to a rope knotted at regular intervals and used to measure the vessel's speed—helped the crew calculate how fast and therefore how far they had traveled. No instrument to measure longitude existed then, but the chief navigator used time of day, the position of the sun at its highest against a previously selected reference point and, deploying the log to check ship's speed and ocean currents, arrived at longitude by dead reckoning.

Nehto realized that while the glossaries in his used books on navigation were helpful, their charts relied on guesswork as much as observation and experience. Cloudy days could throw a ship off course by dozens of miles. So, he attempted to commit to memory each action he saw the chief navigator take. He was thankful he did, because on the fifth day at sea the man failed to appear on deck.

"The captain says the chief navigator suffers from flux, and cannot leave his bunk this morning," the first mate told him. "But the crew whispers that the man is drunk. Either way, you will have to guide us."

"All right," Nehto said, forcing himself to sound more confident than he felt. Yet luck, if that's what it was, again was with him. The seas were calm, the sky nearly cloudless and *The Queen Esther* moved smoothly on a following breeze. From his books the young man knew to let the astrolabe hang perpendicularly to the sea. Next, he aligned the alidade lever with the instrument's two peripheral holes so that the sun's rays shone through. This allowed him to read the angle of the sun's altitude. Consulting his ship's charts, Nehto then called out the latitude.

"Drop the log," he ordered a seaman. Nehto thought he saw the older sailor smile as he did so. The sailor began counting the regularly spaced knots as the log played out. At "sete!" he stopped. *Queen Esther* was making seven knots across the great Atlantic Ocean, at this moment a blue-gray mirror reflecting sunlight off the endless expanse of water, disturbed only by light spray from the ship's prow.

They repeated the processes to determine the ocean's current. The captain, a taciturn old man with weathered brown skin, had watched the pair closely throughout the procedure. "Very good," he said finally as he stopped squinting at Nehto. "Hold your course west by southwest. If such fine weather continues, we will reach Jamaica in a few weeks."

Jamaica! The word conjured an almost fantasy paradise.

For those like himself—Jews, Christian apostates, even a few Moors fleeing their lost *al-Andalus* as Ferdinand and Isabella concluded the *Reconquista* ending centuries of battle and Muslim occupation—Jamaica signaled a sense of freedom, freedom of body and soul. The large, rich island did not belong to Spain, or for that matter any other European power. Recently granted to Christopher Columbus by the Spanish monarchs as partial payment for the Admiral of the Ocean Seas' voyages of exploration, and to his heirs in perpetuity, it was one place the Inquisition and its prosecutorial intolerance did not touch.

Of course, such weather did not hold. A week and a-half out it turned to three days and nights of howling wind, driving rain and battering seas. But by then the navigator had returned to his post and Joao Nehto—twice steadied by Aboab de Aguilar as he slipped dangerously on the rain- and wave-slickened deck—successfully continued his on-the-job training as navigator's mate.

As he did so he also scrutinized the old captain, learning how the man commanded a crew of disparate ruffians, most between the ages of thirteen and thirty. Supported by a first mate who seemed almost a *doppelganger*, the captain used a strong hand, quick mind and a steady voice. By offering incentives or instilling fear and everything in between, he merged the men into a crew working as one. That they melded into such a unit was absolutely necessary, a sailing vessel being very nearly a living thing with the limits of a flesh-and-blood creature.

A ship under sail, even in the best condition and fine weather, must have pumps in the bottom of the hold at the ready, trimmed sails on yardarms across the tallest masts, supplies replenished, ballast carefully placed and seams repatched in a ceaseless effort to keep the vessel intact, the crew healthy and if not happy, then satisfied. All this because a sailing ship did not exist as a human construction apart from its environment. In the worst weather, for example, a single miscalculation as to wind, course and speed that left too many sails unfurled could cause *The Queen Esther*, large and finely-fitted, to over-torque itself and be torn to timber and flotsam. Then again, in long becalmed seas, short of food, out of rum and no indication of a breeze from any quarter, mastering forty or more muttering, soon-to-be seditious men was a matter of life or death.

By the time they reached Jamaica, Joao Nehto, quick student that he was, had acquired more than rudimentary skills of navigation and seamanship. He also had absorbed leadership lessons and, thanks in part to Aboab de Aguilar, developed a plan. He had vowed to avenge Bathsheva, his mother, and kill as many Spaniards as he could. And Portuguese too. Now he was learning how.

In Kingston, Jamaica a dozen *Queen Esther* crewmen jumped ship. Among them were Nehto and Aguilar. Such behavior was not unusual. The city already provided a haven for several hundred Jewish refugees from Iberia and several hundred more *B'nai Anusim*—descendants of Spanish and Portuguese Jews compelled to convert to Catholicism but who had not rejoined the Jewish community. So many such Jews and recent converts or their children had arrived that the Spanish Crown would shortly publish an edict declaring that "Jews, Moors, heretics, *reconciliados* [repentants who returned to the Church] and New Christians are forbidden to sail to the West Indies."

Not that it did much good. A few years after publication, the bishop of Kingston reported to the royal court in disgust that "practically every ship arriving here is filled with Hebrews and New Christians." Further bans were followed by further complaints. Jews kept coming, especially those who previously escaped the Inquisition by voyaging first to Brazil and then to the West Indies, especially Jamaica.

Among them were three men who inspired young Nehto, including one who would combine with him on occasion. They were Moses Cohen de Henriques, Yaakov Koriel and David Abarbanel, the most renowned, feared or despised of the Jewish captains who plied the Caribbean.

Chapter 20

Sometimes they sailed as privateers under Dutch or English letters of marque and reprisal authorizing them to raid Spanish and Portuguese shipping and ports in exchange for a percentage of the booty. Sometimes they set out as pirates doing the same things without sanction of any government and keeping all loot seized from treasure ships carrying Mexican gold and Andean silver back to the lands of the Inquisition.

Nehto and Aguilar, who had become fast friends on the Queen Esther, knocked around Kingston for nearly a year, working as stevedores when they worked, when not sleeping off another night of drinking and visiting those they called "ladies of the port." They loaded and unloaded ships further strengthening their already muscular frames. When not working or roistering, they read. Books about seafaring, about history—European and Jewish—and about Judaism. They searched the city's bookshops for the rare finds that interested them. These they read and re-read.

"Have you heard?" Aguilar asked Nehto one morning as they ate big rolls of Jamaican coconut bread washed down with sweet black coffee. "Moses Cohen de Henriquez is looking for crewmen."

Joao's heart leaped. He jumped to his feet, his chair flying backward. "I'm going to sign on!" he virtually shouted. "This is the beginning, finally! Are you coming?"

"Of course," Aboab de Aguilar grinned.

De Henriquez was famous, or infamous depending on one's monarchical loyalties, as one of the Jewish pirates plundering Spanish and Portuguese bullion. Nehto and de Aguilar found his ship easily enough. Every sailor on shore leave, lounging about the port waiting for the saloons to reopen, knew where it was docked. Small in comparison to the Spanish and Portuguese treasure ships and warships protecting them, the *Sword of Redemption* weighed but 160 tons and carried only 24 guns. But the two young men whistled when they first saw it. The vessel seemed to gleam in the morning sun. Everything about it looked fresh, superbly joined and smartly fitted out.

"It must be fast," Nehto said, admiringly.

"Everyone says so," de Aguilar responded.

The pair spotted a sailor at the top of the Sword of Redemption's gangplank. "We have come to sign on," Nehto shouted to him.

"Have you sailed before?" the sailor asked.

"Yes, I'm a navigator and he's a seaman."

"Then, come aboard, and welcome!" the sailor replied. With that simple exchange, their world changed.

De Henriquez was a Portuguese name, though whether or not the man calling himself Moses Cohen de Henriquez originated in Portugal, one of its possessions or somewhere else entirely remained uncertain. Likewise, his Judaism. Apart from occasionally reading Hebrew texts, he gave no sign of practicing any faith, and many learned men of the time knew some Hebrew, along with a smattering or more of Greek and Latin. But to judge by his vocabulary, de Henriquez was a learned man.

However, he was hardly a cultured one. Big and bluff, he had a habit when drinking wine, which he did often, of swirling the first mouthful around behind closed lips, then spitting it across the deck and bellowing "Good!" or "Worthless!" before imbibing further. He also had developed a habit of slicing a finger off a truculent captive or recalcitrant crewman. His reputation well-established, he rarely needed to reinforce it.

Joao Nehto watched de Henriquez as he had watched *The Queen Esther's* navigator, closely. His scrutiny of the captain helped alleviate the reality of life at sea, one tedious day following another, made bearable for him by anticipation of those sudden if rare days of action to come. In the early weeks of their first voyage on the *Sword of Redemption,* Nehto and de Aguilar could only dream of the coconut bread rolls and hot coffee of Jamaica, not to mention the ladies of the port. On board the food rarely varied—salted fish, salted beef, salted pork (which neither Nehto nor de Aguilar ate), onions, hard biscuits, occasionally lentils, rice, garlic and almonds. And stale water. When available in port, also oranges to protect against scurvy. The afternoon wine ration barely eased the sameness.

His status as navigator's assistant spared him some, but by no means all the wearying labor of an able-bodied seaman. He too could be drafted into climbing the rigging to furl or unfurl sails, going below to restow shifted cargo, re-pitching seams or even swabbing the deck. He had not yet been ordered to join a cannon crew at one of their practices. But as always, he watched and remembered.

Chapter 20

On the edge of sleep one night Nehto felt himself drift pleasantly, mentally and physically as his hammock swayed in the dark, affixed like those of the rest of the crew to beams below deck.

"Joao," a voice whispered in his ear.

"Yes?" he muttered, a little angrily. "Who upsets my dreams?"

"Me, de Aguilar," the voice answered. "Do you know where we are?"

"Of course, idiot! In our hammocks, trying to sleep."

"No, I mean the ship's position."

"Off the coast of Cuba. Everyone knows that."

"No, I mean where exactly off the coast?"

By now Nehto was completely awake, and none too happy about it.

"The captain, first mate and navigator do not tell other crew members any more or less than they need to know. And they think off the Cuban coast is enough information for now."

"Not for me," de Aguilar said, his voice still low. "I know—sailors talk …"

"All the time," snorted Nehto.

"And the wise man learns from everyone," de Aguilar replied.

"So it says in the Talmud."

"Regardless. The sailors say we are bound for the Bay of Matanzas."

"And if we are?" said Nehto.

"Matanzas is where Spanish galleons, heavy with gold and silver, gather for protection, as many as 15 or 20 of them, before making for Seville," de Aguilar said.

"Do these wise sailors of yours think Captain de Henriquez, feared leader that he is, plans to sail the *Sword of Redemption*, good ship that it is, into Matanzas, seize a galleon or two, and make off with the treasure on his own? The galleons are not unarmed, and the bay itself is under the guns of forts on both breakwaters."

"How do you know that?"

"Sailors talk, you said. And once in a while the navigator talks to his assistant."

"Well, it is said we will not be alone. In fact, many of the crew believe we are to join the Dutch Admiral Piet Pieterszoon Hein. As is Captain David Abarbanel."

"Abarbanel?!" Now it was Nehto's whisper that came in surprised admiration. David Abarbanel was nothing less than the most famous, or notorious, again as one's sympathies lay with the English and Dutch or Spanish and Portuguese, of all the Jewish pirates. Or, at this point in the 80-Years War, privateers. Cunning, unpredictable, impetuous but not foolhardy, Abarbanel was the last scion of the esteemed rabbinic dynasty of Iberia and nephew of the legendary Don Isaac Abarbanel.

Don Isaac had been the uncontested leader of Spanish Jewry. He was a scholar. One of his many works was a commentary on the Book of Joshua he wrote in 16 days. A philosopher who differed vigorously with Maimonides on prophecy and the messiah, whom Don Isaac expected soon, that Abarbanel was also Jewish community leader and leading banker. In 1484, Their Majesties Ferdinand and Isabella summoned him to serve as chief tax collector and royal financer. In this role Abarbanel helped the king and queen rebuild their fortunes, depleted as they had been by the *Reconquista*. For eight years only one other man in Spain was more influential at court. That man was Tomas de Torquemada, Inquisitor General of Spain, grandson of a Jewess who had converted to Catholicism to marry one Alva Fernandez de Torquemada. The mostly unspoken struggle between Don Isaac and Tomas continued until the historic year of 1492, when the king and queen, whose ear the Inquisitor General had captured as personal confessor, expelled Abarbanel and his 200,000 fellow Jews.

Of Don Isaac's relative, Nehto and Aguilar knew that David Abarbanel commanded three ships while their own captain, de Henriquez, despite his hard-won reputation for skill and mastery, led but one. He had heard the navigator and first mate talking, so Nehto knew that the *Sword of Redemption* might join Admiral Hein's ships. But he had not heard before about Abarbanel. Either the sailors possessed independent sources of information, or their imaginations knew no limits. As the ship continued making good speed toward Matanzas Bay, Nehto soon would be able to determine which.

At first light, Joao Nehto and Aboab de Aguilar looked south across a placid, aquamarine sea into the Bay of Matanzas on Cuba's northern coast. Like the rest of the crew, though at their tasks diligently now as the appointed hour neared, they stared in awe. There in the harbor nestled into the bay's southernmost point, their sails mostly furled and anchored close together, lay sixteen Spanish treasure ships. Most were large galleons, all of them prizes stuffed with gold and silver and waiting to be taken. Their protective escort vessels, on a wild goose chase to block a nonexistent Dutch and British invasion on the island's south, an invasion based on well-planted rumors, were nowhere to be seen.

Admiral Hein's squadron consisted of six warships, the largest being his own *Delfshaven*, named for his birthplace. A most modern vessel, three-masted and three-decked, it carried 60 guns—four forward, six astern, and 25 on each broadside, nine on each of the two top decks, seven on the third. There were larger ships-of-the-line, of course, some mounting 120 cannons or more, but few were as well-crewed, or as fast and maneuverable as the *Delfshaven*. Five other vessels accompanied it, including the 48-gun *Hollandia* and four smaller yet menacing ships the Dutch called frigates but their British allies condescendingly referred to as "battle yachts." The entire crew of the *Sword of Redemption* now understood that the assault on the Spanish fleet was imminent.

Abarbanel's three ships and the *Sword of Redemption* fell in line aft of the Dutch squadron as it closed on the western of the two fortresses guarding the breakwaters to the harbor. Steering parallel to the stone ramparts, the *Delfshaven's* 36-pounders on the lowest deck began to blast away. This greeting was followed in sequence by the *Hollandia's* 36-pounders, then the 24- and 18-pounders from the frigates and ships of the pirate captains. The fort answered with a curiously ragged counter-fire. Except for the shattered foremast of Abrarbanel's second ship, Nehto saw little damage done to the attackers. It was as if the Spanish, lacking their commanders absent searching for the fictitious invasion force and taken by surprise, could not mount an effective response.

"Nehto, help man that gun!" the first mate shouted at him.

One of the cannon's crew writhed screaming on the deck near a gun carriage. Its recoil having driven the weapon to one side instead of straight back, its wheeled carriage—about 5,000 pounds including the gun—had crushed the sailor's left foot before the thick restraining ropes snapped taut.

"Use this!" one of the other gun crewmen yelled at Nehto, throwing a cannon sponge at him. It was a large piece of fleece wound tightly around one end of a long wooden ramrod. Joao staggered back as he caught it, more from awkward imbalance than the weight of the apparatus. He knew what to do with it, though, having watched the gun crews at practice. Cannon must be scoured after each firing, lest a spark remain in the barrel that might prematurely ignite fresh powder inserted for the next shot. In the confusion and heat of battle cannon occasionally went unscoured. Resultant explosions of the hot artillery could maim or kill the cannon's crew and others nearby.

"Up now, boys!" The ship's doctor, not that he had ever studied medicine apart from a long indenture at sea, and his two doctor's mates, each perhaps fourteen years old, roughly lifted the wounded man, now subsiding into shock as his mangled foot left a trail of blood on the deck. Busy at the gun, Nehto ignored them as they took the man below.

The attackers' line continued forward, crossing the harbor's open mouth and now blasting at the second fortress. This time answering fire was even less effective.

"The Spaniards have stripped the garrison to send reinforcements south!" his gun crew leader exulted. Then the man looked at Joao and laughed. "Boy," he chortled, "if you cover your ears like that each time we fire, they'll go as flat as poor Bartel's foot."

Over in no more than thirty minutes, The Battle of Matanzas Bay would live in history. Admiral Hein, his own captains and the pirate leaders captured thirteen of the sixteen Spanish treasure ships. One galleon and two smaller vessels had managed to lift anchor and squeeze out of the harbor before the attackers had fallen into line off the first fortress. Two others tried the same maneuver too late and found themselves pinned between the breakwaters and the pirate ships.

On board the *Delfshaven*, Admiral Hein ordered the captain-general of the Spanish fleet brought before him. "Sir!" he barked, "I accept your surrender."

"I have not surrendered," the Spaniard responded.

"I have taken thirteen vessels of your fleet, your command ship and you yourself, as you must recognize. So, do you surrender now, you, your crews, ships and all their contents?"

"I have heard the Dutch are lenient," the captain-general said. "At least more so than the British."

"That may be true," Admiral Hein replied. "But best not to presume upon it. Now, do you surrender?"

The Spaniard, pressing his lips tightly, looked about him. That there was no way out, no bargaining position even, was clear. He should have died in battle. More than perfunctory return fire had been required. Not that he was able to give it, most of the soldiers of the forts, their weapons and ammunition off who knew where, to the south. Cuba's governor-general and his advisors, court favorites sent out to enrich themselves on the bounty of mines of New Spain, were the real authors of this debacle. Inefficient administrators, incompetently disdainful of the Dutch and British— "those Protestant heretics, hardly better than the Jews or Moors"—too ill-informed not to bite on insinuating rumor, they and not he should pay. Tomorrow would be another day and he would make his case to Seville, Granada and to Ferdinand and Isabella themselves if necessary.

"I surrender."

"You are wise," Admiral Hein said. "Now, let us have a true accounting of what these vessels contain, and then we may put you and your men ashore to walk to Havana." A most unusual scene followed. The Dutch admiral, flanked by his own captains, sat at small table brought onto the *Delfshaven's* deck. Opposite him sat the Spanish captain-general and his senior aides. They worked diligently over a long paper, unrolled scroll-like across the table. For three hours they listed each captured ship and itemized its contents.

Finally finished, the Dutch admiral looked up. His lips opened to emit a long, low sound somewhere between a sigh and a whistle. "Good God in heaven! It is not to be believed! More than eleven million guilders. I do not exaggerate if I say this may be the greatest treasure capture in the history of seafaring."

"You do not exaggerate," the Spaniard said, with an ironic if defeated sense of pride.

On board the *Sword of Redemption*, a different scene unfolded, a footnote to that taking place on the *Delfshaven*. Having trapped one of the Spanish frigates at the breakwater, Captain Cohen de Henriquez was surprised when the ship tried to escape by ramming his. Pleasantly so, since he always enjoyed what he called "a good joust."

It took only a few moments of close combat for *Sword of Redemption* to compel the Spanish ship's surrender. Out-maneuvered and out-fought, the latter—slowed as it was by its cargo of silver ingots—yielded to the inevitable. Joao Nehto wished the fight had gone on at least a little longer. Pretty sure his cannon had blown apart an entire gun crew on the frigate, eight men plus the little powder boy, he felt a joy—almost a delirium he had not known since before that morning in Castro Marim when Aaron ben-David Ha-Ivri watched his mother, the sainted Batsheva, butchered. He wanted to kill more Spaniards. He needed to feel this day's joy again.

Even after reserving a sizable portion of the booty for their royal sponsors in London and Amsterdam, an amount sufficient to fund all the British and Dutch governments' activities for a year, an unprecedented sum remained for the captains and crews. "What will you do with yours?" de Aguilar asked Nehto that night. "With mine and yours," the other answered. "Combine them, buy and provision a good ship, hire a worthy crew, apply for letters of marque from both the English and Dutchmen, and go into business for ourselves."

"What makes you think I want to do that?" de Aguilar said.

"I have considered it, more than once. And I've concluded that you have not followed me, accompanied me, that is, all the way from Castro Marim until today, through everything, to part ways now. You are my closest friend. And I am yours. But there is something more, isn't there? What is it? I have listened closely to the sound of your voice, and decided years ago it is the same voice that set me running from that accursed square in Portugal."

De Aguilar's eyes narrowed and his expression—often somber—now looked older and, Nehto thought, a bit distant. For a long moment there was silence between them. Finally, de Aguilar spoke.

Chapter 20

"What is it, you ask? The answer is as simple as your name."

"My name? Joao Nehto?"

"Not that one, the name of hiding and survival, but your real name, the Hebrew one."

"Aaron ben David ha-Ivri?"

"Yes, of course. 'Aaron, son of David the Hebrew.' Did you ever think, deeply, about what it means?"

"It means I am Aaron, my father was David, and we are Jews," Nehto replied flatly.

"Of course. But that is only its superficial meaning," de Aguilar said. "It points at the possibility that your father was also a son of David, a ben-David, with lineage stretching back through Saadia HaGoan and the Exilarchs to the last kings of Judah and King David himself."

"If you thought there was even a possibility that was true, why would you have let me go into harm's way and let me run wild in Kingston? That's how you would treat the messiah?" Joao laughed.

"Our assignment is to protect, and in some cases direct, those who might manifest themselves as messiah. But not take over their lives. After all, it is from his life that the Jews will recognize the genuine *Mosiach*."

"Really? And who gave you this job?"

"My superiors in a guild almost as old as Jewish memories."

"Fantastic. Or merely interesting, curious even. But it changes nothing. I am going to get my own ship and kill more Spaniards. Many more. And Portuguese too."

"Of course," replied de Aguilar. "And I am going to help you. And perhaps the Jews will take note. Although you can never tell. We are a stiff-necked lot, as the original Aaron found when he couldn't stop the people's demand for an *egel zahav*, a golden calf."

So it was that the legend of Joao Nehto, captain of *Batsheba's Vengeance* and the Scourge of Spain, spread throughout the Caribbean and beyond. The name itself was enough to cause fear among Spanish sailors. Only in whispers did they speak of his mercilessness toward captured officers. For a dozen years Nehto and *Batsheva's Vengeance*, said to appear and disappear at will, struck terror among the crews and commanders of Seville's treasure ships.

And then the captain and his ship vanished. Some said Captain Nehto had become sated with riches, others than he finally tired of killing. There was a rumor that a freak storm sent *Batsheva's Vengeance*, its captain and crew to the bottom before a single sail could be reefed. More popular was the story that Nehto had purchased a plantation overseen by a veritable wizard of sugar production and settled there with two wives and ten children. But, claimed a few of the Kingston Jews and *B'nei Anusim*, what really happened was that the feared captain had taken his family and riches, his overseer and his family, and sailed off for *Eretz Yisrael*. Some versions had it that only his wife and youngest children made the trip, the older sons preferring to continue sailing the Caribbean and despoiling Spaniards. All the variations on this explanation of the missing Captain Joao Nehto insisted he himself spent his final years studying mysticism with Rabbi Isaac Luria, the saintly Ari, in the holy city of Sefat in the mountains of the Galilee.

A letter written at the time by a kabbalist in Sefat to a relative in Thessaloniki, Greece, now in the archives of the Jewish Museum of Thessaloniki, purports to recount a conversation between one Captain Joao and the Arizel. The museum itself memorializes the history of the Jews of the city, from 200 B.C.E. to 1943.

"Tell me about your life," the kabbalistic master asked. "Has it been well-lived?"

"I will tell, and you will decide," the captain replied. "Know that I killed many Spaniards. Many Portuguese too. They—their kind—had murdered my mother before my very eyes. They destroyed my family. They destroyed the Jewish communities of Spain and Portugal ..."

"Yes, the Iberian cataclysm. I know of it too well," said the Ari, whose name Arizel thus expressed meant lion of God. "But did you kill enough of them, too few or too many?"

"I can't say. God will decide. I can only tell you I became exhausted with killing. And that long before destroying as many of them as they had of us."

"That is good," replied the Lion of Mysticism. "Your exhaustion over causing death, even of our enemies, shows you retained more than a spark of divine goodness."

"Goodness or righteousness? I wonder," said the captain.

"Are they not synonymous?" asked the Ari.

"You tell me," said the captain. "If they meant one thing only, I believe we would not need two separate words."

"The Talmud instructs us that 'if someone comes to kill you, rise and kill him first,'" the Ari stressed. "Such instruction is one route by which we humans are brought to understand God's ways. The commandment orders us not to murder. But the Torah records wars of self-defense, in which killing is not murder but an obligation. Otherwise, we commit the sin of suicide passively."

"God's ways?" the captain responded, a touch of anger within his weariness. "I don't presume to know God's ways. I am a Jew, so I do Jewish things."

"Like study?"

"Yes. That is why I am here in Sefat, with most of my family and my first mate and his family. We intend to study in this mountain air with its evening light that seems to me not only to glow but also to penetrate."

"I see the same light," said the Ari. "Let us study then."

Some scholars cast doubt on the authenticity of the letter, so the Jewish Museum of Thessaloniki keeps it in the archives, puts it on display but rarely, and then with a little notice in curatorese at pains to highlight its disputed status. Beyond dispute is that years later Kingston Jews pointed to truth in the legend of Captain Joao Nehto retiring to the Holy Land. They cited what they had been told was a strange tombstone, near the grave of the Ari himself in Sefat, with a skull and crossbones etched over Hebrew writing, just like several of the markers in Kingston's old Jewish cemetery.

Chapter Twenty-One:
New York City, the Present

On the flight from Pittsburgh back to New York, barely an hour including the long glide into La Guardia waiting for a terminal gate to open, Joshua Golden reflected on his conversation with Dean O'Brien at the Franciscan University of Steubenville. It had been unlike any he had at Columbia while working toward his dissertation. Better than robust, it had been absolutely meaty.

"I have long been impressed with attempts by Rabbi Lord Jonathan Sacks and Rabbi Meir Soloveitchik of Yeshiva University, convincing in my view, to connect the Hebrew Bible—which as the Old Testament comprises the bulk of our Christian Bible, if in somewhat different order—with the American founding. That's something we would like to make explicit in our curriculum here. According to Sacks and Soloveitchik, Moses, as part of his farewell addresses to the Israelites in Deuteronomy, had a futuristic view, nearly 3,500 years in the future when he said 'See, I have taught you decrees and laws as the Lord my God commanded me, so that you may follow them in the land you are about to enter and possess. Take care to keep them, for this will be your wisdom and understanding in the eyes of the nations,'" as the dean read from his King James version of the Old Testament.

Then O'Brien turned to a few loose, printed pages and read, "according to Sacks, Moses believed 'there would come a time when the idea of a nation founded on a covenant with God would inspire other nations with its vision of a society based not on a hierarchy of power but on the equal dignity of all under the sovereignty and in the image of God; and on the rule of justice and compassion. 'The nations' would appreciate the wisdom of the Torah and its 'righteous decrees and laws.'

"Well," said the dean, sitting back and looking at Joshua, "here at Steubenville we believe this happened. It took millennia—the Lord's time is not our own—but it happened in the political culture and language of the United States. What are your thoughts on this?"

What Joshua thought was, the Christian Bible not only changes the order of the Hebrew Bible a bit, it imposes a different, not to say contrary, interpretation on it. What he said was, "Without trying to sound sycophantic, they closely parallel yours. Maybe because we both read Rabbis Sacks and Soloveitchik. And, I might add, in the same vein Rabbi Joshua Berman as in his work on the Hebrew Bible's break with older, top-down king-to-serf, willful gods to humans lacking agency. Berman's *Created Equal* makes explicit the link between Torah and the Declaration of Independence.

"The covenantal nature of the founding still runs like a subterranean stream under U.S. politics and, I hope, culture. That's why President Reagan spoke of Americans as 'one people under God, dedicated to the dream of freedom that He has placed in the human heart, called upon now to pass that dream onto a waiting and hopeful world,'" he recited from memory.

"And it's why President George W. Bush said something similar," Joshua said, pulling up an item on his cell phone. "Bush asserted that 'we are guided by a power larger than ourselves who creates us equal in His image,' and 'from the day of our founding, we have proclaimed that every man and woman on this earth has rights, dignity, and matchless value, because they bear the image of the Maker of Heaven and Earth.' This," Joshua said, looking up, "is, as Sacks insisted, 'explicitly religious language, without parallel in any other democratic society in the world, and it reads like a sustained commentary on Deuteronomy.'"

Joshua went on. "Sacks was hardly the first to note that modern history gives us four experiments in liberty, or what started as experiments in liberty. Two, the English Revolution of the 1640s, and the American Revolution of 1776, were based on ideas rooted in the Hebrew Bible. The other two, the French Revolution of 1789, and Russian in 1917, were based on secular philosophies of Rousseau and Marx, respectively. The first two led to freedom, the latter two to the Reign of Terror in France and the concentration camps of the Soviet gulag."

"Excellent!" Dean O'Brien enthused. "This is what we want you to teach here at Steubenville, with one hand on the Torah, the other on natural law, American-style."

And so it was, Joshua Golden thought as he leaned back in his economy-class seat and sipped an undersized, overpriced Coca-Cola on the return flight, excellent. But, a voice in his head told him—was it hers or from somewhere else? —not quite excellent enough.

Rachel Shapiro, who typically would not drive in the city, picked him up at the airport. She wanted a first-hand report and she wanted it right away.

"So, how did your meeting in Steubenville go?" Her tone was a bit frosty.

Joshua Golden knew she meant it to be that way. His beautiful, brainy beloved—and God, she was all three—had no intention of living in "Steubenville (audible pause) Ohio" as she always put it, a hard, flat emphasis on each word separately, with just enough *hauteur* to be detectable. He decided to give a little of her own back before saying what she wanted to hear. Best not to weaken future bargaining positions by conceding prematurely on this one.

"Great!" he said. "Dean O'Brien turns out to be the kind of department head every tenure-track hopeful wants to have. He's friendly, informal without coming across as fake. And, of course, knowledgeable about natural law and a genuine Judeophile."

"Wonderful," Rachel replied, frost level rising.

Pretending not to notice her annoyance, Joshua continued enthusiastically. "He actually picked me up at the airport in Pittsburgh and drove me the 40 miles to campus himself. The campus itself is attractive, compact, most of the buildings look new or newish anyway, and it's on a hill overlooking downtown Steubenville, the Ohio River and across into West Virginia…"

"Yes, a lot to overlook," Rachel interrupted.

"And the faculty I met, three men in the philosophy and political science departments who in addition to Dean O'Brien seemed pretty smart and enthusiastic about their work."

"Just men, no women?"

"There are women faculty members, of course. These were just the three who happened to be in their offices at the time. And the offices themselves are fine, up-to-date and comfortable. The library too. The main thing though is it's still a university—a place that attempts to nurture scholars inquiring into all manner of knowledge. Universal. Unlike Columbia, to pick a contrasting example out of thin air."

"Joshua," Rachel cut him off, exasperated at his seemingly oblivious, rambling, favorable reaction to this small, passionately Catholic school 400 miles from New York City, "we're not going to Ohio. Not even Ohio State University in Columbus, let alone the Franciscan University of Steubenville!"

"Rachel, I know that," he conceded. "But, at least from my perspective, not because of what it is or what it does. It is most hospitable to Jewish refugees from antisemitism, from places like Ivy League schools. It actually values and encourages intellectual excellence and academic inquiry. But if you're looking for a Jewish environment, and we are, it's not there. Dean O'Brien told me that the Orthodox synagogue and the Reform temple Steubenville once hosted had merged in the '90s—if you can imagine that—due to dwindling congregations. Later even that comingled one closed altogether. A stable, strong, Jewish community is not even down the Ohio River in Wheeling, where a Reform congregation carries on, as does the Marsh Wheeling Cigar Company, oldest in the United States, according to the dean. He promised me a box if I signed on. But for Jewish life, Orthodox Jewish life, we'd have to live in Pittsburgh, in Squirrel Hill, and that would mean a 45-mile drive each way every trip to campus.

"No, I'm going—we're going—to Touro University. It's already accepted me, and I get to design my own courses to teach. In that respect, it'll be like Steubenville could have been. There already are doctoral level classes in 'Maimonides and the History of Jewish Ideas' and 'Jewish Echoes in British Common Law.' But Dr. Pearlstein there, he's Dr.

Edelvitch's friend, remember, who agreed to publish my dissertation, wants me to do what Dean O'Brien wanted me to do in Steubenville—develop and teach classes in the idea of Jewish roots for natural law and the connection between the American founding and the Jewish concept of inherent individual rights as outlined in Deuteronomy.

Joshua was now on a roll. Rachel was rolling her eyes. But she let him go on. "Dr. Pearlstein, just like Dean O'Brien, asked me why I thought that in his first term as president, George Washington would respond to the Touro Synagogue in Newport, Rhode Island by quoting the Prophet Micah. Dr. Pearlstein pointed out that Micah lived in Judea in the eighth century B.C.E., after all. What did he have to do with America just after the Revolution?

"Well, in response to the congregation's good wishes for Washington and the government under the new Constitution, the president famously—or it used to be famous when history still was taught in this country—wrote....wait, wait, I have it right here." Joshua rifled through some papers in his briefcase and pulled out a dog-eared sheet. He read, "'It is now no more that toleration is spoken of as if it were the indulgence of one class of people that another enjoyed the exercise of their inherent natural rights, for happily, the Government of the United States, which gives to bigotry no sanction, to persecution no assistance, requires only that they who live under its protection should demean themselves as good citizens in giving it on all occasions their effectual support ... May the children of the stock of Abraham who dwell in this land continue to merit and enjoy the good will of the other inhabitants—while,' and here Washington quoted Micah, 'every one shall sit in safety under his own vine and fig tree and there shall be none to make him afraid.'" He looked over to her profile as she kept her eye on traffic.

"Very good, Professor Golden," Rachel replied. "Impressive. Seriously, I've been editing your drafts long enough to know where you'll go from there, at least in your introductory classes. You will pivot quickly to the Declaration of Independence and, as you've reminded me, Jefferson's insistence—polished by Franklin and Adams—on the individual's rights, endowed by the Creator, not governments, to life, liberty and the pursuit of happiness. What it pleases you to call the most revolutionary phrase in all of political philosophy."

"How well you know me," Joshua laughed. "But there's one other thing: Since Touro's accepted me, will you? I mean, officially. Rachel Shapiro, will you marry me?"

Almost swerving into the lane next to them, she exclaimed, "Finally! You propose in rush hour traffic in mid-town Manhattan. How appropriate! Well, it's about time! Yes! ... Even though your opus toward an eventual James Wilson Prize for original work on natural rights and the American founding means I'll have to be the primary bread winner in this family. And you thought I wasn't paying attention to your fantasies about a star on the Historians' Walk of Fame!"

That night was the first that Rachel and Joshua dispensed with birth control. "Neither of us is getting any younger," she said.

The next morning Rachel called Rabbi Samson's office to ask for an appointment. She did not tell Joshua.

"What about?" the rabbi's receptionist asked.

"This messiah business, and why he can't be a she," Rachel said.

There was a pause before the reception came back.

"The rabbi says he and his wife will be glad to see you tomorrow, say 6 p.m., after you finish work?"

So quickly, Rachel thought. Is that good, or not so good? "Yes, that will be fine," she replied.

"Oh, and Rabbi and Mrs. Sampson say 'congratulations' also," said the receptionist before hanging up.

Rachel Shapiro clicked off her cell phone. Then she stared at it. How did they know, she wondered uneasily.

"You still have questions about *Mosiach*," Rabbi Samson said to Rachel. It was not a question. "I'm not surprised. You mentioned the topic when we first spoke, though we did not have time to pursue it then. You are, I recognized immediately, a serious person, with an important question that you would like answered."

More than one important question, Rachel thought, but one at a time will do.

"Well, as we touched on before, the obvious and fundamental reason is that for us *Mosiach* is King Messiah. That is, the person who not only presages the messianic era—the footsteps of the kingdom of God on Earth—but also will restore the Davidic dynasty. Yes, in theory a queen descended from King David could do the former. But *Mosiach* must in addition to being a messenger also himself restore the line of Davidic kings," Rabbi Samson said. "So, a man must fill the role.

"For example, in the *haftarah* for the Torah portion Chaya Sarah, which comes from the beginning of Kings I, remember that Queen Bat-Sheva enters to tell the dying King David that his son Adonijah, whose mother was Haggit, was plotting to have himself crowned as David's successor, instead of her son Solomon. That would violate David's earlier promise to her. It also would place her life, Solomon's and that of his supporters, including the Prophet Nathan, in danger should Adonijah's scheme, far advanced at this point, succeed.

"David says to Bat-Sheva, 'By the life of God who has delivered my soul from all suffering! As I swore to you in the Name of Almighty God of Israel, saying 'Shlomo, your son, will reign after me, and he will sit on my throne,' so too I swear today.' The Scribes of Kings record further that then 'Bat-Sheva bowed with her face to the ground and prostrated herself to the King. She said, 'May my master King David live forever!'

"The commentaries tell us that by that she declared the power of David's kingly monarchy—continued through Shlomo, that is, Solomon—was eternal and would be perfected through a King Mosiach, a direct male descendant of David and Solomon. But I can tell you are still not quite convinced," Rabbi Samson said, and waited.

"No, I'm not, but let me think about it. Still, how could you tell I wasn't convinced? I thought I had my poker face on."

"Your poker face for business matters, perhaps," the rabbi said, his eyes twinkling. "But not spiritual ones."

"Hmm," Rachel said. "Okay, but why did your receptionist give me you and your wife's congratulations on the phone yesterday?"

Rebbitzin Samson leaned forward in her chair. Her eyes were twinkling also, Rachel Shapiro thought. Too much *kiddish* wine for the both of them?

"Our receptionist has been with us a long time. She is attuned to those who call. When I asked her what your voice sounded like, she said 'quite positive.' I asked her, 'do you mean 'upbeat?' She said 'no, more like exultant.' So, we took a chance, a small one I think, to offer congratulations on your engagement to Professor Golden. We look forward to the chuppah and subsequent *brit*."

The *brit*, the circumcision. Rachel rolled that around in her head for a moment. They know we're going to have a son? From last night, already?

Chapter Twenty-Two:
New Amsterdam, 1655

"Feels good, doesn't it?" Asher Levi asked his companion after the pair had shouldered blunderbusses for the first time.

"Good? I would say great," Joseph Barsimon replied. "I must tell you now that I never thought we would win our case, not against that Jew-hating little Stuyvesant!" Barsimon spit the man's name.

So it was that the two friends began standing their watch at the wall that gave the adjacent street its name. The pair half strolled, half marched along the wooden palisade that marked the northern limit of their little village. They were the newest, and perhaps proudest members of the watch in New Amsterdam, the Dutch colony at the tip of Manhattan Island.

The great English sea captain Henry Hudson, then working for the Dutch, had purchased the great chunk of granite, thirteen miles long and not quite three miles wide from the Lenape Indians in 1609, whether they liked it or not, or quite understood this bizarre concept of buying and selling land, soil that belonged only to the Great Spirit. Or perhaps it was Peter Minuit who bought the island and surrounding territory from the Munsees, a clan within the larger Lenape tribe, for 60 guilders in 1626. Either way, when 23 Jewish refugees, including Asher Levi and Joseph Barsimon, arrived from Recife in 1654, fleeing the Portuguese who had just reconquered their Brazilian colony, New Amsterdam's Dutch Governor Peter Stuyvesant wanted nothing to do with them.

The Recife Jews' journey to New Amsterdam had been anything but routine, or even much planned. Instead, it resembled an ill-fated flight, until Levi and Barsimon took Governor Stuyvesant to court. As Levi explained to his grandson Elisha David ben-Samson years later:

"When the English seized Jamaica from the family of Christopher Columbus, our ancestors fled to Recife, then a colony of the Dutch. In those days Englishmen had not allowed Jews to live in their glorious green home isles since the York Massacre in 1190, and who knew what would happen in their colonies?

"Meanwhile, the Dutchmen, sturdy sailors and even better merchants, in 1623 had taken parts of Brazil, including Recife, from the Portuguese. The Dutch, who were more tolerant at home than in their colonies, officially barred anyone who was not a member of the Dutch Reformed Church to settle in their New World possessions. Unofficially, the more Europeans who arrived, the better for the rulers in Amsterdam who were interested in commerce at least as much as religion.

"Eventually, there were around 5,000 Jews, many so-called 'crypto-Jews,' in Recife, including your Levi forebearers and those of our friends the Barsimons. In Jamaica we had been free—some of your ancestors free enough to sail against the Spanish and Portuguese for what they had done to our people during the days of Christiani and Torquemada. But under the Dutch in Brazil, our 'neo-Christian' relatives began practicing their ancient faith openly. That is, until the Portuguese returned in 1654."

"Then what happened?" asked Elisha David ben-Samson, an intelligent if excitable twelve-year-old.

"One thing after another, each of which seemed worse than the one before—at the time, anyway," replied his grandfather. "To escape the Portuguese, we took ships back to the Netherlands and Amsterdam. Many others had done so, or tried. But no more than a few days out, a Spanish privateer captured our vessel. The captain, Jacques de la Mothe, offered to take us to New Amsterdam instead—in exchange for all our valuables."

"What did you do?" the boy demanded, barely containing his agitation.

"What could we do? We agreed."

"So, the Spanish pirate brought you here, to New Amsterdam?"

"French. His name was Jacques de la Mothe, remember. In life, it's important to pay attention to names. It is said that the Almighty guides parents even if they don't know it in naming their children. Anyway, a person's name sometimes confirms obvious character traits. More importantly, they occasionally reveal hidden ones," Asher Levi instructed his grandson.

"But yes, de la Mothe brought us here. And then can you guess what he did?"

"Made you walk the plank?!" Elisha David ben-Samson asked, excitedly.

"In a manner of speaking. He sued us in the local court for failing to pay full fare for our passage!"

"Very French," the intelligent young boy said. "But how could you pay any more, since he had already taken your valuables."

"We could not, of course. So that's where Stuyvesant came in, that hateful little official. He seized what bits we had left, except literally the clothes on our backs, and auctioned them. And when that didn't raise what de la Mothe demanded, Stuyvesant threw me and Barsimon into jail and wrote to the Dutch West India Company in Amsterdam asking permission to expel all Jews currently in New Amsterdam and to bar entry to any future Jewish arrivals."

"What did you do then?" the boy demanded.

"If he could write to Amsterdam, so could we," his grandfather said. "We asked the Jews in Holland for help. They petitioned the West India Company, pointing out that Jews were allowed not only to live in Holland but also to invest in the West India Company. The next year, 1655, company directors informed Stuyvesant that Jews must be allowed to live in New Amsterdam 'so long as the Hebrews do not become a burden to the company or to the community.'"

"So, you won the fight and that's why we can live here," the boy stated.

"Not quite," his grandfather corrected. "Just because company directors told Stuyvesant he must let Jews stay in his colony, they couldn't make him treat us as equals. Or so he thought. His next move was to prohibit Jews from serving in the New Amsterdam militia but make us pay a special tax to support others taking our places in the guard."

"That wasn't fair!" young Samson said. "How did you get back at him?"

"We sued him in the colonial court demanding either to be allowed to serve or to be exempt from the tax."

"And you won, right?"

"We won. Although the case took two years to settle. Two long years. But let me tell you, that first night Barsimon and I carried our guns and walked New Amsterdam's walls was a glorious evening! Even if the rain fell."

"Why glorious?" the boy asked.

"Because it meant that we Jews, bearing arms in defense of the entire colony, were finally equal citizens."

"Grandfather, why did Governor Stuyvesant hate us Jews so?"

"Jew-haters give many reasons, Samson," Asher Levi said. "And the reasons often contradict themselves, like saying Jews are greedy and rich, while also that Jews are dirty and poor. Or that we worship the devil instead of God, or, worst of all, that we who must remove all blood from meat secretly kill gentiles and take their blood for matzohs."

"No! They really believe that?" Elisha David ben-Samson was incredulous.

"Some will say they do. It never matters. But deep down, they fear us, this small, different minority that when allowed the slightest amount of freedom, succeeds yet does so without conquering other people. And, although they won't admit it, some detest us because of what we think remains the Jewish people's greatest accomplishment. We brought the Torah with the Ten Commandments down from Mount Sinai. We gave the world God's do's and don'ts, and many have never forgiven us."

"I still don't understand. Why should that make them fear us," the boy wondered.

"Because it makes them ask themselves, even if they don't admit it, if there isn't something about our faith that Christianity—or even Islam for that matter—have not superseded and that therefore they might not automatically be superior to us," his grandfather answered. "Envy and suspicion are universal human emotions, but especially dangerous when focused on a tiny yet successful people."

"Foolish," the boy said.

"Yes," Asher Levi answered. "And therefore, that much harder to defeat."

"And this will go on forever?" the boy asked dispiritedly.

"I don't think so," his grandfather replied. "One day, sooner or later, the Jewish people will live again free and independent on our own land. And then, as the prophets Micah and later Isaiah said in the days of the First Temple, 'And many peoples will come and say: "Come, let us go up to the mountain of the Lord, to the house of the God of Jacob. He will teach us His ways so that we may walk in His paths. For the law will go forth from Zion, and the word of the Lord from Jerusalem."'"

"How do you know so much, grandfather?" Elisha David ben-Samson wanted to know.

"I don't think I know so much," Asher Levi replied. "But life has taught me a few things. And I have faith that the Messiah will come, no matter how long it takes."

"The Messiah," the boy repeated, almost rapturously. "But how will we recognize who he is?"

"When the time comes," Asher ha-Levi said, absently tousling his grandson's hair and his voice carrying a far-away tone, "we'll know."

Chapter Twenty-Three:
Jerusalem, the Present

Rabbi Aaron Yehezkieli put down the Talmud Tractate *Kiddushin*, closed his eyes and sat back in his chair. *Kiddushin*, as even first-year students at Ohr Zahav Yeshiva knew, dealt with the *halacha*, the Jewish law, of engagement or betrothal and marriage. Also, with the obligations of children to parents, and parents to children. His eyelids still closed, a smile played on the rabbi's lips. With the Talmud, even when dealing with a specific topic like marriage, there is always an "also." The "and in addition" approach tested and wearied many a student, but it also agitated their brains, challenging their thinking.

It had been a long time since he had awakened in the New York hospital, a period that included weeks of puzzlement and months of rehabilitation. Much more rehabilitation lay ahead of him, he knew. But he had made considerable progress. He could read and remember again, remember a great deal. Rabbi Yehezkieli also could write and, with some lingering difficulty, speak.

With the constant help of the friendly, concerned woman who seemed to be always at his side, and even now sat nearby typing on a laptop while frequently glancing over at him, he resumed many of his duties as *rosh yeshiva*. She said her name was P'nina. And while she herself did not speak of it anymore, others had told him she was his wife, that they had been married for many years and had children and grandchildren.

How odd, how extremely strange. So much had come back to him since what must have been a very bad accident in New York, but about his family, about this warm, smiling P'nina, nothing yet. The more he tried to remember, the worse the headaches. So, this quiet Saturday night, when most of the students had gone out, only a few still in their rooms studying,

Rabbi Yehezkieli had opened *Kiddushin* and began to read. Maybe something in it would spark a memory.

"When is the marriage formed?" the text asked. "At what crucial moment and in what manner?"

And the text answered: "A family is not created simply by a man and woman living together, or even having children together. Such a relationship might be significant—but it alone is not a marriage. A marriage creates a family when the man and woman, the husband and wife, become, as the Torah states in *Bereshit* [Genesis] 2:24, when they have become *basar ehad*—one flesh. When two distinct but no longer separate individuals become one."

"By what means is the marriage relationship confirmed?" the text asked further.

"By a formal, legal act. This is called *kiddushin*," it answered. "This is a positive commandment fulfilled at the appropriate opportunity. Not a ceremony itself, but rather a contract. Without it the man cannot perform the companion commandment of *peru u'revu*—be fruitful and multiply. This contract signifies the agreement and expressed desire of the man and woman to marry, who are by *halacha* able to marry one another—not close relatives or Israelite and non-Israelite, and witnessed by two other people present. The man may offer the woman money or any other valuable object, stating it is for the purpose of marriage; he may give her a document stating he is marrying her with this contract; or they may perform sexual intercourse for the express purpose of consummating their marriage."

"And can one party dictate terms of *kiddushin* to the other?" the text inquired.

"No," it replied. "Husband and wife each must enter marriage freely. Therefore, they must be intelligent and aware at the time of the marriage. And without witnesses, the marriage is void even if the other aspects are fulfilled."

There was more but this was enough for tonight. Rabbi Yehezkieli was tired. He still had not regained his normal energy, the energy he possessed before the accident, whatever it had been. After a time, he opened his eyes and smiled again at this woman named P'nina, this companion, aide, guardian. As always, she smiled back, her eyes alive with emotion. So, she was his wife? If so, he was fortunate, no doubt more so than most men. But when, oh when would he remember?

There always had been a security guard at the yeshiva's front door, checking bags and briefcases, questioning suspicious looking would-be visitors. But now, on direct order of Prime Minister Alon Meir, there were two at the front door and a third who patrolled the grounds. The prime minister instituted the new arrangement even before Rabbi Reuven Samson recommended it. He knew Samson, head of the JOLO headquartered in Brooklyn, and knew Rabbi Yehezkieli visited him whenever he went to New York. If Samson worried that Yehezkieli needed extra security for whatever reason, he probably was right, the prime minister thought. But if the prime minister had to provide security for every rabbi of note in Jerusalem, there would be no one left to staff the national police or the paramilitary border police. Not enough cops or too many rabbis? Now there would be a good Knesset debate, he told himself.

Chapter Twenty-Three, (continued):
New York City, the Present

"My schedule's become ridiculously crowded," Joshua Golden told Rabbi Samson as they walked to the main door of the Jewish Outreach and Learning Organization. "I don't think I can commit to another session next week, not yet anyway."

Reuven Samson smiled. "I don't think we need to meet in this, let's say, structured manner anymore. It appears we worked together successfully. You defended your doctoral thesis, were appointed a full professor at Touro, and are winning recognition for your work tracing Torah concepts of God and man through the Anglo-Scottish Enlightenment, the barely hierarchical and localized early Presbyterian church, to the American founding. Dean O'Brien at Steubenville republished your thesis on his university press, giving it a little wider circulation. Then there's your weekly podcast, growing in popularity. Most important, you are married to Rachel Shapiro—a true *eshet chayil*, woman of valor—and together the parents of twin boys. And you are what, just thirty-five?"

"Thank God. But thirty-six now," Golden replied.

"Baruch HaShem," Rabbi Samson agreed. "Tell you what," he added, opening the door to Washington Avenue, "If you and your Rachel can arrange it, join my Rachel and me for Shabbat dinner a week from this Friday. Since the twins are so young, no babysitter; bring them. We have room, and the experience." He smiled again.

As the rabbi swung open the door, both men heard a voice booming from the opposite corner, where St. Marks, a small street bordering one side of the JOLO block, met Washington, not far from the Brooklyn Botanical Gardens. A man, standing on the first step of a small step-ladder, shouted through a bull-horn. He was flanked on either side by men in sunglasses, identical tan-colored cargo pants and dark brown bomber jackets, one holding a long pole topped by an American flag, the other an identical pole bearing a white pennant emblazoned with purple crosses and trimmed in gold. A woman in a long white dress and also wearing sunglasses, flowed among perhaps four dozen listeners—white, black, Asian, Hispanic, indeterminant, tattooed, pierced, natural, dreadlocks, bald, this was New York, after all—and distributed pamphlets.

"And this is your million-dollar question," the preacher with the bull-horn shouted. "Will you go to heaven when you die? My friends, have you ever lied, cheated, stolen, taken the Lord Jesus Christ's name in vain, or even lusted—that is, as Matthew Chapter five, verse twenty-eight makes clear—have you committed adultery?

"Because if so, and you die in sin without repenting, you will spend eternity in Hell, your soul forever tortured in the agonies of damnation!" At this the man raised his arms skyward imploringly, then wrapped those arms around himself, letting go a sigh amplified by his bull-horn. "But brothers and sisters, I have good news, the best there is, in fact!

"Though God Almighty sees us as liars, thieves, blasphemers and adulterers, in our hearts if not always in our acts, Jesus Christ paid the price for us. On the cross, His suffering wiped our souls clean! It is as John tells us, Chapter three, verse sixteen, 'God so loved the world that He gave His only begotten Son, that whosoever believes in Him should not perish but have everlasting life.'

"Yes, friends! Jesus fulfilled all the prophecies of the Old Testament, rose from the dead and was witnessed by the multitudes! Repent! Accept Him as the promised savior, and receive the gift of eternal life!"

On the sidewalk now, waiting for Golden's Uber rideshare, the rabbi and the professor caught the preacher's summation. They glanced at each other. Rabbi Samson shook his head. "I believe the good fellow missed our discussion some time back about *Mosiach*, king, redeemer and savior. And if he's reading the Prophets in the original Hebrew, he might be confusing the consonants for vowels."

Just then, the preacher caught sight of the rabbi and Golden. "There, on the sidewalk outside the synagogue of Satan!" he shouted. "There stands the voice of the serpent!"

Holding his bull-horn in one hand as if preparing to use it as a club, the preacher darted into St. Marks Street, his flag-bearers with him, their flag poles now in horizontal lance position. Rabbi Samson and Golden could see that the ends of the poles had been turned to finely sharpened points. Two other men from the little crowd trailed them, whether as participants or spectators was hard to tell, though half a dozen were making cellphone videos of the confrontation. The JOLO security officer at the front door came to Rabbi Samson's side.

The fight, such as it was, was brief. Rabbi Samson almost immediately knocked the preacher's bull-horn away, threw the man to the sidewalk and, one knee on his back, twisted the man's arm up behind his neck. The security officer deftly blocked one flag-bearer's charge. He knocked the pole back into the man's chest, felling him. But the second flag-bearer, running hard, aimed straight for Golden's stomach. Springing to his feet, Rabbi Samson deflected the pole and tripped the man only a few feet in front of Joshua. The remainder of the little congregation scattered, including the other two men who had crossed St. Marks, narrowly avoiding being rundown by a J and J Florists' van in their retreat. Golden thought he saw the woman in the white dress in flight toward the Franklin Avenue subway station.

"Once a collegiate wrestler, always a collegiate wrestler, is that it?" Joshua said breathlessly to Rabbi Samson as he climbed into the Uber. He wanted to be gone before the police, whose sirens could be heard not far off, arrived.

"Once acquired, skills should be maintained. See you a week from Shabbat," the rabbi shot back as his climbed the few steps into JOLO headquarters.

"Report this to NYPD?" the door security man asked.

"Yes, in as much detail as possible. But first ask Uri to review the security cameras' video. See if there's anything we recognize, or anything new we can learn. I'd like to know who this preacher is," Rabbi Samson said. "And good work, by the way."

"A pleasure," the agent said.

Looking at the torn knee and ripped shoulder seam of his suit, Reuven Samson realized it would have to be replaced. Black, navy blue or charcoal gray? Decisions, decisions.

Chapter Twenty-Four:
The Holy Land, 1799

"Now what, Farhi my brother?" Jezzar Pasha, was sitting with his old friend Haim Farhi. Ali Jezzar served the Ottoman sultan in far-off Constantinople as governor of the port city of Acre and surrounding Sanjak Acre, a district or vilayet or province of Damascus. In all the sprawling Ottoman Empire, from Tunisia to Iraq, the Balkans to the Arabian Peninsula, no vilayet, sanjak or kaza was known as "Palestine."

Haim Farhi, as close to Ali Jazzer as an older brother, was the pasha's principal advisor and finance minister. The two sipped Turkish coffee at a small table deep within the high-ceilinged, heavy stone walls of Acre's sea-front fortress. While Jezzar Pasha re-read dispatches rushed to him by messengers from Jaffa, Haim Farhi studied the map spread between them.

Built by Frankish-led Crusaders more than 600 years earlier, the fortress had withstood time and battle since then. The Christian knights lost the imposing structure, and with it their last foothold in the Holy Land to Sultan Khalil and his non-Arab Mamluk army in 1291 C.E. Long an Ottoman stronghold, the building and Acre remained central to the empire's control of what its officials referred to as western Syria. It now would be the scene of history replayed in reverse. Attacking French, led by First Consul Napoleon Bonaparte, would attempt to wrest the place their ancestors had built and lost so long ago from Muslims defending what their forebearers had conquered.

"According to these dispatches," Jezzar Pasha said, "this Bonaparte has produced hell on earth in Jaffa. After four days of siege, the French breached the walls and captured the city. He then broke a promise that soldiers who surrendered would be spared and residents left unmolested."

"That is what I have heard as well," Farhi agreed. "Bonaparte let his troops rampage through Jaffa for two days, pillaging, raping and murdering."

"And they killed three thousand captive soldiers, shooting or bayoneting them on the beach. It took three days," Jezzar Pasha said. "Most of them were Albanians, like myself. He also executed the governor, my brother Abdullah Bey."

"So, what now?" Haim Farhi repeated. "Now we build a second wall just inside the first. If the French do manage to breach the wall along the sea or even inland, they will find themselves caught before the second and ripe targets for counter fire," he said. "In addition, the British navy, having captured many French siege guns in the Battle of the Nile, is bringing some here."

"If they arrive in time, then this Bonaparte—he's not even French, is he? Just some pudgy little Corsican—will find Acre much harder to take than Jaffa," said Jezzar Pasha. "Tell Bassam Daoud Pelegos to make sure the fortress' cannons are positioned and ready to repel French ships. Tell him it is an immediate order from me, though I expect our captain of artillery is at work even now."

Bassam Daoud Pelegos indeed was ready. The artillery officer, a man of long experience and close study, had set to work even before Bonaparte besieged Jaffa. He began preparing for a French assault at Acre the day he learned of their arrival at Cairo. Should the remainder of the Frenchman's fleet, savaged as it had been by the British at the Battle of the Nile, arrive off Jaffa, it would find a surprise awaiting. Two powerful long cannons, the type built to keep enemy infantry at a distance from fortified positions, had arrived from Constantinople. Supplied directly by Sultan Selim III, they were meant to help Jezzar Pasha frustrate French designs. Napoleon Bonaparte grandiosely might want to sever Ottoman possessions, cutting Egypt, Syria and even Arabia from Anatolia and the empire's core and move east to threaten the British in India, but the Turks and English had other ideas.

And Captain Pelegos' ideas differed from even those of his superiors, Haim Farhi and Jezzar Pasha himself. It stood to reason that if the British Admiral Horatio Nelson had destroyed much of the French fleet in Abu

Qir Bay off Alexandria—including blowing Admiral Francois-Paul Brueys d'Aigaillieres' 120-gun flagship *L'Oriente* to splinters and the admiral with it—then Bonaparte, not an admiral but a general after all, would come by land. So Pelegos on his own initiative positioned the sultan's long guns on the city walls facing south. He also moved half the other seaward-facing cannons to cover southern and western approaches. Then another piece of good fortune arrived in the form of a small British flotilla dispatched by Nelson from his fleet and led by Commodore Sydney Smith. The British, Pelegos thought. Even their ordinary names sounded so very proper.

To Farhi, in charge of Acre's overall defenses on behalf of Jezzar Pasha, Smith said, "Tell your artillery officer I will position my ship, *Tigre*, and companion gunboat Theseus, on either side of the citadel. Should the French attempt to close, we will give them the same broadsides they received at Alexandria."

"But Bonaparte will not attack us from the sea," Bassam Daoud Pelegos insisted to Haim Farhi once the British officer returned to his ship. "The main assault will be infantry, coming up the coast through Sanjak Jaffa to Acre."

"Agreed," said Farhi. "But regardless of how Smith deploys his ships, he will help us immensely. After the Battle of the Nile the British captured several French transport vessels headed toward us. They carried siege guns that, at first light tomorrow, Smith will transfer to us."

"Excellent," Bassam Daoud said. "I'll make sure they are well-placed." That night, after promising his wife, Euphrosyne, that Jaffa would withstand any French siege, Pelegos for the first time in months enjoyed the sleep of the untroubled. Euphrosyne was again pregnant. The gypsy who lived in a grand red-and-black tent pitched just inside the western gate had told her, and for only a drachma, one day's wages for a laborer, it would be a boy this time. The forecast's cost was "symbolic only," the gypsy had said, "for such good news." Euphrosyne watched her sleeping husband and beamed.

Captain Pelegos' respite barely lasted past breakfast. "Thirty horsemen are at the gate," his lieutenant of artillery told him. "Their leader demands entrance. He says they have been scouting the French, who are only a day away and he insists on helping us defeat them."

"We know where the French are. The whole countryside does. But did this leader say who they were and who sent them?" Pelegos asked.

"Yes," Lieutenant Demetrios said. Pelegos thought his usually dependable aide looked pale. "He said they came from *Jaysh ein-Galut* and were sent by Allah."

God in heaven! Pelegos swore to himself. Just when all our dispositions are made a pack of fanatics arrives "to help us."

To Demetrios, he said, "bring the leader to me but have the rest of them and their horses confined to the stables. Give them food and water, make them comfortable, but don't let them wander about the city, let alone inspect our defenses."

"Good," said the lieutenant, beginning to look relieved.

Pelegos then reported the arrival of the *Jaysh* contingent to Ali Jezzar and Haim Farhi.

"What do you suggest we do with these troublemakers?" Ali Pasha asked the other two. "Turmoil follows them everywhere. They are worse than the Cult of the Assassins."

"But the Mongols destroyed the Assassins, along with so much else, nearly five hundred years ago," said Farhi.

"All of them?" Ali Pasha wondered. "Some think not. Anyway, the *Jaysh* are real enough, and given their history, unlikely to follow anyone else's orders, even during a siege, and especially not when given by a representative of the Sultan, to whom their allegiance is dubious."

"Yes," Farhi said, "they come and go like the wind, always claiming to act as instructed by Allah, always sharpening their scimitars."

"That makes them unreliable and dangerous," Pelegos added. "Since it would be difficult and hard to explain to some that we expelled men willing to fight for us just before a siege commenced, I suggest we divide them, no more than two or three together, and post them on the walls as far from any cannons as possible. Then, if they help us, good. But if they get it into their heads to act on their own, even try to take command, they will be more easily subdued."

"Sensible," Ali Pasha said. "Have it done."

As it happened, the *Jaysh* men got little time to conspire. The advance guard of the French army appeared early the next afternoon. Kept at a distance by Acre's new long-range artillery, they began digging in far from the city walls. The next morning, March 18, brought the bulk of Napoleon's infantry. At first, the French—13,000 strong—attempted a series of assaults. Ali Jezzar's 5,000 men, reluctantly including the 30 *Jaysh ein-Galut* warriors, directed by Farhi and Pelegos, with the latter's newly-acquired Turkish and captured French artillery on Acre's thick Crusader walls, repulsed them each time. By the end of a long month, Napoleon's men had ringed Acre with fortified positions.

"Now the real siege begins," Ali Pasha said. "Napoleon, frustrated and angry, will try to starve us into surrender."

"He will fail, so long as the British can keep the harbor open," Haim Farhi replied.

"It's wonderful to watch the two British warships blast away at the stray French Navy vessels that try to sneak in," Pelegos added. "Their guns at sea do what ours do on land, disrupt Napoleon's attempts to concentrate a force strong enough to maneuver intact and choke us."

So it went, until late April. Then Napoleon's troops gained a surprising victory. Unfortunately for the great commander, it was dozens of miles from Acre. To block a force sent by the sultan to relieve his besieged garrison, Napoleon detached several thousand men and dispatched them under General Jean-Baptiste Kleber. Though greatly outnumbered, the French crushed the Turks at Mt. Tabor, not far from what Farhi called Lake Kinneret and Pelegos knew as the Sea of Galilee, just where Israelites commanded by the Prophetess Dvorah and her general Barak defeated King Jabin's Canaanite army sometime around 1100 B.C.E.

"Two things will happen now," Ali Pasha said. "One, Napoleon will feel encouraged by the French victory over the Turks. The Turks, such bluster. They would have no empire at all without us, Bosnians, Greeks, Egyptians, Arabs, Jews, all the rest. And two, Napoleon knows time is running out for him. We still eat, thanks to the British navy. But we hear that in the French camp, supplies run short and sickness spreads. So, Napoleon—this Corsican Frenchman with the Italian-sounding name of

Bonaparte—dreaming yet of an empire of his own including that of the Ottomans, will make a last desperate attack on us."

At dawn the next day, May 1, bugles sounded and the French assault came. The first assault. There would be four over the next nine days. On May 9, additional cannons from Egypt finally were deployed along the siege lines. They opened fire on May 10, announcing the fifth and final attack.

"They've broken through the southern wall," Pelegos observed from a parapet. He was calm.

"So, they have," Farhi agreed, standing beside the captain. He too was calm. "Watch what happens next."

The roar of triumph from French forces as they poured through the breach turned quickly to confusion. In front of them stood a second wall, of which they had received no advance warning. Enfiladed by the defenders at short range, Napoleon's soldiers dropped in the hail of bullets, dead or wounded. Survivors fell back. A second attempt several hours later ended the same way.

Surveying the French camps from Acre's walls the following day, Ali Pasha said, "I believe we have won. The only movement from the enemy is a few horsemen and a few wagons headed south."

"From what sources say—farmers, tradesmen, whores, others who do business with the French—that is only the beginning of a full retreat," said Haim Farhi. "With the British still blocking the sea, Napoleon has no way to evacuate his casualties except retreat overland to Egypt. And his losses are substantial. We estimate 2,000 dead, 1,000 wounded, another 1,000 at least too sick to fight."

"And our losses," Ali Jezzar asked.

"Hard to be sure," Farhi answered, "since many defenders are townspeople who simply went home when wounded or ill, but no more than four or five hundred, I think."

So, a victory it was. Except for one curious incident.

"Where is Haim?" Ali Pasha asked Captain Pelegos a day later. "I have not seen him in twenty-four hours."

"Nor I," said Pelegos.

"Have you seen the *Jaysh* men since then?" Ali asked, suddenly agitated.

"No, I have not."

"Find them!" ordered Ali Pasha. "And if you do not find Haim alive and well, bring me their heads!"

Captain Pelegos summoned fifty of the city's best men and before sunset they were riding east, the direction from which the accursed *Jaysh* band had arrived in Acre. Summer came early in 1799 and the May sun, with its accompanying heat, blazed down on Pelegos' troop. Two days later, hot and tired, they camped on the small promontory called the Horns of Hattin, where on July 4, 1099 an Arab army led by the Kurdish commander Saladin the Great annihilated Crusader forces under Guy de Lusignan, King—briefly, as it turned out—of Jerusalem. Looking east, the sun setting behind him, the captain saw the day's last light glimmer off the Sea of Galilee. And at the northern tip of the water the Jews called Lake Kinneret, Harp Lake for its shape, he also saw a line of horsemen still moving, slowly picking their way upward into the Golan Heights. There were about thirty of them, Pelegos estimated. The *Jaysh* band, he determined. Tomorrow he and his men would rise early and ride hard. They would catch these fanatics by mid-afternoon.

So it happened. The *Jaysh* men and their captives—a man, woman and two children—had stopped near the 1,800-foot crest of the Heights. The group dismounted and several men watered their horses at one of the many springs that bubbled up through the basalt crust near the edge of the plateau. The family of four, if family it was, stood to one side, watched by a lone guard. Unaccountably, apparently feeling unthreatened from any quarter, the *Jaysh* had posted no rear guard.

Captain Pelegos halted his men on the upward trail less than two hundred yards behind their quarry. Silently, gesturing with both arms in a forward slashing motion, he divided his force in half, sending one group left, the other to the right. As they moved into position on either side, a horse near the spring whinnied. Suddenly recognizing their peril, the *Jaysh* grabbed their swords. Pelegos nodded and an archer sent an arrow deep into the chest of the man guarding the little family.

"Too late!" the captain shouted. "Surrender! You are trapped!"

"We have the captives!" the *Jaysh* leader shouted back. "Retreat or they die!"

Pelegos nodded again, and three arrows struck the man, two in the chest, one in the neck. He crumpled without a sound. And at that, his remaining men—true believers taught by remnant Assassins in cliffside caves through which hashish vapors sometimes swirled that infidels must submit—nevertheless faced facts. They dropped their swords.

****

"You are well?" Ali Jezzer asked, embracing Haim Farhi. "Yes, quite well now," the latter said. "Though these past two days, before Captain Pelegos here showed up, I had my doubts."

"And you, Leah?" Ali Pasha inquired, looking at Haim's wife as they gathered in Acre's citadel.

"Yes, yes," Leah Farhi said, a little breathlessly. Tall, slender to the point of thinness, her face framed by long, thick black hair, she stood with one arm draped across the shoulder of her daughter, ten-year-old Tzippori, which meant Little Bird, the other on that of her son, fourteen-year-old Solomon ben-Farhi ben-Dovid.

"Good, very good," Ali Pasha said warmly. "Well, welcome back to Acre, welcome back to your home."

Haim Farhi and his wife exchanged quick but discernible glances. They looked concerned. The sultan's governor of Acre city and surrounding sanjak Acre saw immediately that his little homecoming speech had missed the mark.

"What's wrong?" he asked.

"Ali Pasha," Haim Farhi asked, his voice tinged with supplication and urgency. "I wish to relocate my family to Safat."

"Why? What can you have in that poor dusty hill town that you do not have here along the Mediterranean in plenty?"

"Our captivity by *Jaysh*, mercifully short as it was, made us realize we have been putting off something important. Very important. You know that among my people there is the belief that one day God will send, or rather cause to be revealed, our messiah, and that he will be a descendant, if many times over, of King David. ..."

"So, I have heard," Ali Pasha said, as noncommittally as possible.

"... There is a tradition, many generations old, in my family that we are of that line."

"Yes?" Ali Pasha said, struggling with his emotions for this man, so long his aide, no, his partner in governance even though he was a Jew, to remain neutral.

"The past few days forcefully reminded us that no one can count on tomorrow. So, if we are of that line, then it is time Solomon Dovid prepare. In Safat there is a rabbi, a great rabbi, Shlomo Beirav the Younger. Leah and I want our son to study under him, to become learned."

"To get ready, in other words," Ali Pasha said, allowing himself a little smile. "Well, I have heard of this rabbi, who also is a prosperous spice merchant, no small achievement in a place like your Safat, home of Jewish mystics and little else for four hundred years. So, yes, you and your family may remove to Safat. But Haim, whenever I need you, I will summon and you will come?"

"Of course. Agreed. Most definitely agreed."

Captain Pelegos watched the two men embrace again, noticed tears in the eyes of Haim Farhi's wife, and also smiled.

After the Farhi family had gone, Ali Pasha turned to the captain. "Do you have it?" he asked. Without a word, Pelegos turned upside down a small sack he had been holding. The head of the leader of the *Jaysh* men clunked onto the stone floor, rolled, and lay still.

"Good," Also Pasha said. "You have done well." Kicking the head of the recently deceased leader of *Jaysh ein-Galut* in vilayet Damascus into a corner, he added, "have four men accompany Haim and his family to Safat, just to make sure."

Chapter Twenty-Five:
Havana, Cuba, the Present

David ben-Veniste returned to the apartment he, his mother and sister had been crammed into with the Fernandez family. He had been walking city streets for nearly two hours, anxious, searching for an answer. In their room he found his mother crying, his sister distraught.

"What is it?" he asked.

"We no longer must share an apartment," Dinah said bitterly. "Our benevolent government has ordered—I mean, volunteered—mother to Nicaragua for two years to serve *La Revolución* and the Sandinistas, while a new building with a place for us is constructed. I am to stay in school and continue living here while you, dear brother, have been drafted into the Cuban People's Liberation Army Chorus. Someone must have heard you singing, no matter how softly, on the Malecón. Congratulations!" At that, his sister began crying also.

This news gave David ben-Veniste his answer. He knew now how to inform his mother and sister.

"That would be terrible news, if true. But it is not," he said quietly.

"What do you mean?" his mother Channah asked, wiping her eyes once more.

"I mean, we are leaving this prison country tonight. …"

His mother looked at him wide-eyed. "My son, are you ill, feverish?"

"Or delusional?" Dinah added.

"No, please listen. You remember the Americans I told you about, the ones who periodically bring supplies for the pharmacy?"

"Those old Jews from B'nai B'rith?" his mother hissed, in a whisper.

"They are not all old. And not all from any Jewish organization we ever heard of. One is a man named Uri Stein. Mother, he knows about our family, that father's middle name was David, as was his father's and so on. 'All the way back,' he said. And that his organization got the first Soviet Jews out, and the first Ethiopian Jews. He said we must be on the beach at Playas del Este just at sundown. ..."

"For what!" his mother demanded.

"That's when the helicopter will arrive and take us to Key West," David said quietly.

"Are you crazy? Anyone who would tell you a story like that either is crazy himself or a government agent trying to trap you. Trying to trap us!"

"No, mother, I am not insane. And I don't think he is a spy for El Jefe," David said sarcastically, using the title Cuba's current leader liked to hear applied to himself. "Here, he gave me these," David said. With that, he handed Channah and Dinah two small boxes with hinged lids. Inside, on dark blue velvet, were necklaces, small stars of David, 14 kt. gold on matching chains. He pulled an identical necklace from under his shirt. Inside the lid of each box was written in Hebrew and Spanish, "Am Yisrael Chai l'Olam." The People Israel Live Forever." On each Magen David, engraved in nearly microscopic script, one nevertheless could squint and read the words "Made in Jerusalem."

Channah ben-Veniste turned the necklace over in her hand. It was real enough, she knew. "Still, it could be a trap," she muttered. "Though El Jefe and his little people don't possess such finesse." Dinah already had her necklace on.

"Yes," David said. "It could be a trap. But it also could be our chance, our one chance."

Dinah felt a wave of dread, followed immediately by a thrill of anticipation. She made up her mind. "Come with us, mother," she said.

"Stein said not to bring anything we would not take with us on an evening stroll," David added quickly. "He said everything would be provided to start our new lives."

"Our real lives," Dinah said.

"This is insanity," Channah replied.

Her son began to sing. In a soft voice, he repeated the words of a song he had heard one of the B'nai B'rith groups sing in answer to the pharmacy staff's thank you as they completed their visit. "The whole world is a narrow bridge," the refrain went. "The main thing is not to be afraid at all." *Kol Ha'olam kulo gesher tzar/ Veha'ikar lo lefajed klal.*

When he finished, he said, "they told me it came from a partisans' song during the war. During World War II. They said it meant that even in the worst moments, even if a Jew has lost faith, no longer believes in God, a Jew must still have hope, hope that the words of the God he no longer believes in will be fulfilled nevertheless."

Channah felt the goosebumps raise on her arms. "Your father used to say the same thing," Channah told her children. Then she smiled.

The last orange rays of the setting sun lit the horizon out beyond the beach at Playas del Este, a Havana suburb favored by tourists who did not mind vacationing in someone else's tropical jail. Most of the beach-goers—Europeans, Canadians, even some Americans—had withdrawn, headed for nighttime entertainments. These would be cheap for foreigners with real currencies. Three people, a mother, her teenaged son and teenaged daughter walked slowly along the surf, toes in the water, holding their shoes in their hands. They seemed in no hurry. But inside, all three were nervous, more anxious than they ever had been before. It was hard to walk slowly and not raise their eyes to scan the horizon for whatever it was they were waiting. Channah, most of all, knew that if it was a trick, they would be declared traitors and dealt with accordingly. Long prison terms for the children, quite probably execution for her.

They heard it as the orange horizon turned purple. The sound came up suddenly and quite nearby, the throp, throp, throp of a helicopter rotor. It was a most unusual sound for any Havana beach. Startled, they ducked involuntarily. And then there it was, just in front of them, hovering a foot or two above the sand, a gleaming, streamlined-looking helicopter.

A door opened and a stocky man half jumped, half stepped down from the machine and onto the beach. "Hurry!" he shouted, beckoning with one arm. Bent over, they ran toward him, sand swirling in their eyes. As they reached the door, the man lifted first David, then his mother and finally Dinah inside. His movements were quick, agile, efficient. The helicopter immediately slid up and over the bay in a northerly direction.

A beach guard—not a lifeguard for swimmers but a sort of sentry over beachgoers—came running. He raised his rifle toward the machine but the helicopter tore out over the water almost as if it were an alien spacecraft. The beach quickly vanished behind them before Dinah had managed to buckle her seatbelt. As for the gaping sentry, he fired his weapon in the general direction of where the helicopter had just been, but knew it was pointless even as he felt the recoil.

"Welcome, welcome!" shouted Uri Stein from the co-pilot's seat, turning to face David.

The teen recognized him immediately. "How fast?" David managed to shout above the noise in his excitement, before his breath failed him.

"Faster than commercial helicopters. Almost as fast as the newest military ones, about 250 miles per hour," Stein said. "Put on these helmets. They have microphones so you can talk."

Channah ben-Veniste spoke in Spanish. "It's barely 100 miles to Key West. So, we should be there in less than half an hour." Her children thought their mother's voice remarkably matter-of-fact, considering their extraordinary circumstances.

"Unless we must maneuver to avoid the largely outmoded air force of your now-former country," Stein said, sounding unconcerned.

"Won't they try to shoot us down?" David wanted to know.

"If they detect us, they no doubt would like to try. But this helicopter is quite stealthy. Plus, we have counter-measures, jammers and such, what defense manufacturers in America like to call 'state-of-the-art,'" Stein said. "Cuba's *Defensa Antiaérea y Fuerza Aérea Revolucionaria* might be able to tell there's an aircraft somewhere in its aerial exclusion zone, but not exactly where nor what kind. And if it were to send up one of the last three or four Russian MiG-29s it has the money to maintain, we have software not even the U.S. Air Force has perfected yet. We just might take control of an air-to-air or ground-to-air missile fired at us and send it back to the unlucky comrades who pressed the launch button."

"I'd like to see that!" David exclaimed.

"So would I," Stein said. "But we're safe enough up here, even from radiation that dishes operated by the *Dirección de Inteligensia* aim at the American embassy and sometimes cause debilitating neurological symptoms in diplomats—symptoms the State Department has confirmed but the CIA insists, for undetermined reasons, result from unknown causes. News media call it 'the Havana syndrome.' In any case, the simulations we've run in New York suggest the radiation bursts quickly fade." Simulations directed by the Chacham, when he was in town. The man was a genius as well as troublesomely elusive.

Looking at his watch, Stein added, "given the smooth flight so far, I think we'll be touching down in the United States of America in a few minutes."

Channah addressed Stein. Her Russian was better than her English, having studied in Moscow at the Peoples Friendship University for a semester, but she could make herself understood in either language. "Mr. Stein, I must ask you: Why us? Why rescue my children and me instead of some other Cuban Jewish family, a family more religious, more involved in community life, than ours? Or even a non-Jewish family of leading dissidents, people opposing the regime at the risk of imprisonment or worse? Not that we are not grateful beyond words, but it simply makes no sense."

Uri Stein smiled. "Yours may not be the first family we have taken off the island," he said. "Certainly not the first we have helped leave a number of Egypts for promised lands elsewhere. In any case, you and your children may be more important to the Jewish people and the Jewish Outreach and Learning Organization than you might guess. For example, we believe, given his remarkable talent, that with the right opportunities David could well develop into a popular and influential voice, in more ways than one, for the Jewish people and its mission. Dinah is an intelligent young woman of almost unlimited potential. We want to open doors for her. And you, in addition to being their mother, of course, are a trained physician. We can expect your continued professional development under better circumstances."

"Mr. Stein, that is all well and comforting. Encouraging, certainly. But I am no naif, no *ingenuo*. This organization of yours, is there anything it doesn't know or cannot do? It sounds a little too good, too good to be true, or completely true," Channah said.

"It does, doesn't it?' he replied. "I used to wonder about that myself. But the longer I've worked for the organization and the greater responsibilities I've been assigned, the more I've learned that we have our limits and our human failings, just like any other group of imperfect people working for a common mission. Considering our goal, we actually are small and understaffed."

"But, judging by this helicopter and the audacity of your operation, not under-financed?"

"No, not under-financed. You could say we operate with a large and very old endowment."

"This mission of yours: what do you mean by that? The one my parents used to whisper about, the thing about being 'a kingdom of priests' and 'a light unto the nations'?" Channah asked. "One of the many things the party taught us was propaganda from the *Yanqui* imperialists?"

Stein almost laughed. "Not Yankee imperialism, but rather Jewish universalism."

After landing at JOLO's little Key West heliport, the family was hurried off for the night, a night in which they barely slept. The next morning, the ben-Venistes breakfasted with Rabbi Chaim and Rebbetzin Sarah Berliner and Uri Stein.

"Of course, you might feel a little overwhelmed now," Stein said. "We don't expect you to make any decisions right away. Spend a week here with Rabbi Chaim and Rebbetzin Sarah. We are all part of JOLO. Ask them any questions you have—and no doubt that will be a lot—and just take things easily. Reorient yourselves, you might say. I will be back in a week, and we can move on from there."

"Mr. Stein," Channah ben-Veniste said with some force, "I've been thinking about you and this JOLO of yours since last night on the helicopter. I would like you to tell me in one sentence what the organization does. What is your product, so to speak?"

"Fair enough. I hope I would ask the same if I were in your position," Stein replied. "Well, we've been described, both by friends and detractors, as Jewish missionaries to the Jews."

"Go on," Channah said. "Another sentence or two."

"Basically, we work in education. We try to bring Jews, whether observant or non-observant, connected in some way with the Jewish community or completely unaffiliated, young, old, middle aged each closer to Jewish knowledge, practice and community."

"Laudable," Channah said, almost dryly. "But why go to so much difficulty, to risk yourselves, to free us? Because David can sing?" Channah was skeptical, to say the least. Having lived her entire life in a police state, she had learned not to trust neighbors, even friends. Being reported by a member of the ubiquitous CDRs—neighborhood watch groups—as "counter-revolutionary," for anything from playing music too loudly to questioning the wisdom of El Jefe could mean trouble, serious trouble.

"Mrs. ben-Veniste, David is more than a just a singer. We have had several first-hand reports about David's vocal ability from visitors who were good listeners. And one specialized part of JOLO's educational mission is to find and develop Jewish talent in many spheres, including music. We believe that is worth doing for its own sake and that the greater the talent and the more trained it is, the more likely it will be able to carry Jewish messages in any number of fields and not only to Jews but to any and all who might be listening. And thereby the organization helps fulfill the Torah's instruction to the Jewish people—to make the profane sacred." All this was true, of course, but Stein stopped there. The greater reason David and his family were rescued was for that morning left unsaid.

Two days later David and Dinah were walking through Key West's business district. They passed jewelry stores and art galleries, taverns and restaurants, coffee shops and bakeries. Even a gas station with no lines. They saw shaved-headed women and men with elaborate hair-dos, men in suits and women in bikinis, the young and well-muscled, the old and well-tanned and well-wrinkled.

Key West presented to the siblings such a contrast to the Havana that had been their home, their life until a few days ago. The latter was drab, crumbling and coerced, the former vivid, vibrant if a little disorderly.

"This Key West seems like a strange place for an Orthodox Jewish synagogue," Dinah said.

"Yes, but the Jews are a strange people," David replied, stopping in front of a store window. A colorful poster inside announced, "Free Concert, Saturday Night! 'Songs of the Caribbean,' performed by Kol Ami Olam Band, Rabbi Chaim Berliner on lead guitar! Right after Havdalah."

"Voice of the World People Band," Dinah said. "I suppose we're going?"

"Of course," David said. "Rabbi Jaime told me I could sing a song or two, if I liked."

"If you liked," Dinah snorted. "The rabbi knew you would like and so you do. What will you please the audience with?"

"I think 'Joshua Gone Barbados' and '*Henai M'tovuh M'nai'im,*'" her brother replied.

"Safe enough," his sister said. "Do you think they will like it?" she added, emphasizing the word "they."

"Who?" David asked, bewildered.

"The two young men following us. Don't turn around!" Dinah hissed. "They trail along behind us half-a-block or so, pretending to shop."

"How do you see such things?" David asked, impressed once more by his sister's powers of observation.

"How do you not, my brother? Never mind, I know the answer: your heart is in the clouds, mine is right here on Earth. Anyway, I don't think these two are from the secret police. They probably are friends of your Mr. Stein."

Back at *shul* Channah ben-Veniste was speaking with Rabbi and Rebbitzin Berliner. "So, if the question is where would you rather be, Miami or New York—or somewhere else—how will you decide?" the rebbetzin asked.

"I think I've already decided," Channah answered. "You were right when you said Miami might provide an easier assimilation, integration. Yes, there are plenty of Jews, plenty of refugees from the great Cuban motherland in Miami. And so many Spanish-speakers from all over what you call Latin America. But in a way that's what we have escaped, what you rescued us from. Not the Jewish part, but the Cuban, even the Spanish part. The sooner David, Dinah and I become Americans, speaking English comfortably on the streets, free to be Jewish in ways we want to be, free of that part of our past—a big part—that was life under surveillance, in a big virtual prison, the better. And for that, I think New York City is where we must go."

Chapter 25

"Either would have been a good choice, I think, but you are no doubt right—New York will be better for you and your children," Rebbetzin Berliner said.

"I suspect JOLO has given some thought as to how and where in the city we will live, at least to start," Channah ben-Veniste said to Rabbi Berliner, her head cocked to one side, eyebrows slightly arched.

"You suspect correctly," he nodded. "Uri told me there's an apartment waiting for you in the Fort Greene neighborhood of Brooklyn. Small, only one bathroom, but three bedrooms—one for each of you. A living room-dining area and small kitchenette. The apartment and building have been upgraded recently."

"Upgraded," Channah said, drawing the word out and smiling a little. "Such an American sounding word. I'm sure we will love it."

"As to how you will live, if you decide on this, one reason the organization secured a place in Fort Greene is that the Brooklyn Music School is nearby. Though David's talent is immediately recognizable, he lacks the formal credentials that would help open the door at the Brooklyn Conservatory of Music. Both schools are well-established, each more than a century old. And either school can provide the formal musical education unavailable to him up to now, the training that would polish his talent. But the Music School still operates as something of a community institution, drawing students from the neighborhood as well as around the world and often generously supporting those who might not otherwise be able to afford it."

"What about for Dinah?"

"I told Uri that she just lately said to you she thought she wanted to be a police woman, a detective actually. Undercover work even. That the idea excited her. Also, that she told you she immediately spotted the two JOLO men assigned to watch her and David while here."

"That girl!" Channah said in mock exasperation. "But is that a realistic possibility?"

"Quite realistic," Rabbi Berliner answered. "Uri had someone check. Kingsborough Community College in Brooklyn offers a two-year associate's degree in criminal justice. Mostly class work, but there's a three-month internship involved with a local police agency. If she decides she likes the program and wants to continue, she could either go two more years at a four-year college for a bachelor's degree, or apply directly at any number of police departments.

"You haven't asked about yourself yet," the rabbi finished.

"First the children. As for me, I'm already at least half-way through my professional career, and I'm sure it's quite difficult, if not impossible, for a second- or third-world doctor to just start practicing in America," Channah said.

"When you put it that way, yes. It would be difficult. However, given your training and experience, and knowing the regime in Havana tends to dispatch its better physicians abroad to earn cash for the government, we think you most likely could requalify in a couple of years. Meantime, Uri says you would have little difficulty qualifying right away as a physician's assistant."

"Again, it all sounds almost too good to be true," Channah said. "But there's one more thing. At least one more thing. What about the children's Jewish life, their Jewish education? They, we, really know so little, confined and limited as we were."

"As you can imagine, in New York—the most Jewishly-populated city in the world, even more so than Jerusalem or Tel Aviv—the opportunities are limitless. But to narrow them conveniently, also in Brooklyn is the main campus of Touro University. Your children and you will be able to choose from a smorgasbord of options. And, of course there are synagogues and a Jewish community center nearby that offer all kinds of formal and informal courses. I would say that Jewishly, Brooklyn is your oyster, but they're not kosher. So, let's say Brooklyn will be you *cholent*." Rabbi Jaime was pleased with his Jewish culinary substitution.

"What's *cholent*?" Channah ben-Veniste asked.

Chapter Twenty-Six:
Burlington, Vermont, 1901

I must be an unusual sort of immigrant, Chaya Alperovich thought to herself as she trudged through calf-high snow in a pine forest that straddled the U.S.-Canadian border. How many saw the Statute of Liberty in the New York City harbor twice in three days? She had. The first time, of course, was when the *S.S. Friesland* steamed toward Ellis Island a week ago Monday. The second time was when it steamed out two days later headed back to Antwerp, by way of Halifax, Nova Scotia, and the Europe she had determined to escape.

For the 1,127 third-class passengers, many of whom who traveled thanks to the Hebrew Immigrant Aid Society, the voyage had been cramped, smelling of diesel fuel, and sustained by meals of salted beef, steamed cabbage and stale bread. Danzig temporarily closed by order of Kaiser Wilhelm II himself, Jewish escapees from the Russian Empire often spent most of whatever money they had left to reach HIAS' hastily-organized Antwerp collection point. On Ellis Island, more than three score had been held "for isolation and future disposition." Isolation usually was decreed for health reasons, particularly quarantine for suspected tuberculosis. But it could be for lesser maladies as well. Myopia, for instance, as in Chaya's case. Or imbecility, as in that of her seven-year-old son, Samuel. Disposition almost always meant return to the erstwhile immigrants' ports of embarkation.

As for myopia, Chaya had glasses, several different lens prescriptions. And Samuel, of course, was no imbecile. He already spoke Yiddish, Russian and Hebrew and could read in them as well. But around strangers, especially in strange places—Ellis Island, for instance—he would refuse to speak to anyone except his mother. To the immigration officials they encountered, that made silent Samuel an imbecile and his entry into the

United States illegal. As for Chaya's near-sightedness, a mild case worsened by ill-ground glasses and overtiredness, the drops prescribed by her doctor back in Minsk usually did the trick. But generally, not until the third day's dose. By then, however, she and Samuel would be sailing back toward a God-forsaken life in West Prussia, by way of Canada.

But mother and son faced another challenge in addition to near-sightedness or extreme shyness. Their sponsor, a cousin of her ex-husband, had failed to show up in New York. Mr. Joe Green, Yosif Grinshtyn in the old country, even forgot to sign the government form pledging he would not let mother and son become a charge on the state. So, after two days in isolation, officials bundled Chaya and Samuel back onboard the *S.S. Friesland* for its return passage.

Chaya Alperovich had other plans. At Halifax she and her son jumped ship. Nothing daring, really. Abandoning most of their luggage, carrying only one small bag each so as not to arouse suspicion, they just strolled down the gangplank as sweet as you please in a clot of other disembarking passengers and, after asking directions, walked to the nearest synagogue. There she implored the rabbi for aid. "I must join my husband and daughter in New York. Won't you help me?"

Not that she had a husband or a daughter anymore. When Judah ben-Dovid Alperovich hesitated to emigrate, even after the pogrom in which their daughter Bella had been murdered by neighbors, Chaya had demanded a divorce. It took pressure, even being roughed up a bit with a promise of more to come, from her brothers and their friends but Judah Alperovich finally agreed. He gave her a *get*, a Jewish divorce decree so she could remarry by Jewish law and even acquiesced to requesting that his cousin Yosif Grinshtyn act as sponsor. Still, entering America and getting to New York City now tested her unlike anything before.

The rabbi in Halifax had seen other such cases, too many in fact, but arrangements were soon made. "A congregant will drive you and your son to Sackville. There you will transfer to another car and be taken to a spot near the border. It's a long trip; you and your son probably will sleep much of the way. Your second driver will show you where to walk into the United States. You'll follow a path for about a mile to where a truck will be waiting. On the doors it will say, 'Miller's Second-Hand Furniture.'

Miller—I knew his father as Meyerson, a true *mensch*—will take you to Bangor, Maine. From there, you'll get a train to Boston, transfer, and go to New York City."

Chaya could only stare at the man. Uncertainty must have shown on her face, because he said, "Don't worry. We've done this before, many times. Everything is in order. And before you cross the border, you'll be given train tickets and enough money in U.S. dollars to get to New York. So don't be concerned. The hardest part of your journey already is over. In New York, you'll join your relatives."

Chaya simply nodded. No point in telling the good rabbi they had no relatives in the great city, at least none she knew of. They already had guardian angels though, so to speak. The rabbi, their drivers in Canada, and the man Miller all belonged to the Free Sons of Israel, one of the many *Landsmannschaften* formed by Jewish immigrants to the United States, Canada, Mexico and elsewhere in the New World. Modeled along the lines of the Free Masons, they provided fellowship, insurance, unemployment relief and even sickness care for new arrivals struggling to establish themselves in their big, opportunity-filled but impersonal new countries. In the case of the Free Sons of Israel, they provided something else, not only assistance but also protection when necessary for certain male immigrants and their families.

Early the next morning with dawn barely glimmering and after the two car trips promised by the rabbi, Chaya and Samuel slogged through the snow. Chaya was once more was conscious of her wet, freezing feet. In all her preparations for their journey, she had not thought to bring waterproof, insulated footwear. Not that she possessed any.

"*Emma*," Samuel cried. "I'm cold!" She felt him shivering next to her. "And hungry. How much farther? How much farther?" She heard his question as a plea.

"Not far my son, not far," she said, and stroked his head. When was it permissible to lie to a child? she wondered. What did the Sages say? "Dear God," Chaya began to pray, then stopped. Up ahead a truck sat, its engine idling, at the edge of a road, no more than a logging trail really, about two hundred yards ahead where their path met gravel pavement. "Not far at all. In fact, we're almost there."

Milton Miller was a small man, brown hair balding on the top of his head. He wore a heavy, brown overcoat that looked to be a size too large over a black suit that might have been a size too small. At this hour of the early morning, for Chaya thought she glimpsed light on the horizon, he nevertheless also wore a tie. All Americans cannot be this formal, she suspected. Perhaps only the Jewish ones, like the German Jewish "*yekkies*," so-called by their non-German brethren, especially in British Palestine, for always appearing to be dressed in jackets and ties.

Noticing her staring at his clothes, Miller said, "I've been busy since the rabbi telegraphed from Halifax. We had a lot of arrangements to take care of." With that he handed her a new purse.

"Look inside" he said, glancing at her just long enough to emphasize his words.

The purse was made of fine black leather. In it were bills totaling more than $35, train tickets and immigration papers. In the name of Chaya Alperovich and her son Samuel, they attested to the fact that mother and child had been cleared through Ellis Island, sponsored by Milton Miller of Maine, and suffered no disqualifications of politics—neither syndicalists or anarchists, for example—lack of sponsorship or poor health. Under the health certification, eyesight category, Chaya's papers stated simply, "normal." Samuel's documents, under health, intellectual level, read "above average." "Baruch HaShem," she breathed under her breath.

A small apartment awaited them on Stanton Street three blocks west of Hamilton Fish Park in the Lower East Side. Chaya found work as a seamstress, twelve hours a day, six days a week. She enrolled Samuel in the Rambam School, located on the first three floors of a nearby tenement building. Chaya chose it because Rambam taught secular as well as religious subjects, and she wanted her son to be both knowledgeable in his Judaism as well as at home in his new country.

"But you already have work," the principal at Rambam told her when she applied for a job six months later.

"I do, Mr. Goldstone," she said. "I squint at a needle and thread six days a week, from morning to night, with only Shabbat to myself and my son. I need more time for him and for me."

"Have you ever taught before?" he asked.

"How is my son, Samuel, doing in your school?" Chaya inquired.

Taken aback by what he considered to be her non-sequitur of an answer, Mr. Goldstone said, "He is progressing quite satisfactorily in all his subjects—arithmetic, English, American history, Torah, Talmud, Hebrew. In fact, he is one of our best third-grade students. But what does that have to do with you seeking employment here?"

"Judging from my son's experience and what I hear in the neighborhood, you run a good school, Mr. Goldstone. But you are not teaching literature to the upper grades, not Yiddish or Hebrew. Before the new generation forgets the *mama loshen* altogether, with its richness and all its memories and stories of our people, you must start to fill the gap, Mr. Goldstone. I will do that for you and your school."

Shimon "Sy" Goldstone stared at this determined, well-spoken and, to be frank, not unattractive woman sitting across the desk from him. He considered. Her point about Yiddish literature and the need to perpetuate it, to pass not just the vernacular of street vendors but also the language of a thousand years of thought, romance and yes, hardship of their experience in the European *galut*, the European exile, to the next generation was well-taken.

"There is a place for Yiddish literature here at Rambam," he conceded. "But do you know it?"

"Do you mean do I know Sholom Aleichem, I.L. Peretz, Mendele Mokher Seforim and the rest? Which would you like to discuss first?" Chaya's first, normally well-hidden, love always had been literature.

"You may know them," Shimon Goldstone said, conceding a bit while trying to decide whether he should feel affronted or not, "but can you teach them? You haven't said you have any teaching experience."

"Mr. Goldstone," Chaya responded, in a softer tone of voice, "you yourself have said my Samuel is one of your best students. I do appreciate all the teachers here at Rambam have done and are doing, but I always have been my son's principal teacher."

Chaya Alperovich got the job. Also Shimon Goldstone. Barely more than a year later, they became the parents of a baby boy, whom they named David Miller Goldstone. As an adult, he would change his name to Golden. He too would father a son.

Chapter Twenty-Seven:
Las Vegas, Nevada, 1979

What the hell am I doing here? Liri Gilboa asked herself, and not for the first time. Not for only the second or third time either.

"Higher, Liri, higher!" the chorus line master shouted, also not for the first time. "Kick it like you mean it!"

I'd like to kick your butt somewhere up around your ears, she thought to herself.

Liri Gilboa, Miss Israel at 18, lead dancer and second female singer in the Israel Defense Forces entertainment troupe for two years after that—two years during which she heard over and over that "you've got to go to Hollywood! You're a show business natural!"—now hoofed in the second dance line of showgirls at The Sands Casino and Resort. She had been there since arriving in Las Vegas by Greyhound Bus Line in 1976. Temporarily out of funds but not out of determination, Liri's application at the first casino she entered generated a headline. "Jewish Warrior-Princess to Dance at The Sands," announced the ten-paragraph article in *The Las Vegas Review-Journal*. The byline was that of Jimmy Goldstein, summer intern from Arizona State University's school of journalism. Of course it did not read "summer intern," but *"Review-Journal* Staff Writer." Jimmy eventually had that clipping laminated.

He idolized all things Israeli, even hoped to visit the Jewish state someday. Israelis seem more heroic somehow that his parents, uncles and aunts. Yes, some of them had served in the U.S. military during World War II, but now they sold insurance, real estate or patent medicines and filled prescriptions at drug stores. They golfed and played bridge and their Judaism was more the delicatessen sort than the Israeli citizen-soldier variety. So, when City Editor Carmine "The Red" Videnzo told Jimmy to "get over to The Sands and interview that new chorine the entertainment director keeps touting," he jumped on it. (By the way, no one in the *Review-Journal* news room knew for sure how all-business Carmine came by his nickname but curiously for a place full of journalists, no one asked him.) Videnzo went on, "I hear she's straight from the Israeli army and not only can handle a gun but has looks that'll stop a tank. I'll send a photographer with you; I'll want a full body shot of her in costume as well has a head shot."

Jimmy already assumed, based on the few photographs he had seen, that most Israeli women looked like a cross between Gina Lollobrigida and Bridget Bardot. Backstage with Liri Gilboa in her small dressing cubicle, he felt overwhelmed by beauty, by admiration and by sheer animal attraction. So, he didn't know quite where to look when he spoke with her. She was in costume all right, what there was of it. From top down it consisted of a big, feathered headdress, outrageous yet alluring eye makeup, a flesh-colored skintight garment that looked like a one-piece bathing suit cut low over the chest and high over the hips, glittering fringed gloves up to the elbows, and long, shapely legs sheathed in mesh stockings over impossibly high heels. So, wherever summer intern Jimmy Goldstein looked, there was plenty of Liri Gilboa to see. Ms. Gilboa not only could dance in that outfit, she sang too. And it was not only that chest, those hips, the legs that could stop a tank, but also her face, which seemed without intention to flash to every passerby, "Hollywood. Starlet."

But that headline on young Goldstein's article, from which City Editor Carmine "The Red" Videnzo had excised three paragraphs of what he called "sheer gush," was the only one chronicling Gilboa's presumed rise to silver screen fame. Three Rosh Hashanas, three Yom Kippurs and three Passovers had come and gone and the former Miss Israel Liri Gilboa still sweated away in the second chorus line at The Sands. Well, she told herself, also more than once, if the Israelites had to return to the desert, at least this time it was air conditioned.

Life so far had taught Gilboa to be honest with herself. She recognized that Las Vegas overflowed with women still young or youngish who had been told most of their lives and not without reason that Hollywood called them. She herself had grown up in a cramped apartment in the Kriyot, the adjacent small cities of concrete mid-rise apartment buildings just north of

Haifa. These were Kiryat Motzkin, Kiryat Yam, Kiryat Ata and Kiryat Bialik, all basically next door to Israel's biggest chemical refinery. Distillate fumes chronically drifted over the Kriyot. The family home, with Liri, her parents and two brothers, was pleasant enough. But by God, where could one turn around, let alone high kick, or erupt—on key, of course—into "Hello Dolly?"' After high school but before selection to the IDF entertainment corps, Liri served six months as a guard in a women's prison, vaguely planning on joining the Border Police. So, yes, she'd seen enough to be honest with herself.

"That's better, Liri!" the dance master shouted. "Much better!"

Danny Delahanty had mixed feelings about Liri Gilboa. As a showgirl, she was good enough, passable. She possessed talent, and a solid work ethic. And, of course, she was beautiful, even without the fantasy costume that transformed pretty girls into womanly objects of male desire. But Vegas was full of hoofers like her. On what basis could he justify moving her to the first line, let alone giving her a singing lead? That he was head-over-heels in love with the woman, had been since he first laid eyes on her? Promoting her would have been unprofessional, and he could not risk that, especially not with old Haim Wineman, his assistant—a man who in his younger days had danced professionally with Israel's Batsheva Dance Company Youth Ensemble and after that in the Philadelphia Ballet—scrutinizing his every move. What was it with these Israelis? he wondered occasionally. Not just Liri and Wineman, but in The Sands alone a blackjack dealer and a casino bouncer. That little country must be too small to hold them all. Sort of like his grandparents' Ireland, he supposed.

And, of course, there was his wife Marjorie, who danced at The Tropicana under the name May Wu. May Wu, where did she come up with that? She didn't even look Asian. When she announced her new stage name, Danny had said, "Why not May Woo Wee? That's even funnier." Marjorie had just glared at him. Some days Danny suspected she would love nothing more than to sue him for alimony. So, it was all he could do sometimes just to yell "Kick higher, Liri! Higher!" God, what legs she had. And everything else. "Life," as The Sands' Israeli bouncer once had informed him, "are hard."

Liri had turned down marriage proposals in Hebrew from the bouncer and blackjack dealer and a third in English accented straight out of Staten Island from Louie "The Mailman" Sardini. The Mailman because, it was said, if instructed by any of the heirs of the hard men who founded the Vegas strip, heirs who now wore custom suits and ties and spoke of return on investment and leading versus lagging economic indicators instead of sleeping with the fishes, he would send you away, permanently. To the blackjack dealer and bouncer Liri had replied, in their native Hebrew, "*shtuyout!*" that is, nonsense! To The Mailman she said, politely, "I'm flattered, Mr. Sardini, very flattered. But I don't think I'm ready for marriage yet."

"That's okay, babe," he replied. "When you change your mind, call me." And he handed her a business card. Printed on an expensive, thick white stock with embossed black letters, it read: "Louis Sardini, Corporate Assignments, (702) 555-0101."

Very nice card, Mr. Sardini, she thought to herself, tucking it into her Louis Vitton knock-off clutch purse. A little too nice, all things considered.

So, though she wasn't in the market for suitors as she told another dancer, Felicity Vonn—real name, Fanny Jo Harlow from Hot Springs, Arkansas—one day after rehearsal, when William Burton Silver proposed, Liri felt the time if not the man might be right. Though the fact that all Nevada recognized the Silver name did not hurt. She wasn't getting any closer to Hollywood and, noticing the start of tiny crows' feet at the corners of her eyes while wiping away stage make-up one night, she wasn't getting any younger.

Mr. Silver did not set her heart aflutter, she admitted to herself. He was around 35 years old, his hair starting to go thin on top, yet fit in every other way. He had asked her out three times already, after introducing himself post-performance one evening. He took her to dinner, to the national touring company performance of "A Chorus Line"—which made Liri wonder if she should have headed for Broadway instead of Hollywood—and even to Wayne Newton's show at the Frontier. Newton was known in town and nationally as "Mr. Vegas" for drawing audiences larger than those that went to see Sinatra or Elvis.

"What did you think of Wayne Newton's big production?" he asked her afterwards.

"Well, he certainly can sing—just as good live as on his records. It's a little strange at first, seeing and hearing a man as big as he is sing with such a high voice, but it's a strong voice and I believe he has perfect pitch," Liri said.

"He does," Silver said. "My father had him to the house to entertain for his 75th birthday last year. For a man who started with a little department store, my father knows a lot about music. Dad is pretty well known in Vegas, but not too many people are aware that he plays clarinet in a jazz combo after-hours here at The Sands every Sunday night. In fact, that's how I first saw you. I play bass guitar in the same group, at least I fill in when the regular bass player can't make it. I was early one Sunday about six weeks ago, and caught the end of your last show."

"It's hardly my show," Liri laughed.

"As far as I'm concerned, it is," Silver said. He proposed a few days later.

What to do? That little department store Silver's father founded half a century earlier when Las Vegas was hardly more than a desert outpost was now a state-wide chain with more than a dozen outlets. His father was still chairman but William Burton Silver served as chief executive officer. Everyone in the state it seemed knew of the Silver family, either from shopping in its stores, benefiting in some way from its philanthropy—the Silver Arts and Cultural Center downtown rivaled anything similar in Los Angeles—turning to it for political fund raising, or all three.

Yet Bill, as he insisted she call him, put on no airs. He treated her with respect just as he did waiters and waitresses, parking valets, blackjack dealers and anyone who recognized him and said hello. He also stood about six feet tall, was square shouldered, handsome, and well-spoken. So, what was not to like, she asked herself?

Bill's great-grandfather had emigrated from Germany, he told her. "He'd been a rabbi of some sort back there, my dad said once, but here he nearly went broke prospecting for silver. Funny about that; he had changed his name from Hirsch to Silver. The American dream, I guess. Thank goodness his wife, my great-grandmother, knew a thing or two about running a boarding house. He's buried in a cemetery in Carson City. My aunt, who's into genealogy, has a family scrapbook with a picture of his tombstone. It's engraved in both English and Hebrew. His Hebrew name, according to her, was Meir ben-David Hirsch. Apparently, there was some sort of Hirsch rabbinic dynasty in Germany. Anyway, one of his sons, my grandfather Jonas, married Elizabeth O'Reilly, newly arrived from County Cork by way of St. Louis. And, three generations later, here I am."

And here I am, thought Liri. This was after their fifth date, when Liri Gilboa, former Miss Israel, former Israel Defense Forces singer and dancer extraordinaire, three years in the second dance line at The Sands, turned to William Burton Silver, clasped his hands in hers, and said, "Yes." Shortly after, the Israeli bouncer at The Sands, saying something about getting a new job in Brooklyn, quit the casino.

Chapter Twenty-Eight:
New York City, the Present

A non-descript man—or rather a quite common-looking type of man in that neighborhood at that time—sat on a bench outside a high-rise full of medical offices in lower Manhattan. He had been there before. Somewhere between five-feet eight inches and five-feet ten in height, hair dark brown, or perhaps black, and his eyes brown, or maybe hazel, he appeared relaxed as he scrolled through cell phone messages. In the slowly dimming late afternoon light his suit looked to be charcoal gray. Or perhaps it was navy blue. Certainly, his shirt was white and his tie dark blue. No, maybe hunter green.

In any case, the man, barely noticed by those hurrying out of the building to hail a cab, catch an Uber or make for lower Manhattan's Fulton Street subway station, continued studying his phone. As he did so, a petite, middle-aged woman, quite striking in appearance, passed quickly behind him, waving at some vehicle in the street. How, the fellow wondered for the umpteenth time, could women walk in those shoes?

Her spiked heels clicked on the pavement as she strode to the curb. The shoes themselves actually were booties, black suede with a delicate silver chain looping above the ankle. Unusual as they were for office wear, they complemented the rest of her outfit: deep purple blouse whose collar peeked out from a short black jacket and a snug black skirt. The clothes repeated the color scheme of the woman's thick hair, wavy black with purple tips.

How she could walk in those shoe-boots was less a question than would he trust her as his shrink, Sidney Schwartz thought. Many others did, otherwise she could not afford an office in this neighborhood. A car pulled to the curb beside the woman, its flashers on. So, Schwartz realized, she had not been hailing a cab. The driver, in a sort of concierge uniform, exited and nodded as the woman slid behind the steering wheel. He then headed toward the office building. As for the woman, she slipped off the emergency flashers and at the first slight opening, nosed her Jaguar F-Type, a two-seater going for north of $60,000, British racing green, of course, into uptown traffic. As she pulled away, Schwartz read the read New York state license plate. It was a vanity tag reading "Purple." The doctor must be obsessed with the color purple, he decided.

Schwartz touched an icon on his cell phone. "She's gone," he said.

"What about the security systems?"

"Building access, no problem. The usual 'state-of-the-art' stuff, easily distracted by our software," Schwartz said.

"Cameras included?"

"Yes," Schwartz said.

"And her office security?" the voice at the other end demanded.

"Even easier. Five years out of date. Like that at most professional offices."

"Okay, it's a go. Now," replied Benjamin Ross. "Copy Meyer's file, leave everything as you found it, and get out as we planned via the utilities' tunnel. Just to be extra certain, no in-and-out images on the doctor's building security if there's back-up. Gal is with you?"

"Yes," Schwartz said. "And H." H. for Hubert Himmelfarb. No one called him Hubert, let alone Hubert Himmelfarb, other than his parents, and they were gone now. H. never would answer to his given name to anyone else even when they were alive, not after sixth grade and that fight with Kenny Ferlinghuysen over Shelly Gross. Not even to Sidney, Gal or Benjamin now.

"Good," Ross said. "We'll meet as arranged."

In the office building's lobby Schwartz passed a fob over the reader at the top of a security turnstile and headed for the elevators. Running a second fob over a small glass circle between elevator doors, he watched a light glow yellow, then cycle through red to green as a door opened. He punched the button for floor number 15 and rose to the office of Dr. Karen Kimberly Levine, psychiatrist. And therapist to one Gerald Emmanuel Meyer.

Pocketing the fobs, he pretended to insert a key into the door of 15-D, Karen K. Levine, M.D., as the nameplate announced, and entered. The door, already unlocked, opened as he turned the knob. Inside he found Gal, in the uniform of building maintenance, seated at the receptionist's desk scanning patients' computer files.

"Where's H.?" Schwartz asked.

"On patrol, covering this floor, the stairwells and watching the elevators," said Gal, whose full name was Gal Rotem. One Hebrew meaning for the paired words, "exalted wave, strong desert plant," might be confusing. However, those who met her quickly understood. They recognized an athletic, intelligent, beautiful and above all determined woman. She made Ross' little platoon hum.

"When you find Meyer's file, let me know. I'll look for its paper duplicate."

Schwartz knew that more than a few psychiatrists and psychologists—though rarely doctors accepting Medicaid patients—filed patients' documents not by last or even first names but middle ones to obstruct unauthorized access. So, he started with Emmanuel and quickly discovered Gerry Meyer's folder. Photographing as he skimmed, he recognized the first few phrases: "delusions of grandeur," followed by a question mark; "narcissistic personality disorder" and "oppositional defiant disorder," followed by no question marks; and "deeply ambitious, increasingly risk-prone." New to him was "late sexual compulsive. Attempts to justify behavior: simultaneous relationships with two followers as symptomatic of late onset ADHD. Fashionable excuse for sexual indulgence."

Then, at the bottom of the final page, in a doctor's nearly illegible scrawl, "not an official disorder, according to Diagnostic and Statistical Manual of Mental Disorders-5," but "'messianic complex,' functionally, for sure."

Yes, Schwartz said to himself, that's our boy.

"Did you hear that?" H. asked, slipping into the office. Sidney and Gal stopped what they were doing, which was putting Dr. Levine's office back in order after copying Gerry Meyer's files, and looked up.

"Someone's outside?" Schwartz whispered.

"No, further away, the sound of a crash."

H.'s sense of hearing was acute. So was his sense of smell and taste. If someone had smoked a cigarette in an otherwise well-ventilated no-smoking room six months previously, H. could tell. Likewise, whether citrus from Florida or Chile produced his fresh-squeezed orange juice. As for hearing, the cry of a rabbit in the jaws of a coyote close to half a mile off awakened him one night during an impulsive weekend in Palm Springs. More than once these peculiarities contributed to the success of a mission. Like that time he exposed as an infiltrator at JOLO a skilled actress, a consummate professional who had played countless roles in theaters on three continents, but whose Egyptian accent H. detected far beneath her otherwise flawless Brooklynese.

"A crash?" Gal asked.

"It sounded like sheet metal crumpling. Probably one idiot driver smashing into another," H. said dismissively. "The city's full of them—either foreigners who never drove until they got here, or the natives certain no one else has the right-of-way but them." Still, he felt a sense of unease.

"It doesn't matter," Schwartz hissed. "Let's go!"

Less than an hour later they sat at a dining room table in a small brownstone in Brooklyn's gentrified Park Slope neighborhood. Benjamin Ross placed four paper cups on the table, the containers reading "Wizzotsky's Original New Old World Tea Shop." On a plate were sliced bagels and a slab of cream cheese.

"Help yourselves," Ross said. "H., I already dropped an ice cube into your coffee, to protect your highly-tuned taste buds."

"Appreciated," H. replied. "Especially since I never got such after-mission consideration from that Menschnikov guy."

"What have we got?" Ross asked Schwartz.

"Mostly confirmation for what we already know, or think we know. His psychiatrist is pretty certain Meyer has narcissistic personality and oppositional defiant disorders, and thinks he probably suffers delusions of grandeur. She sees him as an obsessively ambitious person, more and more prone to take bigger and bigger risks. Also, as something she calls a 'late sexual compulsive' having affairs simultaneously with two women and pursuing a third. Meyer attempts to justify this as a form of attention deficit/hyperactivity disorder. Anyway, at the end of the file she wrote 'messianic complex.'"

"That's not a formal psychological category," Ross snapped.

"She knows that," Schwartz replied evenly. "She scrawled 'not an official disorder the DSMMD'. But it fits with delusions of grandeur."

"Does this rule Meyer out as a possible *mosiach*?" Gal Rotem wanted to know.

"I'm pretty sure it does for the moment, though Rabbi Samson will make that call. I suppose one could argue that if Meyer changed, evolved from his negative behaviors to positive ones only while retaining and expanding his obvious charismatic qualities, then maybe."

"Sid, you told me when you arrived that you saw Dr. Levine get into a green Jaguar and drive north just before you entered her building."

"Right, a beautiful F-Type, not 'green' but the essential British racing green."

"I stand corrected," Ross said, his impatient "as if it mattered" understood though unspoken. "And H., you said you heard a car crash while you were in the doctor's office."

"It sure sounded like a crash."

"It was," Ross said. "Just before you got here, WINS Radio reported that 'prominent psychiatrist Karen Kimberly Levine' was involved in an accident in TriBeCa. Apparently, a stolen Ford F-150 pickup truck ran a red light at speed and broadsided the doctor's car. Luckily for her, the side as well as the front air bags deployed. She managed to climb out the passenger side door on her own, before being taken by ambulance to Presbyterian Hospital with bruised ribs and facial lacerations."

"Stolen Ford F-150," Schwartz mused. "Did the report identify the driver?"

"He ran off but collapsed not far away. Witnesses were quoted as describing him as either Middle Eastern-looking or Hispanic."

"*Jaysh ein-Galut*, or Knights of the Chalice? Take your pick?" asked Schwartz.

Again Ross snapped: "We haven't proved that Jaysh exists anymore, at least not since their failure at Acre more than 200 years ago, let alone that it was behind the shooting outside Meyer's operation. As for the

Knights, their last confirmed sighting was in Pecos, Texas in 1883, when they tried but failed to kidnap the son of the general store owner, Jesse Davidson. There were three of them, and attempting to escape they apparently died of thirst in the Chihuahuan Desert a dozen miles out of town."

"Apparently?" Gal asked, eyebrows arched.

"That's how the coroner's report read," Ross said, managing one of his rare smiles. "It seems extreme dehydration can leave small holes in the skull just above the spine," he said evenly.

"Cover-up," H. said flatly. "I can smell one a mile away. The Elders of Zion, again. No doubt."

"That's some schnozz you got there," Gal put in. More seriously, "what did JOLO call itself then?"

"'*Shomrim*,' Watchmen, the name we've gone by, at least among our predecessors, for more than a thousand years," Ross said. "But people, are we missing the most likely? Put Occam's razor to it. In detective work, in science, hell, even journalism, look for the logical explanation with the fewest parts. It's the opposite of conspiracy theory, the antithesis of a Rube Goldberg machine; the less convoluted, the more direct, the more likely."

"Okay, give us yours," Sid challenged.

"Maybe it's right in front of us: Meyer has a messianic complex, he's carrying on with at least two of his followers, and he presents an oppositional defiant disorder. Which, by the way, is four times more common among convicted felons than among the adult population in general. One reason rehabilitation is elusive. The Chacham told me this once. Most young boys, and many girls, go through a 'you're-not-the-boss-of-me!' phase. But they grow—or are trained—out of it. Not repeat criminals though. Deep down, they hold a nearly unshakable belief that rules are for suckers, not for superior types like themselves. This also can leave them cold to others' emotions and feelings, even getting enjoyment from other peoples' pain. Sociopaths."

"And this is Gerry Meyer?" H. was dubious. "Whatever he is, or has been, the man's no career criminal."

"Late onset," Ross said flatly. "He talks about his problems, his challenges and desires, mid-life crisis. And judging by his sermons, interviews and the rest, the man loves to talk, especially about himself. So, Dr. Levine knows all about him, or nearly all. There's the old saying about the secrets a man keeps from the world, those he keeps from friends and family, and finally, those he keeps from himself.

"Anyway, it dawns on our self-recognized *mosiach*, quite recently from the looks of things, that he has talked too much, especially to his shrink. He knows his affairs, in particular, could threaten his growing movement if they were exposed. But late sexual compulsive that he is, combined with a growing appetite for risk—the gambler's thrill as the roulette wheel spins—and delusions of grandeur, he won't desist but can't chance exposure. Karen Kimberly Levine knows too much, so she's got to go. Forget about the apparitions of *Jaysh* and the Knights."

"So, he hired 'a Middle Eastern-looking man' to attempt a potentially suicidal attack by truck?" Schwartz was doubtful.

"Through a cut-out. Probably two. The first, another follower, someone completely loyal but none too bright. The second, a street thug known somehow by the first cut out. Meyer staged-managed it, of course, but others implemented it."

"What would the driver have to be offered for such an attempt?" H. asked.

"Money, of course. A lot of it. And plenty of captagon, for example," Ross said. "There are a lot of Middle Eastern refugees knocking about New York who would, after thinking about themselves, their families, their limited prospects and the city's crushing prices, consider taking the money. And they would know about captagon, the amphetamine-like drug the former Syrian regime grew rich on, trafficking it throughout the Middle East and beyond. It's said to provide users with at least a short-term sense of invincibility. Some of the Hamas butchers of October 7, 2023 reportedly dosed themselves with it."

"So, Gerry Meyer tried to kill his own psychiatrist to protect his messianic career?" Gal Rotem asked. "Sounds a bit far-fetch," she said, looking around the room at the others, who did not return her gaze.

"Well, that's what I'm going to tell Rabbi Samson," Ross said. "Not in person, of course."

Before sunrise and morning prayers the next day, a courier delivered a large envelope, unmarked except for the recipient's name and address, to JOLO headquarters. Rabbi Reuven Samson read the anonymous report and studied the attached photographs. For the third time. Finally, he called in Uri Stein.

"Uri, the retreat is available?"

"Everything is ready, as you requested, just in case."

The retreat, a few hours from Brooklyn by car in the low hills of the Catskill Mountains, had been used by JOLO for special seminars and study sessions. Also, during two weeks in the spring, two in the fall, for training and refresher courses by a variety of organization personnel. Surveillance, surveillance avoidance, martial arts, marksmanship, chess competition and physical fitness, including, of course, swimming. As it is said. And evening discussion sessions about Torah and current events, on alternate nights. A popular resort in the mid-twentieth century for middle class Jewish families escaping the city's hot, congested summers, the retreat now offered comfortable if spare quarters, basic kosher cafeteria food and, most importantly, seclusion.

"Well, just in case has arrived," the rabbi said.

Soon after, a bequest greatly surprised Gerry Meyer. But not enough to look a gift horse in the mouth. An anonymous donor gifted his Jewish Revival Institute with a pleasant retreat in the Catskills. He began spending more and more time there, giving talks on Jewish subjects ancient and modern, inviting liberal-minded Talmud scholars to conduct seminars, and leading what he called Jewish meditation sessions himself. He purposely restricted attendance at each overnight or multi-day retreat, which helped keep the institute's steadily growing membership clamoring for admittance. And he assigned Judith Krakower and Lisa Lenkowitz, alternately, to supervise enrollment.

"The retreat," Rabbi Samson said to Uri Stein some time later, "may prove to be the rope Gerry Meyer needs to hang himself with."

"How so?" Stein asked.

"For one thing, it should make his dalliances with the Krakower and Lenkowitz women more frequent and therefore more difficult to hide. For another, it keeps him out of the city more often, which might lessen his hold over at least some of his followers," the rabbi said.

"Maybe," replied the other. "But we know he is charismatic and engenders strong loyalty. What we think of as followers are quite often true believers."

"Yes, unfortunately," Samson said, "in the Cult of Gerry Meyer."

Chapter Twenty-Nine:
Efrat, Israel, 1998

"Rabbi Riskin, come quickly. There's a young Arab man at the front door, and he's crying." Two men, both worshippers, approached the rabbi as he stood at the rear of the sanctuary, speaking with congregants after Friday evening services. One was Ramon LaValle, formerly the go-to lawyer for Manhattanites in bankruptcy proceedings, now president of this burgeoning Judean congregation. The other was Niles Wallace, previously a sergeant with the Glasgow, Scotland police and now a member of the synagogue security team. Wallace wore a black T-shirt, khaki cargo pants and a black knitted *kippa* on his head. The strap of an M-16 carbine crossed his shoulder and each leg pocket of his pants held an extra 30-round magazine.

Rabbi Sholom Riskin, formerly Rabbi Steve Riskin of Lincoln Square Synagogue on Manhattan's Upper West Side, was founder of the growing settlement of Efrat—better the long-delayed, by about 2,000 years, reconstructed Efrat. Having outgrown village status, the still expanding new town already counted nearly 6,000 inhabitants. It stretched along a ridge on the edge of the Judean Desert a few miles southeast of Jerusalem, a few miles northeast of Bethlehem and next door to Herodium. Herodium was the fortress palace King Herod the Great occasionally retired to when knives in the capital got too sharp, even for him.

Riskin had decamped for *eretz Yisrael* with a good chunk of his New York congregation in the early 1980s. As Efrat had grown, so had Riskin's reputation as a leader in modern Orthodoxy, though like most modern Orthodox he didn't care for the term. Sort of a theological Tevye, although with texts instead of a fiddle, he would rather put it that Tradition really was traditions, not one tight garment but several well-stitched ones from similar yet not identical patterns. In addition to leading his ever-expanding congregation, the rabbi taped a weekly radio commentary on the Torah portion, delivered an annual lecture that drew standing-room-only crowds to the Great Synagogue in Jerusalem and perhaps most importantly, served as Efrat's de facto city manager.

Erev Shabbat, sabbath evening, in Efrat was always special. Seen from the center of the new town, which crowned a low hill, the setting sun resembled a large red ball dropping into the Mediterranean roughly 30 miles west. To the east, the day's last rays glimmered off the Dead Sea, no more than 10 miles distant but two thousand feet lower, most of that below sea level in the great rift valley of the Jordan. The light, comingled with the atmosphere—warm dry air of the day beginning to cool—helped make the congregants' prayers feel unique to the moment.

But a young Arab man standing outside the *shul*, crying? This was novel, Riskin thought. "Let's talk with him," he said.

The young man stood just outside the synagogue's front door, flanked by a dark-skinned fellow in civilian clothes and another member of the security team, dressed in black and khaki as was Wallace.

"We've patted him down," one said. "He's been cooperative."

"What's his name? Where is he from?" Riskin asked the two congregants in Hebrew.

"My name is Pelegos, Yusuf Pelegos," the young man answered in Arabic-accented Hebrew. "My family lives in Jerusalem, in the Christian quarter of the Old City. We have lived there for generations."

"Pelegos," said Wallace. "There is a Pelegos who runs a fish restaurant at the marina in Acco. Any relation?"

"That is my father's cousin," Yusuf Pelegos answered.

"What is your father's name?" the rabbi asked.

"Yassa," the young Arab said.

"Yassa," Riskin repeated thoughtfully. "And what does your father do?"

"He is an assistant to Patriarch Diodoros."

"Diodoros," the rabbi said, half closing his eyes. "We have met. He has a difficult job, maintaining the Greek Orthodox position at the Church of the Holy Sepulcher, given the rough-elbowed competition from the other clergy." Rabbi Riskin thought of the other Christian sects in the church: Roman Catholic, Coptic, Syriac, Ethiopian and Armenian. "Plus, his flock is small in number and spread across Israel, the territories and Jordan."

"Yes, my father is always busy," Yusuf answered.

"Tell me, why did you come to us this evening?"

Young Pelegos, whose tears had stopped by the time Riskin first approached him, began to weep again. The five men around him waited. Finally, drying his eyes on a red handkerchief that looked large enough to be a bandana, he said, "Because of the music."

"The music?" Riskin asked.

Softly, haltingly at first, then more steadily in a not-unpleasant voice, Pelegos began to sing. "*L'cha dodi, l'ikrat kala, p'nai Shabbat n' kabalah. L'cha dodi, l'ikrat kala, p'nai Shabbat n'kabalah ...*"

Sung every Friday night, in nearly every synagogue in the world, *L'cha dodi*—"Come, My Beloved"—whether sung mid- or up-tempo, to the traditional tune or local improvisations, let the Jewish voice welcome Queen Shabbat, bride of the One God on the Holy Throne, as She opened the sacred weekly day of rest. Composed in the 1500s by Shlomo Halevi Alkabetz, one of the great mystics of Safat, the lyrics contained several layers. Perhaps the most fundamental one encoded the Jews speaking to God and asking for the start of the messianic era.

The other four congregants, eyebrows raised, glanced at Riskin. The rabbi looked at Yusuf. "You heard this as a child, when your mother lit candles and sang it on Friday nights at home?" Riskin's words were as much statement as inquiry.

The young man looked at him in surprise. "How did you know?"

"It would not be the first time such a thing has happened," he said, "especially in Jerusalem. A secular, Jewish Israeli woman, infatuated with a young Arab man, marries him, moves a few neighborhoods from where she grew up, basically cuts ties with her own family, with her roots. West meets East, you might say; western Jerusalem and eastern Jerusalem.

"Years later, her son, to all appearances a young Arab, Christian or Muslim, passes a shul on *erev Shabbat* and hears a half-forgotten melody. The tune and the lyrics remind him of his mother, who never really said much about her past or this song and those candles, but whose tenderness when she sang never failed to move him. And you are here because you want to know why?"

"Yes," the young man said.

"All right. But why here and not at a synagogue in the Old City? That would be much more convenient for you."

"In the Old City I would be recognized going into a Jewish place. That could cause problems for my father. Maybe even for me. Besides, some of the rabbis near us are not so friendly. I have heard that you can explain things, that you are a good teacher."

"Well, I do my best to explain some things," Riskin said with a smile.

"I will come back Monday morning, if that's all right. I don't have any classes then. I am in my second year at Hebrew University."

"What do you study?" the rabbi asked.

"General subjects now. I must decide on a major this year. I have a course in comparative religions. It's just an elective, but I enjoy it."

"Do you have time to stay for Shabbat dinner? You are welcome," Riskin said.

"No, not now. I must go home."

"There are no cabs or buses running on Shabbat," the rabbi said.

"That's all right. I can walk. It's not so far to Beit Jala, and there will be cabs there. But I will come back Monday morning." Beit Jala, an Arab settlement, lay between Efrat and Jerusalem.

"Good," said Riskin. "Then we'll compare. Oh, one more thing. What is your mother's name?"

"Nitzevet," Yusuf replied.

"A good name," Riskin said. "A very good name." In fact, Nitzevet was a Hebrew name borrowed unchanged by Arabic. The name of King David's mother, the rabbi thought. Just as Yassa was Arabic for Yishai, in English Jesse, David's father. The Pelegos family has been here a long time, a very long time, the rabbi thought. Almost as long as mine.

****

July 31, 2002: Efrat, Israel

"How were this season's digs?" Rabbi Riskin asked the Chacham as they sat on the terrace outside the Aroma Café in Efrat late Wednesday morning. If one measured by local extent only, the Aroma chain was the Israeli equivalent of Starbucks, the American coffee shop phenomenon gone international. Though other than for convenience of countless locations, the comparison unjustifiably elevated Starbucks. Aroma really was a coffee-forward restaurant with shops in all Israeli cities and many towns. Though the menu was limited, sandwiches offered were excellent and the soups heavenly. And Aroma's primary beverage managed to be robust without over-roasted burnt notes. None of which could be said for the giant Starbucks chain.

"Hardly a season," the Chacham laughed. "I was on site for only nine days. But I'll tell you this: I'm more convinced than ever that Eilat Mazur was right—what she first called 'the Great Stone Structure' is indeed what she insisted it was, King David's palace. The location fits the biblical reference to David leaving his palace and 'going down to Jerusalem'—that is, going inside the citadel walls—when he heard of the Philistines' approach, and more of what was recovered this year. That includes fragments of balustrades carved to a high level and of cast glass and metal grillework—a window treatment that would have been a luxury item in that place and time. In other words, in Jerusalem 3,000 years ago, only in the king's palace."

"Nine days as 'supervising observer.' Is that what they call you in the field?" It was the rabbi's turn to laugh.

Amused, the Chacham nodded. Then he took the conversation in an entirely different, though hardly unexpected, direction.

"So, what do you make of this Pelegos?" he said.

"I ought to be asking you that question," Riskin said. "You're the one with the uncanny ability to see what the rest of us apprehend only later." The rabbi smiled but the Chacham looked somber.

"Yes, a curse of sorts I've been aware of since I was fourteen."

"Why curse?" Riskin wanted to know.

"You would think such foresight—not the ability to make specific predictions like, say, the stock market's going to be up fifty points today or Congress will defund the United Nations next week, but the almost unerring sense of how people and trends are going to coalesce and roughly when—would be a great help in life. For a manager of a large, impersonal bureaucracy, no doubt. For a human being with emotions, not so much."

"What do you mean?" the rabbi asked.

"For example," the Chacham started, his voice wistful, "there was this girl once. A young woman. I was infatuated. Those were the happiest weeks of my life. It was like the lyricists write—the sky was bluer, food tasted better, sights and scents brighter." He began, if not to sing, then chant: "'I have often walked/ Down that street before/ But the pavement always stayed beneath my feet before …'

"Yet even then I saw somehow, in actual pictures as if I were watching a video, how and why our relationship would unravel—no, crash—and how quickly. The happiness turned to pain *before* she told me we had to have one of those 'We have to talk' conversations. Which I knew already she was going to tell me."

"And what did she tell you?"

"That she was getting engaged to an old flame."

"Why?"

"Because he was 'safe,' he would give her a solid, protected life. And none of what attracted her to me as she ticked off a list of flattering attributes, some of which I didn't know I possessed, was 'safe.' And I had known, in detail, this was going to happen beforehand. Like I knew right after his inauguration but days before the attempt, that Reagan would be shot. Shot but survive. There are countless such examples. Countless."

"One more," the rabbi requested, "current."

"All right. I'll tell you now what I told our friend Rabbi Samson in Brooklyn, one of the Jews' auxiliary capitals. Some years from now his little JOLO operation will have to deal with a messianic candidate—more likely a false messiah—in his own backyard. And doing so will require extraordinary measures, both to protect the fellow and to contain him. At one point, Samson will consider that the man can be rehabilitated, only to find he is mistaken."

The two sipped their coffee. Time passed. Finally, the rabbi said, "Pelegos' lineage, as far as I can tell, is good. He's Greek Orthodox, of course, but most likely the family did not convert until late in the fourth century, not long after the visit to Jerusalem by Constantine's mother,

Queen Helena, on her self-appointed mission to identify New Testament sites. The Pelegos family, like so many others, arabized following the Muslim conquest by Caliph Omar ibn al-Khattab in 637 C.E. So, Hebrew to Greek to Arabic. Israelite-Jewish to Greek Orthodox to Arab Greek Orthodox. But still the Davidic lineage, it seems."

"Yes, it's not just the continuity of names in the family," the Chacham said, "but the physical evidence as well. The DNA sample your Ramon LaValle took from young Pelegos' tea cup the last time he studied with you is consistent with others we've obtained from potential candidates in recent decades. Nearly all point to a common male ancestor nearly 3,000 years ago. But lineage alone is hardly sufficient, is it?"

"Of course not," Riskin said. "But he studied with me for two years, through his undergraduate work at Hebrew University. He's nearly completed a doctorate now in comparative religions, focusing on the Jewish roots of the early church. And he has organized an informal discussion group in Jerusalem for young Jewish and Greek Orthodox professionals. They meet monthly to hear a speaker, discuss his or her presentation, and get to know each other across their many divides. I'm not sure I would want any of my children to attend regularly, but for a multi-ethnic city, fraught with competing religious, national and emotional claims, probably not a bad idea. It certainly shows his heart is in the right place."

"Hmm." The Chacham exhaled more than spoke. Pensively, he wondered, "is this part of Pelegos' path back to us, or his opening a door through which some young Jews might leave?"

"You of all people already know it could work both ways," Riskin replied.

As they finished their coffee the radio playing in the café sounded the familiar beeps. It was 11 a.m., time for hourly news on Kol Yisrael, Voice of Israel radio. On the hour the beeps sounded from countless speakers throughout the little country, heard by a people whose local news often made international headlines.

"*Mechablim* have bombed the cafeteria in the Frank Sinatra International Student Center at Hebrew University's Mt. Scopus campus," the announcer stated, referring to terrorists. "The cafeteria was crowded with students on campus for summer session final exams. Perhaps a dozen are dead, many more wounded. Ambulances continue to come and go from the center." Here the two men heard the sounds of sirens as part of the news cast, then of people wailing in the background.

The announcer continued: "In Gaza City, a masked spokesman for Hamas claimed credit at a celebration attended by more than 10,000 people. He said 'this operation is part of series we will launch from everywhere in Palestine.' At his request, the entire crowd knelt to pray that future attacks 'would succeed against the enemies of God.'

"United Nations Secretary General Kofi Annan and U.S. President George W. Bush in separate statements condemned the attack. So did the Palestine Liberation Organization in a release that blamed Israeli Prime Minister Ariel Sharon for the bombing, calling it a response to Sharon's 'provocative' policy of targeted killings of terrorists. Hamas said it would pay stipends to the families of anyone arrested for the attack."

It would be a few hours before Rabbi Riskin and the Chacham learned that not a dozen but nine people, Jews and Arabs, had been killed in the blast, though more than 100 had been wounded, many seriously. Among the dead was Yusuf Pelegos.

Chapter Thirty:
New York City, the Present

The morning when Gerry Meyer had awakened from an unusually restful sleep to find himself stretching pleasantly on a new sofa in his office at Beth Aaron/Jewish Renewal Institute remained vivid in his mind. He had returned late the night before from another study seminar at the institute's Catskills retreat. Now he looked around himself with pleasure. If the retreat was serviceable, comfortable even, the remodeled synagogue headquarters of his movement had been remade as premium worship space.

He noticed many changes, some small, some larger but all significant. Water-stained acoustical ceiling tiles had been replaced with new ones. Solid metal-framed doors with double-, or was it triple-glazed glass—bulletproof? —replaced the older, splintered wooden frames. Security cameras perched relatively unobtrusively at the corners of the building, relaying pictures to two banks of monitors, one in his office wall opposite the desk, the other high on the back wall of the sanctuary, visible to whomever stood on the *bimah*. Panic buttons on the floor under his desk and at the reader's table in the sanctuary connected directly to the New York Police Department. Outside, sturdy-looking bollards stood ready to prevent a car or truck plowing through the doors. And interior lighting, in the sanctuary, reception hall, classrooms and offices had been upgraded to provide bright yet warm illumination. New furniture, including padded benches in the sanctuary, was everywhere.

And checking out back, he saw that no sign of the deadly shoot-out remained. Someone had erased them, going so far as to power-wash blood stains from the pavement. The building itself looked like it had been sandblasted, decades of grime removed to reveal the sandstone beneath that, thanks to quartz and feldspar embedded within it, gleamed in both early morning and late afternoon sunlight.

Who had gone to such trouble, and why, he asked Judith Krakower late one night after the first study session with his old class.

"We thought you had ordered it," she said, keeping her legs clasped tight over his buttocks. Feeling himself ever-so-satisfyingly spent physically yet a bit troubled mentally, he replied only, "well, I suggested to a few members that we needed to upgrade this place, but the conversations never got much further."

"Someone heard you," Judith Krakower said, breathing huskily. "Yes, they did." She ran her hands down his back, then slipped them between her belly and his. "Yes, indeed," she sighed.

Gerry Meyer felt but barely heard her. He was trying to figure out who had paid for the synagogue's upgrades—hell, who had the clout at City Hall to get those bollards embedded in municipal sidewalks—and how soon could he see Lisa Lenkowitz again. Outside of class and Friday night activities, that is. Lisa, Judith, Michael the Obsessive, Ido Tabatchnik, Simon Peltz and the others returned to class as soon as word spread that Meyer was back from the latest retreat. Returning his attention to the passionate woman beneath him, that maddening sheen of salty perspiration again showing on her skin, Gerry Meyer told himself, "Compartmentalize. Compartmentalize!" It worked with Judy, he knew. Her adoration was almost embarrassing, when it was not satisfying, deeply satisfying. Still, it troubled him that Lisa Lenkowitz seemed to be growing suspicious. He could sense it.

****

"I would think such behavior, not to mention the speeding tickets trailing his new Ferrari, automatically disqualifies Meyer as one of our candidates," Rabbi Samson was saying to Uri Stein. "Yet his little outreach enterprise has grown from a couple score attendees in a remodeled drug store to nearly five hundred sometimes at the old Beth Aaron synagogue on Bragg Street here in Brooklyn. You say that he thinks anonymous donors funded the upgrading of the place, which you tell me Ido reports now looks magnificent, inside and out. Thankfully, no paper trail exists on that. His message—discounting coy intimations, never direct—that ours is the messianic age Jews long awaited seems to have inspired a great many. No one else in this generation, certainly not in New York, has spurred more Jews to keep kosher than this fellow. So, perhaps it's still too soon to expose, to deny him."

"Seriously, a would-be murderer?" Uri Stein said.

"You yourself say you suspect, but cannot prove that," Rabbi Samson answered.

"Not yet. We're working on it," Stein said.

****

Soleiman Tabataei was not happy. "The Jew, Meyer, has more followers than before. My sources say he creates more enthusiasm than most other rabbis in New York. And a more dangerous enthusiasm. He hints, no, more than hints, he practically suggests that the Jews' *messiah*—as if, by Allah, they were to have one—is about to appear. And implies to his followers that it is he. This cannot continue!"

"How many times, Soleiman, how many times have I tried to tell you not to say 'the Jew' this and 'the Jew' that? We're in New York City, for God's sake," Professor Noam Lustner responded. "There must be a million and a-half Jews in the metro area. Or more. Including me. For the umpteenth time, say 'Zionist.' 'The Zionist' Meyer, for example. Then you'll even get some Jews on your side."

Prof. Lustner, occupant of the Sylvia and Arnold Balzberger Chair in Political Science, Columbia University, was beginning to doubt that Soleiman Tabataei would ever get the message. Hard to believe that Tabataei was a retired diplomat. A former Iraqi diplomat, then—briefly—governor of the Central Bank of Lebanon, the post going to a Shi'ite Muslim at that particular period, now ostensibly put to pasture as chairman of the Imam Sistani Capital Management Fund, offices in Doha, Brussels and New York. One would think, Prof. Lustner said to himself yet again, that Tabataei at least could grasp the nuances and subtleties of the environment in which he hoped to succeed.

This Lustner. If we were in Beirut, let alone Baghdad, I would finish with him quickly enough, Soleiman Tabataei was thinking. And he calls himself a Jew. It's a wonder the Zionists let him make such a nuisance to themselves, writing Op-Eds in *The Times* and appearing on CNN, always spouting off against Israel. At least that's to my benefit."

The third man in the small but well-appointed conference room of the ISCMF offices slouched in a corner, one leg draped over his Herman Miller fully-adjustable Aeron titanium-framed office chair, retail price $1,299. He rebuffed them. "Okay, you two. Enough of the nomenclature debate. Soleiman, this time Noam is right. Stop with the Jew stuff. Remember who's paying you. I'm a Jew, too, though so many of my tribal associates wish it otherwise. So, it's Zionist, Zionist, Zionist, not Jew, Jew, Jew. Your actions must be accompanied, and therefore explainable, contextualized and ultimately justifiable, by the right words."

"Okay," Tabataei muttered. "Okay, Henry."

Henry was Henry Joseph Havesi, by some accounts the world's third-wealthiest individual. Second, third, fourth, what did it matter? To a man with homes in Los Angeles, New York and Zurich, with what he called his little get-away places in Bali and now, to gratify his gratifying third wife, ever so déclassé Monte Carlo, not much. What mattered was that Henry Havesi was the silent—actually undiscovered—partner and founding principal investor in the Imam Sistani Capital Management Fund, with nearly $1 trillion in total assets, not far behind the headline-seeking Blackstone Funds. Born into a wealthy European Jewish family, Henry became a bar mitzvah at thirteen, then was shunned and twice beaten up at Magdalen College, Oxford, and rejected as a suitor in his early twenties by none other than the beautiful, brilliant, oddly devout Naomi Dreyfus Rothschild.

But all that was long ago. Now eighty and universally known as H.J. on the pages of *The Financial Times* and *Wall Street Journal*, he had not seen the inside of a synagogue since. He visited Israel once, just days after the Jewish state's providential victory in the 1967 Six-Day War. He had just turned twenty-one. The country's triumphant enthusiasm threatened him. For the first and only time in his life, it made him ask, who am I? No answer came. Relentless sunshine at the plaza in front of the Western Wall nearly blinded him. A brief feeling of dizziness followed. He vowed never to feel so unsettled again.

"But," Tabataei was saying, "the Jews—I mean the Zionists—really do run the United States. Trump's grandchildren are Jewish; Spielberg, the movie person, is Jewish; what's his name, the senator, Schumer is a Jew. And there was President Roosevelt …"

"Which one? Franklin or Teddy?" Professor Lustner jibed, feeling exasperated with his obtuse comrade.

"Both!" Tabataei shot back.

"It doesn't matter," Havesi said, overruling them. "Just tell me what you're going to do about Gerry Meyer."

"We are going to blow up his damned synagogue, with him in it!" the Iraqi shouted.

"Soleiman," H.J. Havesi said softly, almost soothingly, "who is we? Not, I hope, operatives like those Mexican gangsters you subcontracted the last time. The ones police found shot dead—and by whom we do not yet know—behind Meyer's place more than a year ago. Not more of the drug-addled Syrian refugees like the incompetent who smashed Meyer's psychiatrist's car."

"No," Tabataei answered. "This time it will be men from the Iranian Revolutionary Guard Corps, from the al-Quds Force itself. They trained in Lebanon and fought in Iraq and Syria. Their predecessors rid us of the Jews' embassy and their community center in Buenos Aires in the '90s, a busload of Israeli tourists in Rome in 2011, and nearly finished off the accursed Trump, among other liberation operations. These lessons have been learned and repeated throughout the Middle East and Europe. Soon, praise Allah, also in America. These men know what they are doing."

"Good," said Havesi. "But Soleiman …"

"Yes?" the Iraqi cut in, unable to contain his frustration with these associates.

"… make sure the strike comes when only Meyer himself is in the building, or with just a few others. Not on a Friday night or on a Saturday morning when the place is filled. That would be too much for the police and press to downplay. Politicians and even some of the public, and not just here but all over the country and beyond, would demand an investigation and arrests.

"Of course," Tabataei said, almost calmly. As if minimizing Jewish deaths mattered.

"How soon?" Havesi asked.

"Very," the Iraqi replied.

"And Noam, what can you contribute?"

"Plenty," the professor said. "Our coordinating committee—faculty members, administrators, a few officers of campus-related unions, clergy, some graduate and undergraduate student activists—at Columbia, NYU, City College, Hunter, Medgar Evers College in Crown Heights, SUNY Maritime University in the Bronx, you name it—have the next wave of anti-imperialist, anti-racist, anti-Zionist demonstrations ready to go. Thanks to steady funding from your Progressive Humanities Foundation, I must note.

"Assuming the troublesome Gerry Meyer meets his just reward some quiet, weekday evening, the next morning the streets of this great city will be filled with good citizens demanding reparations for all oppressed people of color, foremost among them the Palestinians. Morning rush hour will be paralyzed on the streets, sidewalks and in subway stations, in the name of social justice. And the end of Mr. Meyer almost immediately will be forgotten, a one-day story as we in all righteous rage flip the script."

"Distracting attention, official resources and investigative focus. Very good, professor," said Havesi as he rose, collected his Saint Laurent trench coat, wool and cashmere felt in black, $7,000 retail, slightly more custom fitted, and headed to the private elevator. He had feared that he ultimately might have to use his personal security people to finish Meyer. Embedded with Professor Lustner's gaggle, they had, after all, if not eliminated then virtually silenced the accursed, so-called saintly Rabbi Yehezkieli. And now there was this noisy Meyer person, Havesi thought. He could not bear one more cutesy *Daily News* or *New York Times* feature story on this minor league Jewish Billy Graham, Jewish Joel Osteen or whoever the religion beat reporter compared him to. Such Bible-thumpers made his skin crawl, always had. Especially Torah-thumpers. Well, this one, who seemed to be getting noisier by the month, had to go. And when H.J. Havesi decided it was time someone had to go, they went.

****

"Ido, are you coming?" Gerry Meyer was a little agitated. Here it was the third Wednesday evening study session since his return and Lisa Lenkowitz was not there and Ido Tabatchnik seemed to be dawdling. The rest of his original regulars—including Simon Peltz, Michael the Obsessive, and of course Judy Krakower—already were seated, joined by more than forty others, ten more than last week.

"Sorry, have to hit the men's room," came Tabatchnik's voice from the hallway. "Be there in a minute."

The big man opened the door to the men's bathroom, let it bang closed, but did not enter. Instead, he returned quietly to the main entrance and stepped outside. Down the sidewalk about fifty yards, a little red light blinked on and off in three short bursts. Glancing across the street, Tabatchnik signaled to a man standing in a recessed doorway, holding what looked like a guitar case. Reaching into it the man withdrew a tube several feet long with what appeared to be a trigger-apparatus near one end.

Standing but a few feet away at the edge of the curb, Lisa Lenkowitz was looking down, deep in thought. Oblivious to what was taking place around her, she noticed neither the man just behind her in the doorway, Ido Tabatchnik as he dropped to one knee outside the front door of the Jewish Renewal Initiative/Beth Aaron Synagogue and withdrew a huge handgun, in fact a .45 caliber Smith & Wesson 460XVR. Used by wilderness guides and big game hunters as a back-up to their rifles, it generally needed only one round to stop a charging bear, two for a rhinoceros. Some called it a hand-cannon. The woman who had flashed Tabatchnik the red-light signal did the same.

Lisa Lenkowitz made up her mind. She was going to JRI/Beth Aaron all right, but not to pray or study. She was going to expose Gerry Meyer, and that unbearably foolish Judith Krakower in the process. Let him flit back and forth from the synagogue to his new retreat, with barely a word for her, and then try to say how much he missed her, how much he needed her! This while bedding Krakower again and salivating over the young blonde who showed up at the Wednesday night sessions a month or two ago. Not anymore, Lisa Lenkowitz told herself. Not if I have anything to say about it, and I most certainly do, she thought.

"No!" the man behind her shouted, grabbing her by an arm just as she started to step off the sidewalk and cross the street. He whirled her back into the doorway. Stunned, she started to protest. The sound of a truck accelerating toward them drowned out whatever words she tried to utter. The explosion as a rocket-propelled grenade and a fusillade of gunshots tore the hood off the approaching truck and shattered its windshield filled the block. On fire and careening from one side of the street to the other, the truck overturned just beyond JRI/Beth Aaron's front door. Ido Tabatchnik and his two companions ran to the driver's side door but not in time to stop the dark young man crushed against the steering wheel, blood streaming across his face and one arm dangling uselessly, from pushing a capsule through clenched lips with his good hand.

"Ido!" Lisa Lenkowitz had recovered enough to shout that one word. And to see Tabatchnik, the man with the tube-like weapon and a woman climb into a black SUV that rolled up to collect them in the middle of the street.

The next morning, acting on an usually detailed if anonymous tip, New York law enforcement, accompanied by FBI agents and U.S. Treasury Police, raided the offices of the Imam Sistani Capital Management Fund. They were seen, *The New York Post* reported in a front-page story, removing box loads of documents, computers and, to the surprise of the Treasury Police spokesperson, handguns, AK-47 rifles, explosives and detonators. A news brief in *The New York Times* did mention the documents but not the weaponry.

Two days later, authorities received permission from a superior court judge to enter the Columbia University campus over objections of the school's chancellor and president. Students and faculty who had been blocking both the main gate and entrance to Hamilton Hall with its administrative offices, unmolested by campus police, were pushed aside. But by the time city cops, the FBI and Treasury Police got to his office, Professor Noam Lustner was gone, along with his computer hard drive.

"I did find these Post-it notes on my computer terminal," a secretary—her desk nameplate read "Administrative Assistant"—told police. "There are four Post-its but it's all one message."

"Janice," the instructions read, "have my teaching assistants take over my Poli. Sci. 301 and 415 classes. You know, 'Voting Patterns of the Privileged and Oppressed' and 'Global Capitalism as Colonial and Gender Exploitation.' Only a week left before finals, they can follow my syllabi. Final exams in the class file. My one-year sabbatical at the National Autonomous University in Mexico City starts Wednesday and I need to get down there. Best, Prof. Lustner."

"Turns out Lustner does have a sabbatical scheduled in Mexico," the FBI special agent in charge said to his NYPD and Treasury Police counterparts over coffee in his mid-town Manhattan office the following day. "But it doesn't start for four months."

"Any idea where he really went?" Lieutenant John O'Hara asked.

"Not yet," FBI Special Agent in Charge Vivek Sudarman said. "But if he ever does show up in Mexico City, we have an extradition policy with the Mexicans."

"Don't worry," said the Treasury Police's James Quinton Smith. "If he charges anything to a credit card, or pays cash for anything that generates a receipt with his name, we'll find him."

"James Smith. That's your real name?" Sudarman asked, bemused.

"As real as yours," came the reply. "Doesn't Vivek mean Jim in Hindi?"

But Treasury, to the astonishment of all three men, would turn up nothing. The outward-bound Professor Lustner needed to buy nothing, not in his own name. H. J. Havesi had seen to that.

As for Soleiman Tabataei, by the time authorities began removing material, incriminating or otherwise from the ISCMF office, he was reclining in a first-class seat on a Qatari Airways flight to Doha. He planned to change planes there enroute not to Baghdad or back to Beirut but for his original hometown, the holy city of Qom in Iran. While he was still enjoying an inflight meal of wild duck breast a l'Orange—despite, he considered, perhaps just a bit too much black pepper—the fund issued a statement, posted on X. It read:

"Given recent market slowdowns, the fund has decided to go in a new direction. Directors have named Butros Shenouda Butros, chairman of the economics department at Cairo University, as chief investment officer.

Professor Butros will be based in ISCMF's New York City office and focus on both emerging opportunities in tech and U.S. blue chip equities. The board thanks outgoing New York chief Soleiman Tabataei for his years of versatile service."

"Versatile service, indeed," Tabataei thought as he pocketed his cell phone and began to exit the departure gate at Hamad International Airport in Doha. That was when two men—rather large men, Tabataei considered—moved next to him on either side. He could not see their eyes since they wore sunglasses like those favored by airplane pilots. He did notice their elegant, well-tailored dark suits, rich silk ties and highly shined black shoes. He noticed how their shoulders nearly reached the top of his head, and how thick were their necks. And he noticed how they began to press against him, subtly redirecting his steps away from the baggage carousel area and toward a small, surprisingly dark hallway.

Days later, FBI Special Agent in Charge Vivek Sudarman would be informed that no passenger manifest attested to any Soleiman Tabataei transferring to Baghdad, back to Beirut or anywhere else from Hamad International Airport.

On the southwest coast of Bali, atop the 200-feet cliffs of Uluwatu, Henry Joseph Havesi leaned back in his chaise lounge. What he called his "little place," which it was, compared to the one in Los Angeles, sat a quarter-mile away from the other palaces of what the natives—H.J. corrected himself, the locals—referred to as "Billionaires Row." At poolside, he sipped from a tumbler half-filled with 30-year-old Macallan single malt Scotch whiskey. Too bad about Soleiman, he thought, but when certain things had to be done, they had to be done, that was all. Tabataei had become not only a man who knew too much but one who could stand up against too little.

As for Lustner, no doubt the professor was enjoying himself in Caracas. If past performance was any indicator of future returns, then Lustner would make of Simon Rodriguez National Experimental University his personal playground. No matter that only a few dozen demonstrators had turned out the previous morning at New York City subway stations, in a couple of intersections and on a handful of sidewalks, several of them being arrested and held by immigration authorities for deportation proceedings. A trifle, in the bigger picture. And H.J. Havesi always looked both at the details and the bigger picture. In any case, he reminded himself, the important thing was that Venezuela lacked an extradition treaty with the United States.

"Gorgeous, isn't it?" asked his wife. She had slipped up beside him, her own drink—an Apple Jack, straight from Prohibition, as she liked to say—in hand. Yvette Albanese, wife number three, had startled him.

"I was just thinking how smooth, how rich this Macallan is. Of course, I would be too if aged 30 years in sherry-polished oak casks," H.J. said, telling himself yet again that he indeed did look a decade younger than his 80 years. Everything is gorgeous here, he thought. This roseate sunset, the indigo-colored water below highlighted by the white foam of low breakers lapping the beach. And, of course, my wife. Hard to believe that she is sixty-two years old.

In a white bikini artfully constructed from the Lycra Spandex equivalent of half-a-dozen shoe laces, displaying her even and extensive tan, its color between buff and copper, Yvette Albanese could have passed for forty-five. But then, she benefited from personal trainers on-call, the finest dietician-chefs and, when occasionally necessary, elite cosmetic surgeons.

"I'm not sure even 30 years in a sherry-oak cask would mellow you," she laughed. "But it couldn't hurt. Apropos of nothing we're looking at now, what do you think of the yen? Hold or sell?"

"Great question," Havesi said. "We sold just before I poured this Scotch."

****

The next Saturday morning Lisa Lenkowitz took care to arrive early. She reddened briefly at the two armed security guards now posted at the main entrance. They nodded in recognition and she walked resolutely into the sanctuary, choosing an aisle seat on the second row. She had thought about what she would say since last Wednesday, that fateful night, typed it on her computer and then printed it. After reading it aloud several times, trying to get her pacing and inflection just right, she stood in front of a mirror and rehearsed. But only a couple of times. She wanted to sound spontaneous as well as genuine.

Gerry Meyer had just started his remarks as he called them—"not a sermon, just remarks"—a well-modulated if tightly edited recollection of what he had studied most recently at the Catskills' retreat and how that intersected with the weekly Torah portion, when Lisa Lenkowitz stepped into the aisle, turned and began to speak, loudly.

"My friends," she said, "please excuse me. But I have a relevant question to ask. What kind of Jewish teacher, what kind of Jewish leader, sleeps with two members of his congregation while chasing a third?" The four hundred or so attendees went completely silent. No one coughed. No one rustled in his or her seat. She had their total attention.

"What kind of man playing at these leadership roles races a red Ferrari through Manhattan—to the extent it's possible to race any car through this city—collecting speeding tickets he forgets to pay, then calls a friendly judge to get them erased? What kind of leader does not and maybe cannot say where the money came from for all the upgrades of this synagogue? Or who paid for our new retreat upstate? And what kind of Jewish teacher, what kind of leader, speaks of the messianic era to come and simultaneously hints, and none too reservedly, at himself as *Mosiach*? All the while womanizing and breaking the law? What kind?! What kind?! We must demand an answer! Now!"

Judith Krakower, who had been sitting only a few rows behind Lisa Lenkowitz, rose and, sobbing loudly, bolted up an aisle and out the front door. Gerry Meyer, who had stood mute—frozen was more like it—during most of Lenkowitz's outburst—pointed at her and, face red, said with controlled fury, "This is neither the time nor place for such scandalous allegations. Please leave my temple!" Then, losing control, he threw a *siddur* at her.

Only six people showed up the following Wednesday evening for class. The following Shabbat morning, fewer than one hundred and more than a few of them the curious, thrill-seekers hoping for more sensation. Lisa's denunciation of its leader opened fissures in the Jewish Renewal Initiative's cultic wall.

Chapter 30

"Spiritual searchers can swallow a lot of fantasy, believe a great deal of demagoguery, even pay for and submit to endless forms of indoctrination," Rabbi Samson was saying. Sitting with Professor Joshua Golden in his office at JOLO headquarters, the rabbi spoke quietly, almost as if reminiscing. "From Hollywood celebrities in the Silent Screen era attending seances through poor families the so-called Reverend Jim Jones gathered at his People's Temple in Guyana to drink the Kool-Aid of devout suicide to today's followers of 'Palestinianism,' people in crowds will do what they as individuals would never contemplate—as long as it's properly packaged and always in the name of a larger cause, a higher good."

"Niche versions of the Bolsheviks, Italian Fascists, German Nazis, Chinese Maoists. The list is endless. Eric Hoffer nailed it in *The True Believer*," Professor Golden said.

"But if a few dissenters eventually lead to a critical mass of skeptics recognizing self-aggrandizement, corruption, futility as well as brutality in their movements, then all bets are off," Rabbi Samson concluded. "Hitler knew this, so the Gestapo's ruthlessness knew no limits. Stalin too, so the GRU and NKVD murdered dissidents from Moscow to Mexico City. And Mao, Mao slaughtered tens of millions of fellow Chinese to silence any questioning of the Communist Party gospel. Today, internet mobs try viciously to overwhelm and silence any contemporary Paine or Orwell."

"And as a micro example, Gerry Meyer knew it too. Maybe that's why he hurled a prayer book at Ms. Lenkowitz," Joshua Golden observed.

Their conversation took place some weeks after the confrontation at JRI/Beth Aaron synagogue. A few days after the "Building for Lease" sign went up in front of the structure.

****

"Given that he came with little English and even less Hebrew, he's made rapid strides. His teachers say he has an ear for languages as well as for music. He's diligent enough in Torah and Talmud studies, and has taken to wearing teffilin at morning prayers. But it is music, both singing and playing the guitar, that captivates him and at which he excels," the head of JOLO's security reported.

"What about secular studies?" Rabbi Samson asked. "When we have the opportunity, which does not always arise, we must train any candidate as thoroughly as possible."

"He spends three afternoons a week studying at Touro. A little math, some science and political science. He is said to soak up astronomy."

"You know, Uri, it's funny, perhaps unprecedented. In the history of this organization, and its predecessors, going back 1,400 years now, I am not aware of a generation in which one candidate instructed another," the rabbi said. "I understand that young ben-Veniste takes a course from Joshua Golden."

"Well, based on the respective sizes of their followings ben-Veniste is the star," Stein said. "He is starting to attract followers to his music on social media, which not surprisingly he has become quite adept at. It is being said that he inspires many, and not just among the young, to become more involved in *Yiddishkeit*. Then there is his self-assurance, which is balanced by humility. He begins to approach messianic expectations as much as anyone we've seen in recent generations."

"All that is so," Rabbi Samson conceded. "But let's not get ahead of ourselves. Professor Golden is by no means disqualified. His writings, lectures and podcasts on the Torah roots of early American natural law concepts and how they influenced the Declaration of Independence and Constitution are being noted—supported, opposed, debated, but the main thing is they are attracting attention—in academia and beyond. He seems to be not only popular but also influential among students, and his first book, his doctoral dissertation revised for the general public, continues to sell modestly. Perhaps just as important considering the subject at hand, he and his wife Rachel, your new chief of informatics—whatever in HaShem's creation that might be—are the parents of twin boys."

"What about Rabbi Yehezkieli?" Uri Stein asked. "Does he no longer qualify as a candidate? We are still protecting him in addition to the others."

"The man is a saint," Rabbi Samson said. "Of that there was never any doubt. As to his candidature, doubt remains. He has recovered his memory, certainly most of it, as you well know. Not long ago he resumed direct leadership of Or Zahav yeshiva, though I understand he leans heavily on his wife, the indispensable P'nina. But that portion of his memory not yet recovered relates to P'nina and the rest of his family. He greatly appreciates all she does for him, but has no recollection of their life together before the assassination attempt, no recall of anything prior involving their children or grandchildren. And his speech is still slow. Apparently, he has some form of aphasia. From his writings and reaction to speech by others, his understanding is as keen, as insightful as ever. But not his ability to articulate, to vocalize ..." Here the rabbi trailed off.

"Moses called himself heavy of tongue," Stein reminded him. "So, he needed his brother Aaron as spokesman. But he led."

"Yes. Of course, he also spoke directly with God. Which I'm pretty certain is not the case for the fourth of our original quartet of candidates," the rabbi said. "What is the latest with Mr. Gerry Meyer, our self-proclaimed 'historic figure,' though not, we must be fair, not yet at least self-proclaimed *mosiach*?"

"Since his congregation, or following—whatever we call it—fell apart, he's kept a low, no, make that somewhat lower, profile. Traded the red Ferrari for a black Porsche two-seater, started oil painting—takes lessons—and is studying to renew his real estate license. One other thing: he apparently aspires to work as a stand-up comedian. He's done at least three open-mic sessions at local comedy clubs. Riffs on religion and sex, mostly. He gets laughs. For example, 'A rabbi gets into an elevator at the twenty-fifth floor and presses the button for the lobby. Two floors later, the elevator stops, the door opens, and a naked woman steps in ...'"

"I've heard it," Rabbi Samson said. "'My wife has an outfit just like that.' Most rabbis have heard it, probably since Rodney Dangerfield, or maybe even Henny Youngman came up with it."

"Okay, speaking of resurrecting Henny Youngman, Meyer also gets a few laughs with 'my wife and I go out two nights a week. She goes out Tuesdays, I go out Wednesdays.'"

"Again, not original. Uri, stick to security," Rabbi Samson advised.

****

"Professor Golden? May I come in?" A young man, tall, slender with dark hair and an olive complexion, stood at Joshua Golden's office door.

He carried a back-pack slung carelessly across one shoulder stuffed not only with books, a water bottle, and an iPad, but a small automatic pistol, a ghost gun fabricated almost entirely of plastic on a 3-D printer, wrapped in a towel at the very bottom.

Golden, seated at his desk, marked a student's essay on the semester's research topic, "Adam Smith's *The Theory of Moral Sentiments* and *The Wealth of Nations*: Conflict or Complement?" It was after five. Rachel and the twins—now old enough to be out and about in their double stroller, which they enjoyed—were coming to meet him around 5:30. They would then get dinner at Vezzo's. Finish this paper and he would be ready to go.

Glancing up, he did not recognize the person at the door. He looked like a student, of course, but Touro was a big place. Joshua Golden knew his own students, about forty total in two classes per semester, by face and by name. But even with that relatively small number it usually took about three weeks into the term to be certain of each of them. This fellow definitely was a stranger.

Osgood Garvey started work as a janitor at Touro the same day Professor Golden began teaching there. Coincidentally, he previously had been employed as a janitor at Columbia, in the same building in which Golden worked. Now, furthering the coincidence, Garvey somehow had been assigned to the building that housed the political science department where Joshua Golden landed after his encounter with Professor Sybil Rothgott-Marquand and the Columbia thought police. Some Chasidic masters insist there are no coincidences. This was a belief Professor Joshua Golden could not take seriously since it meant that neither apparently random evils and or apparently random blessings were not accidents. It was a belief about which Osgood Garvey was both professionally and personally agnostic. Regardless, Garvey just now happened to be pushing a broom slowly past Golden's door. He too did not recognize the young man waiting tentatively.

"Come in," the professor said, and, gesturing to a chair opposite his desk, "Sit down. What can I do for you?"

"Well," the newcomer said, shifting the backpack to his side, "I'd like to ask you about your recent podcasts."

Chapter 30

"What about them?" Joshua asked, adding "I'm actually on my way out for the day." He tried to recall specifics of the twenty-minute sessions, distillations of his classroom presentations for busy or distracted listeners—categories that seemed to include far too many people.

"Specifically, what you say about the Anglosphere and progress. I have some questions."

"Are you a student here at Touro? I don't think I recognize you."

"I go to Brooklyn Community College, part-time."

"And what else do you do?" Joshua Golden asked.

"I'm a baker at Sahadi's in Brooklyn Heights."

Joshua knew the place. He and Rachel shopped there occasionally. Great breads, Middle Eastern specialty dishes, cheese and yogurt, spices, olives, coffees and teas, dried apricots and figs, and reasonable prices, too.

"And you listen to podcasts?"

"Not many," the young man conceded. "But yours are very interesting." Actually, the young man started listening to Professor Golden's podcasts two months previously, after reading about their hateful anti-Palestinian messages on the GlobalIntifadaNow! website. But what he heard did not really accord with what GlobalIntifadaNow! said about them. This left him confused, since two of his co-workers at Sahadi's swore by the website.

Just outside the office door, Osgood Garvey was taking his time emptying a trash container in the hallway. A good listener, Garvey heard what sounded like a pleasant conversation coming from within.

"Well, I'm glad you think so," Golden said. "Tell me, what's your name?"

"Paul. Paul David Pelegos. My family's from the Bronx. Not originally, of course. Way back, from Lebanon. I was there once, when I was about ten. We visited relatives one summer."

Pelegos, Golden thought. Sounds like a Greek Orthodox name. Lebanese, too. My podcast audience must be growing. He said, "so, what are your questions? I'll do my best to answer them."

"Well, the way you talk about this Anglosphere, the English-speaking countries—especially England and the United States, but also Canada, Australia, New Zealand, even sometimes if I understand you right, other places the English colonized, like India—it almost sounds like they're superior to everywhere else …" he trailed off.

Joshua again tried to explain. "No, not superior if by that someone misunderstands that I mean the people there are somehow better. Rather, that for the past few centuries it is from the Anglosphere and, you are right, especially the United Kingdom, adding Scotland to England on your list, and the United States that have advanced the ideas and put them into practice earliest that underlay human progress toward freedom and prosperity. Inherent rights of the individual like freedom of religion, free elections, private property, capitalism, limited government, rule of law, ordered liberty and so on. These are known now pretty much world-wide, though hardly practiced that extensively and opposed aggressively by various authoritarians. And they came, starting with the Magna Carta in 1215, and by long forward and backward struggle, out of Britain and then its colonies and successors, especially America.

"Put it less theoretically: three hundred years or so ago, most human beings lived as the vast majority of humans always had lived, at the subsistence level, working from dawn to dusk, usually for a master of some sort, a duke, prince, king, czar, or emperor with life expectancies short and poverty and famine not uncommon. Today, the reverse is true. Why? Because of the ideas and behaviors that took root first in the Anglosphere and largely were spread by it."

"But that seems to exclude everyone else, or make them second-class," Paul David Pelegos objected. "Will you do podcasts on 'the Sino-sphere,' or 'the Hispanic-sphere,' or 'Arabic-sphere?'"

Joshua Golden thought he heard anger in the young man's voice. But he answered quietly. "On one hand, those are fields of study separate from my own and I'm sure have podcasts of their own. There are, after all, podcasts on everything, from fly fishing and do-it-yourself plumbing to cryptocurrency and cryogenics. But think of it this way:

"Distinct civilizations of China and its offshoots, or Spain and its former New World possessions, let alone the culture that came out of the Arabian Peninsula to conquer and influence much of the Middle East, North Africa, Asia, even parts of Europe, deserve their own close scrutiny. There has been significant overlap and cross-cultural fertilization, of course, but in modern times the English-speaking West has been, to paraphrase other scholars, ahead of the rest. The rise of China in the past forty or fifty years—borrowing, appropriating, stealing from or copying the West, the United States in particular—may change things. But I have attempted to describe where things stood between say 1500 and 2000 and how we got here."

"What happened to the Arabic-sphere?" Pelegos asked. "Uncle Constantine, one of my father's five brothers, is always talking about the lost glories of the Arab world. How for centuries after Mohammad and his armies made their great conquests the Arabs had the most advanced civilizations in government, military affairs, astronomy, literature, especially poetry, even mathematics, like Arabic numerals. What happened? How did these glories get lost and who lost them?" Pelegos demanded.

"Well, again, in very abbreviated form: For about three centuries after the Arab-Muslim conquests in the sixth and seventh centuries, Muslim leaders, often aided by Christian and Jewish translators, administrators and advisors, did rule much of the world. Their societies did make outstanding contributions in the fields your uncle mentioned. Though you might tell him one day that the numbers we today call 'Arabic numerals' came to them from India. Human progress often has combined local social-cultural initiatives with borrowed influences. For example, the lowly tomato: it seems everyone on the planet today uses ketchup and eats pizza, but the essential red, ripe tomato started as a little, green barely edible thing high in the Andes Mountains. Cultural appropriation, or experimentation, exchange and progress?

"In any case, around 900 C.E., Arab intellectuals and especially Muslim theologians turned inward. Their worldviews stopped expanding, became rigid, even reactionary. So, when the First Crusaders showed up in the Near East just before 1100, conquering Jerusalem and much of the Holy Land, it was quite a shock. Likewise, the long *Reconquista* by Christian kings of the Iberian Peninsula—Spain and Portugal—from Muslim rule, ending in the late 1400s. Then, European imperialists in the late nineteenth and early twentieth century treated much of the Middle East as colonies and in the process destroyed the Ottoman Empire and caliphate led by the last Turkish sultans in World War I.

"These calamities, topped by a tiny minority, the Jews, recreating an independent state in the region, fueled a reaction, sometimes pan-Arab, including Christians, sometimes pan-Islamic, largely excluding them. Sunni Islam gave birth in Egypt to the anti-Western, anti-Christian, anti-Jewish Muslim Brotherhood, mother ship of movements like al-Qaeda, the Islamic State in Iraq and Syria and Hamas. Shi'a Islam featured the Iranian revolution of the Twelver Shi'a waiting for the emergence or return of the messianic Twelfth Imam and meanwhile, imposing a previously minority view, *Velayet-e Faqih*, rule by Islamic judges, the mullahs in Iran, and derivatives like Hezbollah in Lebanon.

"So, instead of Washingtons and Lincolns, Churchills and Reagans, Henry Ford or Bill Gates, Arab and Islamic societies produced Nasser and Ghadafi and Saddam Hussein or Osama bin Laden and Ayatollah Khomeini. As one consequence, you had a series of annual United Nations Reports on Human Development from 2002 through 2005, for example, compiled mostly by Arab specialists, that listed a series of 'deficits' in Arab countries. These shortages included individual and political freedom, education, women and minority rights, religious tolerance, economic growth, research, artistic output and so on. Reasons given were corruption, oppression, religious fundamentalism. Not mentioned was the obsession with fighting Israel rather than emphasizing domestic development, but no doubt it contributed."

"That seems harsh," Pelegos said. "Very harsh."

"Where do your father's brothers, your uncles, live?" Joshua asked.

"Uncle Constantine and his family are here with us," the young man said. "He and my father are partners in Sahadi's. Uncle Yiannis lives in Paris, Uncle Linus went to London and Ozias, the oldest of the five, died in the civil war. He was an officer with the Lebanese Forces and one day a bomb exploded in his Tyre office. I wasn't born then."

Assassinated, either by the Syrians, Hezbollah or a rival Christian militia, Golden thought. He said, "I'm guessing, but based on the one hundred and fifty-year evacuation of Arab Christians from their ancient Middle Eastern homelands, one reason your father and uncles Constantine,

Yiannis and Linus don't live in Lebanon is due, in some ways, to those 'deficits' the U.N. reports cited. Lebanon, by the way, is the ancient Phoenicia. Its port of Tyre is noted in the Bible and was important through Roman times. It's only a dozen miles north of Israel."

"Uncle Constantine says that we're not really Arabs anyway, that we're Phoenicians, or their descendants. But then he'll say that doesn't really matter now and go back to talking about the lost glories of the Arabs."

"Look, something similar happened with China in the 1400s as with the Arabs by 1000. China then possessed an advanced civilization, materially ahead of Europe, and the world's greatest navy. It had sailed far across the Pacific to the east and far across the Indian Ocean to the west. It was, geographically anyway, on the verge of discovering the New World. Then a new emperor came to the throne, ordered the navy dissolved, and China, seeing itself as the superior and self-sufficient Middle Kingdom, non-Chinese as barbarians, turned inward. This led eventually to stagnation and vulnerability. That left it to the Europeans—and their Anglosphere offshoot—to begin, a few decades later, the Age of Discovery and five hundred years of world leadership if not domination. China now, headed by its Orwellian communist party, challenges America and the old ideals of the Anglosphere. What the Arab-Islamic sphere will do, if and when the question of Islamist fundamentalism, as seen in Iran and the Muslim Brotherhood, is answered, remains to be seen."

"This is why I listen to your podcasts. I find them interesting ... and disturbing. I am studying business management now, but I'm not sure. Political science also interests me," Pelegos said. As he spoke, he made a decision.

"Well," Golden smiled, "just keep in mind it's not a science, really, more in the 'arts and crafts' category. Also, that there are plenty of political scientists but only one Sahadi's."

"That's what my father says," Paul David Pelegos remarked ruefully as he rose to leave.

"Anyone in here?" Rachel Shapiro Golden asked, pushing the twins in their stroller through the office door.

From the hall, Osgood Garvey finally finished lining a trash can with a new plastic bag. "Anything for me today, professor?" he asked, sticking his head into Joshua's office. He watched the young Pelegos walk away. Not a student here, Garvey knew.

Outside the building, at the nearest trash can, the boy dug deeply into his backpack and withdrew that thing wrapped in a hand towel. Glancing around, satisfied that no one saw him, he shoved the object down amongst the refuse. He had decided he could learn something from this Professor Golden.

Chapter Thirty-One:
Jerusalem and New York City, the Present

Music came softly from the background. The aural quality was excellent, especially considering the small size and age of the Bose Wave System IV radio and CD player producing it. The machine had been a gift a few years back from a young member of Columbus, Ohio's Schottenstein family, the discount department store clan behind both Value City Arena/Jerome Schottenstein Center, home to the Ohio State University's men's and women's basketball teams, and the 15-year, $40 million, 73-volume English translation of the Babylonian Talmud.

An older man with a white beard sat at a polished wooden table on which books were stacked to one side. Through an open window the sound of water plashing in a stone fountain at the center of a small courtyard could be heard momentarily each time the CD player cycled between songs.

Aaron Yehezkieli propped his head up with one hand while once again poring over the famous, more than a few said foundational, prophecy made by Micah in the eighth century B.C.E., repeated by Isaiah in the sixth:

"And many nations will come and say, 'Come, let us go up to the mountain of the Lord, to the house of the God of Jacob. He will teach us His ways, so that we may walk in His paths.' For the law [Torah] will go forth from Zion and the word of the Lord from Jerusalem."

Yes, but when? The older he got the more he desired, even against his will, a hint, a signal, a sign. Had Maimonides himself not warned against trying to calculate the coming of *Mosiach*, but then attempted to do so? At that moment he suddenly became conscious of the music playing in his study. A young man's voice, extraordinarily pleasant and moving, floated behind—no, all around him—while one clear note after another sounded on guitar. The voice sang in Hebrew, moving seamlessly from the Prophet

Micah to the words of the Prophet Habbakuk, "though it takes time, wait for it; because it will surely come and it won't delay." The bearded man listened, astonished.

Rabbi Yehezkieli had never forgotten those lines of Habbakuk, proclaimed after the words of Micah but before those of Isaiah. He had learned them as a child and repeated, or heard them repeated, countless times since. Turning to his wife, who sat nearby, Rabbi Yehezkieli said, "It *is* you, P'nina, isn't it? I mean, not just a person whose name I've been told is P'nina, but you, my wife." He smiled almost quizzically and said, "please turn the radio up a little. That is a heavenly tune and a most heavenly voice." Then, tears in his eyes, he stood to embrace his wife.

****

"That was quite a crowd at Citi Field last night," Rabbi Samson said.

"If I had not been there, I would not have believed this morning's news coverage," said Uri Stein. "Nearly 40,000 people, almost a sell-out. And by no means all Jews, coming to hear a young man sing songs of Jewish mysticism, some of the tunes hundreds of years old, the lyrics first uttered thousands of years ago. Unprecedented."

"A bigger crowd than the Mets usually draw," Rabbi Samson mused. "I'm told his music is especially popular with young people."

"It's true," Stein responded. "My son says his first album has gone platinum, whatever that means, and that his latest release, 'The Mountain of the Lord,' was last week's most-often downloaded pop music single."

"It is remarkable, doubly so when we consider that half of his recordings are in Hebrew, with the other half in Spanish and English," the rabbi said.

"Well, regardless of language, the word goes out. So, where does that leave us now?" Stein asked. "Persian friends tell us Soleiman Tabataei never reached Iran. And he hasn't turned up publicly anywhere else, not Lebanon or Iraq, not even Paris or Rome. And somehow," he said, smiling a little, "Professor Noam Lustner has managed to get himself a long prison stay. In Venezuela, yet. He's been convicted of drug-running and trafficking in underaged girls. Not even the regime's judicial stooges could deny the photographs and documents that suddenly appeared on the

Caracas' high court's website. Nothing like a cutting-edge tech squad and artificial intelligence to accelerate things. And for that, by the way, much thanks are due Rachel Shapiro. Her previous experience at that cybersecurity risk management company has proved invaluable. Put her near a keyboard and the woman's a marvel.

"But as for Henry J. Havesi, he travels above our reach, above the reach of most governments. They grant him a wide berth as a seemingly necessary pillar of international high finance, no matter how self-seeking and potentially dangerous to themselves and their currencies he may be."

"Uri, didn't you tell me not long ago that Havesi's wife, number three, that is, has exquisite taste and expensive desires?" Rabbi Samson said.

"Yes, but she is more than a materialistic bauble to Havesi. Unlike his first two wives, this one is not mere arm-candy. She behaves more like a partner and he accepts her that way. The former Moira O'Shaughnessy, she now goes by the name Yvette Albanese. She was a translator at the International Monetary Fund—that's how she met Havesi and displaced wife number two, the still flamboyant former French actress Lolita LeGrande. Not just a translator, but one of the IMF's best, fluent in English, Spanish, French and Arabic. And now, having proven her utility in ways linguistic, personal—let us say—and organizational, Albanese directs her husband's Progressive Humanities Foundation as chief operations officer. She is the power behind his feckless older son Jean-Louis, who occupies, just barely, the president's seat. Unlike LeGrande, Moira O'Shaughnessy-turned-Yvette Albanese seems more interested in power than possessions—not that she distains the latter. She apparently could squeeze Havesi for much more, but it looks like she is content with the villa he bought her in Monaco, high on the hillside looking down on the casino and harbor filled with mega-yachts. Anyhow, the deed is in her name."

"Perhaps her psychology, a drive for power that grows with her acquisition of it, might eventually provide us with an opening. Look for it," Rabbi Samson said.

"As for Gerry Meyer, with all good wishes for his success as a real estate comedian, we can withdraw his team and reassign its members to those already watching ben-Veniste and Golden."

"What about Yehezkieli?" Stein said."

"Even fully recovered from amnesia, now finally from the curious lacunae regarding his wife and family, we don't believe he has enough time left, not for the messianic mission as we consider it. Still, he also meets, so far, every messianic qualification. So, continue protecting him, along with the security provided by the Israelis themselves. Especially since it's been arranged thanks to Professor Pearlstein and others at Touro University that young ben-Veniste will spend his semester abroad studying with Rabbi Yehezkieli in Jerusalem. For us the overriding consideration is that we must free more personnel for increased protection of ben-Veniste and his family, and for Professor Golden and his."

"Golden?" Stein questioned.

"Yes. Only Ha-Shem knows what tomorrow will bring. And in any case, there are his and Mrs. Shapiro's twin boys. If not ben-Veniste in this generation, perhaps yet Professor Golden—his podcasts led to an invitation for him and Rachel to attended the White House state dinner for Prime Minister Meir. He, like ben-Veniste, has been selected by *The Algemeiner* for its most recent list of the Top 100 People Positively Influencing Jewish Life. And if neither of them, then maybe one of the twins in the next generation."

"Baruch HaShem," Stein said.

"Baruch HaShem," Rabbi Samson responded. Blessed be the Name of the Lord.

No sooner had Stein left than Samson pushed an intercom button and said, "Yitzi, please ask Rachel Shapiro and one of her staff, Audrey Haber, her name is, to see me."

Once seated, Rachel asked, "what did you want to see us about, Rabbi Samson?"

"You know who H. J. Havesi is?" he said.

"Who doesn't? One of the world's richest men and an international currency speculator feared by central banks, finance ministers and big investors around the world," Rachel answered.

"And, surreptitiously, the world's most dangerous anti-Jewish Jew," the rabbi said. "Scrub the news media-applied sheen off the leftist non-profits he funds in Europe, North and South America and Asia—groups

Chapter 31

like Democracy in Crisis, Social Justice Universal, Progressive Humanity Foundation and Middle East Equity Now!—and you find the fronts, pass-throughs and coordinators of a great deal of anti-Zionist antisemitism on four continents. Wouldn't it appear to be a miracle if one morning Havesi awoke to find that his most audacious bets on currency devaluations, bond yields and stock short-selling had all failed, based on misleading data and instead of being one of the world's wealthiest individuals, he now faced debts greater than all the resources even he could muster?"

Rachel Shapiro looked at Audrey Haber. Audrey nodded. "Rabbi Samson," she said, "do you remember news reports that while Israel and the United States were bombing Iran's nuclear weapons facilities, a mysterious cyber-hacking group that called itself 'Predatory Sparrow' was draining $100 million from Nobitex, Iran's largest crypto-currency exchange, and shutting down Iran's Bank Sepah, which served Tehran's military?"

It was the rabbi's turn to nod.

"Well," Ms. Haber said, "I've always had a strong interest in ornithology."

Rachel turned back to the rabbi and said, "You know the old Yiddish saying, Rabbi Samson, that 'all things can be found in algorithms?' Our experiment with movements of the Japanese yen and Havesi's reaction to it the other day suggest the miracle you imagine can be arranged. Give us a week."

"It's yours," Reuven Samson smiled. "Although, I'm not familiar with that old Yiddish saying. By the way, how are the twins?"

"Growing like crazy," Rachel Shapiro said.

"I'm not surprised," the rabbi answered, thinking of one of his favorite prophetic passages, Isaiah 11:1-2: "And a shoot shall spring forth from the stem of Jesse, and a twig shall sprout from his roots." And so it did, from Jesse's son David, to David's sons and grandsons. Many times removed.

-the end-

References used in this work included but were not limited to *A History of the Jewish People*, edited by H.H. Ben-Sasson; *Judaism on Trial, Jewish-Christian Disputations in the Middle Ages,* by Haym Maccoby; *Jewish Pirates of the Caribbean*, by Edward Kritzler, "New Amsterdam's Jewish Crusader (1655)," by Michael Feldberg, Ph.D., Jewish Virtual Library. Also, Jewish Virtual Library for the 2002 Hebrew University terrorist bombing and other incidents.

www.ingramcontent.com/pod-product-compliance
Lightning Source LLC
Chambersburg PA
CBHW070936230426
43666CB00011B/2460